The Princeton Review®

2 Practice Tests for the

ACT®

The Staff of The Princeton Review

PrincetonReview.com

Penguin
Random
House

The Princeton Review
110 East 42nd Street, 7th Floor
New York, NY 10017
Email: editorialsupport@review.com

Published in the United States by Penguin Random House LLC, New York, and in Canada by Random House of Canada, a division of Penguin Random House Ltd., Toronto.

ISBN: 978-0-375-97796-1

ACT is a registered trademark of ACT, Inc.

The Princeton Review is not affiliated with Princeton University.

The material in this book was previously published in *1,471 ACT Practice Questions,* a trade paperback published by Random House LLC in 2017.

Editor: Aaron Riccio
Production Editor: Kathy Carter
Production Artist: Deborah A. Weber

Printed in the United States of America.

10 9 8 7 6 5 4

First Edition

Editorial
Rob Franek, Editor-in-Chief
Casey Cornelius, Chief Product Officer
Mary Beth Garrick, Executive Director of Production
Craig Patches, Production Design Manager
Selena Coppock, Managing Editor
Meave Shelton, Senior Editor
Colleen Day, Editor
Sarah Litt, Editor
Aaron Riccio, Editor
Orion McBean, Associate Editor

Penguin Random House Publishing Team
Tom Russell, VP, Publisher
Alison Stoltzfus, Publishing Director
Amanda Yee, Associate Managing Editor
Ellen Reed, Production Manager
Suzanne Lee, Designer

Acknowledgments

The Princeton Review would like to recognize Sara Kuperstein, Kathy Carter, and Deborah Weber for their swift and attentive work on this title.

Special thanks to Adam Robinson, who conceived of and perfected the Joe Bloggs approach to standardized tests, and many of the other successful techniques used by The Princeton Review.

Contents

Get More (Free) Content

1 Go to **PrincetonReview.com/cracking.**

2 Enter the following ISBN for your book: 9780375977961.

3 Answer a few simple questions to set up an exclusive Princeton Review account. (If you already have one, you can just log in.)

4 Click the "Student Tools" button, also found under "My Account" from the top toolbar. You're all set to access your bonus content!

Need to report a potential **content** issue?

Contact **EditorialSupport@review.com**.

Include:

- full title of the book
- ISBN
- page number

Need to report a **technical** issue?

Contact **TPRStudentTech@review.com** and provide:

- your full name
- email address used to register the book
- full book title and ISBN
- computer OS (Mac/PC) and browser (Firefox, Safari, etc.)

Once you've registered, you can...

- Take a full-length practice SAT and/or ACT

- Get valuable advice about the college application process, including tips for writing a great essay and where to apply for financial aid

- If you're still choosing between colleges, use our searchable rankings of *The Best 384 Colleges* to find out more information about your dream school

- Print out additional bubble sheets

- Check to see if there have been any corrections or updates to this edition

- Get our take on any recent or pending updates to the ACT

Chapter 1
Introduction

So you think you need more practice? In this book, you'll find the equivalent of two full ACTs to help you get your best possible score on this beastly test! After all, the harder you practice, the better you'll be on test day.

Here is a breakdown of the "tests" on the ACT.

1. English Test (45 minutes—75 questions)

In this section, you will be given five passages that contain a variety of errors in grammar, punctuation, and sentence structure. Most questions will refer to an underlined portion of the passage and ask you to either fix the error or indicate that the original is correct as written. Other questions will ask you to weigh in on the structure of the passage and decide where words, sentences, and paragraphs should go and whether ideas should be added or deleted.

2. Math Test (60 minutes—60 questions)

These are the regular, multiple-choice math questions you've been doing all your life. The easier questions tend to come in the beginning and the difficult ones in the end, but the folks at the ACT try to mix in easy, medium, and difficult problems throughout the math test. A good third of the test covers pre-algebra and elementary algebra. Slightly less than a third covers intermediate algebra and coordinate geometry (graphing). Regular geometry accounts for less than a quarter of the questions, and there are four questions that cover trigonometry.

3. Reading Test (35 minutes—40 questions)

In this section, there will be four reading passages of about 800 words each—the average length of a *People* magazine article but maybe not as interesting. There is always one prose fiction passage, one social science passage, one humanities passage, and one natural science passage, and they are always in that order. One of these passages will consist of a dual passage in which the *total* length of the two passages will still be about 800 words. Each of these four sections is followed by 10 questions.

4. Science Test (35 minutes—40 questions)

No specific scientific knowledge is necessary for the science test. You won't need to know the chemical makeup of hydrochloric acid or any formulas. Instead, you will be asked to understand six or seven sets of scientific information presented in graphs, charts, tables, and research summaries. In addition, you will have to make sense of one disagreement between two or three scientists. (Occasionally, there are more than three scientists).

5. Optional Writing Test (40 minutes)

The ACT contains an "optional" writing test featuring a single essay. Be sure to check whether the colleges you'll be applying to will require this, as the last thing you want is to be forced into taking the whole ACT over again, this time with the Writing test. The essay requires that you consider a socially relevant prompt and three perspectives on that prompt. The essay is scored by two graders who will each assign a score of 1–6 for a total score of 2–12. This score will NOT factor into your Composite score.

If you are unsure about any of the sections or if you want more strategies for conquering these kinds of questions, you can find more information at PrincetonReview.com or you can review our *Cracking the ACT* book. One thing to definitely keep in mind is that the ACT is a multiple-choice test that does not penalize wrong answers, so don't leave any questions blank!

What you should also know is that the key to raising your ACT score does not lie in memorizing dozens of math theorems, the periodic table of elements, or obscure rules of English grammar. There's more to mastering this test than just improving math, verbal, and science skills. At its root, the ACT measures academic achievement. It doesn't pretend to measure your analytic ability or your intelligence. The people at ACT admit that you can increase your score by preparing for the test, and by spending just a little extra time preparing for the ACT, you can substantially change your score on the ACT (and the way colleges look at your applications). After all, out of all the elements in your application "package," your ACT score is the easiest to change.

That being said, we have included in this book two complete practice ACT exams. Rest assured that these tests and questions are modeled closely on actual ACT exams and questions, with the proper balance of questions reflective of what the ACT actually tests. You'll also find scoring tables after each test—although the curve varies from test to test, this information should help to give you a rough approximation of your score.

A final thought before you begin: The ACT does not predict your ultimate success or failure as a human being. No matter how high or how low you score on this test initially, and no matter how much you may increase your score through preparation, you should never consider the score you receive on this or any other test a final judgment of your abilities. When it's all said and done, we know you'll get into a great school and that you'll have an incredible experience there.

The Princeton Review

Chapter 2
Test 1

Please turn to page 65 to find the bubble sheet for this test.

ENGLISH TEST
45 Minutes—75 Questions

DIRECTIONS: In the five passages that follow, certain words and phrases are underlined and numbered. In the right-hand column, you will find alternatives for each underlined part. In most cases, you are to choose the one that best expresses the idea, makes the statement appropriate for standard written English, or is worded most consistently with the style and tone of the passage as a whole. If you think the original version is best, choose "NO CHANGE." In some cases, you will find in the right-hand column a question about the underlined part. You are to choose the best answer to the question.

You will also find questions about a section of the passage or the passage as a whole. These questions do not refer to an underlined portion of the passage but rather are identified by a number or numbers in a box.

For each question, choose the alternative you consider best and blacken the corresponding oval on your answer document. Read each passage through once before you begin to answer the questions that accompany it. For many of the questions, you must read several sentences beyond the question to determine the answer. Be sure that you have read far enough ahead each time you choose an alternative.

Passage I

The Record

The moment I had been anticipating finally came on a seemingly routine Monday. I arrived home to find a flat package; left by the delivery man casually leaning against the front screen door. Reading the words *Caution! Do not bend!*

scrawled on the top of the box, I immediately recognized my uncle's sloppy handwriting. I quickly ushered the box

inside, and my heart skipping a beat (or two). I knew what the box contained but still felt as anxious as a child on Christmas morning. Could this *really* be the old vinyl record?

My hands trembled as I opened the box, of which I was thrilled to see that it did indeed contain the record I had been seeking for years. To an outsider, this dusty disc with its faded hand-written label would seem inconsequential. To others, on the other hand, it was worth something far greater. The record was a compilation from the greatest musician I had ever known—my grandfather.

1. A. NO CHANGE
    B. package, left by the delivery man
    C. package; left by the delivery man,
    D. package, left by the delivery man,

2. F. NO CHANGE
    G. were scrawled on
    H. scrawl on
    J. scrawled

3. A. NO CHANGE
    B. inside,
    C. inside and
    D. inside, when

4. F. NO CHANGE
    G. box that
    H. box, and
    J. box

5. Given that all the choices are true, which one would most effectively illustrate the difference between outsiders' perception of the record and its actual significance to the writer's family?
    A. NO CHANGE
    B. In fact, the recording was not heard by many people outside my family.
    C. To my family, however, it was a precious heirloom.
    D. The disc would be in better condition had my uncle stored it in a sleeve.

GO ON TO THE NEXT PAGE.

Several years before he married my grandmother,

Papa <u>would make</u> his living as a folk singer in a
   6

band. <u>Performing</u> in music halls and local festivals. He recorded
    7

a single <u>album produced by Great Sounds Records</u> before
       8
giving up his professional music career to pursue business. This

record was all that remained of his life's passion—<u>in fact,</u> there
                              9

<u>had been</u> only one surviving copy since Papa's death 10 years
 10

earlier. It took many years of <u>begging and pleading</u> to convince
                 11
my uncle to pass the record down to me.

   I brought out my old record player from the attic and

gently placed the disc on the turntable. As soft, twanging notes

filled the room, I was transported to my grandfather's cabin,

<u>located at the foot of the mountains.</u> My cousins and I would
            12
gather around the campfire every night to roast marshmallows,

cook hotdogs, and listen to my grandfather's old stories.

<u>Of the many familiar favorites, Papa would pick up his guitar</u>
                            13
<u>and play all of our familiar tunes.</u>
          13

   When the record started playing one of my favorite songs, I

struggled to hold back my tears. It was a bittersweet reminder of

6. **F.** NO CHANGE
    G. would have made
    H. would have been making
    J. had made

7. **A.** NO CHANGE
    B. band; performing
    C. band, which he had performed
    D. band, performing

8. **F.** NO CHANGE
    G. album, produced by Great Sounds Records,
    H. Great Sounds Records album
    J. album

9. **A.** NO CHANGE
    B. even so,
    C. since,
    D. for example,

10. **F.** NO CHANGE
    G. had been about
    H. is
    J. was to be

11. **A.** NO CHANGE
    B. begging
    C. pleadingly begging
    D. begging the plea

12. At this point in the essay, the writer wants to suggest the significance of his grandfather's cabin to the writer's upbringing. Given that all the choices are true, which one would best accomplish that purpose?

    F. NO CHANGE
    G. where I had spent many childhood summers.
    H. which I still remembered well.
    J. a family property for many generations.

13. **A.** NO CHANGE
    B. Playing all of our favorite songs, the many familiar tunes and guitar would be picked up by Papa.
    C. Papa would also pick up his guitar and strum familiar tunes, playing all of our favorite songs, of which there were many.
    D. Picking up his guitar, Papa would also play strumming familiar tunes all of our favorite, of which there were many, songs.

GO ON TO THE NEXT PAGE.

the man I loved and <u>missed,</u> Papa's gentle voice on the record,
₁₄

14. **F.** NO CHANGE
    G. missed for
    H. missed.
    J. missed

however, assured <u>me,</u> that he was still with me, both in spirit
₁₅
and in song.

15. **A.** NO CHANGE
    B. me
    C. me—
    D. me;

Road Trips Back Home

During my junior year of college, it became a kind of ritual
for a group of us to hop in a car and "discover" a new suburb
every month. At first, we all agreed, we had come to college in
this major city to escape what we thought were our boring lives
in our various places of origin, but after a time, we realized that
it would be impossible for us to turn our backs on our old <u>lives</u>
₁₆
completely. <u>I grew up in Pennsylvania, many parts of which</u>
₁₇
<u>look like the ones we drove to.</u>
₁₇

16. **F.** NO CHANGE
    G. lives,
    H. live's
    J. lives'

17. Given that all the choices are true, which one best supports
    the point that the narrator and his friends all shared a com-
    mon background?

    A. NO CHANGE
    B. Many suburbs have become as populous as the cities
    they surround.
    C. The first major migration of families from the city to
    the suburbs occurred in the late 1940s and early 1950s.
    D. Our hometowns were all over the map, but they all
    shared a palpable likeness.

The first stop was typically some old diner, which
reminded each of us of one from our various hometowns. There

we'd usually sit, chat with the restaurant's <u>owners</u> drink a cup
₁₈
of coffee, and figure out which new and exciting place we'd
be driving to next. Even now I can remember one diner in
Maryland, whose sign we could see flickering from the highway
as we turned off <u>looking forward to it in anticipation.</u> Although
₁₉
we had all agreed that it had to be a new town each time, we

18. **F.** NO CHANGE
    G. owners;
    H. owners'
    J. owners,

19. **A.** NO CHANGE
    B. in anticipation.
    C. excited and looking forward to it.
    D. in anticipation and expectation.

GO ON TO THE NEXT PAGE.

tacitly agreed a few times to break the rules and come back to this place. ⬚20

After we had taken nourishment (usually a grilled cheese sandwich, a patty melt, or something similarly nutritious that could be ordered from the menu) for our "big night out," we would then drive on. We got to know the lay of the land so well that we could usually just follow our noses to the kinds of places we liked to visit in these towns, typically stopping by the biggest retailer we could find. There we'd buy industrial-sized packs from childhood of instant noodles, huge packs of soda, and other types of foods we all remembered but which we were either too embarrassed to buy in front of other people at the University market, or which were too expensive in the city, where there is a lot more variety.

Going to as many places like this as we could, we were always sure to happen upon something strangely familiar to us. The place—whether it was one of a million grocery stores, movie theaters, or fast-food restaurants—were unimportant; it seemed that everywhere had something special for at least one of us,

20. At this point, the writer is considering adding the following true statement:

   Many diners have been forced to shut down to make way for larger, national chain restaurants.

   Should the writer make the addition here?

   F. Yes, because it provides important contextual information relevant to the passage.
   G. Yes, because it helps readers to see why the narrator was drawn to this particular diner.
   H. No, because it interrupts the flow of the paragraph, which is primarily a personal reflection.
   J. No, because it alters the focus of the paragraph from a discussion of driving to a discussion of specific places.

21. A. NO CHANGE
    B. whom could be ordered from
    C. whom could order
    D. that were ordering

22. The best placement for the underlined phrase would be:

    F. where it is now.
    G. after the word *noodles.*
    H. after the word *soda.*
    J. after the word *remembered.*

23. Which choice most effectively supports and elaborates on the description in an earlier part of this sentence?

    A. NO CHANGE
    B. where prices for such basic foods were steep.
    C. where we didn't like to drive the car.
    D. where most of us had only small refrigerators.

24. Which of the following alternatives to the underlined portion would NOT be acceptable?

    F. As we went
    G. While going
    H. While we went
    J. We went

25. A. NO CHANGE
    B. was
    C. have been
    D. are

GO ON TO THE NEXT PAGE.

and even now, many years on, I still think of these trips fondly.
²⁶

Looking back, I'm still not sure why we took these trips.

Nevertheless, I have been living in an urban environment
²⁷
now for almost eight years, and should I ever have to move

back to the suburbs, I will certainly go reluctantly. Sometimes,

though, even now that I live in a different city, I'll still sneak

out to those kinds of places once in a while and just drive

about the town. I guess, in a way, many of those early memories
²⁸
are like that diner sign we could see from the highway; most

people would never notice that old sign, but to those of us who

cherish it in our hearts, we all harbored a great hope that it
²⁹
would still be burning the same as we remembered every time

we drove by or came back.
³⁰

26. Given that all the choices are true, which one most ef-
    fectively signals the shift in focus that occurs when moving
    from this paragraph to the next?
    F. NO CHANGE
    G. we all remained friends until we graduated.
    H. I regret not having spent more time in the city when I
       had the chance.
    J. I haven't been back to any of those places since I
       graduated.

27. A. NO CHANGE
    B. Therefore,
    C. Nonetheless,
    D. DELETE the underlined portion.

28. Which of the following alternatives to the underlined por-
    tion would NOT be acceptable?
    F. among the town.
    G. about.
    H. around.
    J. around the town.

29. A. NO CHANGE
    B. have a great fondness for it
    C. have strong feelings of adoration for it
    D. cherish it

30. F. NO CHANGE
    G. we were coming back.
    H. were returning.
    J. there was a return by us.

GO ON TO THE NEXT PAGE.

NO TEST MATERIAL ON THIS PAGE.

Passage III

> The following paragraphs may or may not be in the most logical order. Each paragraph is numbered in brackets, and question 45 will ask you to choose where Paragraph 3 should most logically be placed.

The Palio of Siena

[1]

Siena is an old, picturesque city located in the hills of Tuscany. <u>Even though</u> its inhabitants live modern lives, many
₃₁
historical markers from as far back as medieval Italy still

remain throughout the city. 32 Another remnant from Siena's rich history that still plays a very prominent role today is the tradition of *Il Palio*.

[2]

Il Palio di Siena is <u>a biannual horse race that is held</u>
₃₃
<u>twice a year,</u> once in July and once in August. A field of ten
₃₃
bareback horses races three laps around a dangerously steep track circling the city's central plaza, the *Piazza del Campo*, <u>each with two dreaded right-angle turns.</u> Even though *Il Palio*
₃₄

31. Which of the following alternatives to the underlined portion would be LEAST acceptable?

A. Although
B. While
C. Though
D. When

32. Which of the following true statements, if inserted here, would best connect the first part of Paragraph 1 with the last part while illustrating the main idea of this paragraph?

F. Like most Italian cities, Siena is very serious about soccer, a modern sport codified in England in the 1800s.
G. Cobblestone streets and Gothic architecture are blended with modern sidewalk cafes and trendy designer stores.
H. The city of Siena is certainly a mixture of ancient and contemporary practices.
J. Siena is a major cultural center that offers numerous examples of art and architecture by Renaissance masters.

33. A. NO CHANGE
B. a biannual race that is held two times a year,
C. a horse race that is held twice a year,
D. a biannual horse race, held

34. Assuming that a period will always be placed at the end of the sentence, the best placement for the underlined phrase would be:

F. where it is now.
G. after the words *horses races* (setting the phrase off with commas).
H. after the word *laps* (setting the phrase off with commas).
J. after the word *plaza* (setting the phrase off with commas).

GO ON TO THE NEXT PAGE.

lasted only about 90 seconds, its importance in Siena goes far
beyond the race itself.

[3]

Members are fiercely committed emotionally, socially,
and financially to their own *contrada*. Because the members
voluntarily tax themselves to support their own *contrada* and to
invest in a good horse and jockey for the biannual race. Jockey
salaries for a single race often exceed 250,000 euros! This
is, however, a small price to pay to achieve victory at *Il Palio*.
Seeing the colors and arms of their *contrada* in the winner's
circle is the most glorious event—even more so than getting

married for many Sienese citizens. Old men weep openly out of

sheer joy, and elated adults and children parade. Throughout the
city with their newly won silk banner, also called the *palio*.

[4]

The brief race is a spectacular culmination of an entire way
of life in Siena. Every citizen belongs to one of seventeen city
districts, collectively known as the *Contrade*. *Contrada* is the
term for a single district that has its own color and arms, such
as the *Aquila* (the eagle) or *Bruco* (the caterpillar). A *contrada*
is the source of so much local patriotism that every important
event; from baptisms to food festivals, is celebrated only within

one's own *contrada* and fellow members, who become more
like family.

[5]

After the actual race day, the *Palio* festivities continue for a
minimum of two weeks. Thousands of visitors from around the

---

35. A. NO CHANGE
   B. will last
   C. lasts
   D. had lasted

36. F. NO CHANGE
   G. Though they
   H. In addition, they
   J. They

37. A. NO CHANGE
   B. moreover,
   C. for instance,
   D. therefore,

38. F. NO CHANGE
   G. married—for
   H. married, for
   J. married; for

39. A. NO CHANGE
   B. parade; throughout
   C. parade throughout
   D. parade throughout,

40. F. NO CHANGE
   G. *Contrade*
   H. *Contrade,*
   J. *Contrade* yet

41. A. NO CHANGE
   B. event, from
   C. event: from
   D. event—from

42. F. NO CHANGE
   G. for whose
   H. whose
   J. whom

GO ON TO THE NEXT PAGE.

world travel to Siena during the summer; not only to witness
                                    _____
                                         43

the exciting race but also to attend the after-parties were thrown
                                                         _____
                                                              44
by the locals. While the *Palio* is not as important to outsiders
who do not live in Siena as it is to the Sienese, the race and the
festivities that follow are a spectacular experience.

43. A. NO CHANGE
    B. summer. Not
    C. summer not
    D. summer, not

44. F. NO CHANGE
    G. thrown
    H. were threw
    J. threw

> Question 45 asks about the preceding passage as a whole.

45. For the sake of the logic and coherence of this essay, the best placement for Paragraph 3 would be:

    A. where it is now.
    B. before Paragraph 1.
    C. before Paragraph 2.
    D. before Paragraph 5.

Passage IV

> The following paragraphs may or may not be in the most logical order. Each paragraph is numbered in brackets, and question 59 will ask you to choose where Paragraph 2 should most logically be placed.

Sherwood Anderson the Pioneer

[1]

Sherwood Anderson saw his first novel, *Windy McPherson's Son*, published in 1916, but it was not until 1919 with the publication of his masterpiece *Winesburg, Ohio* that Anderson was pushed to the forefront of it in American
                                                    __
                                                    46
literature. The latter book, something between a short-story

collection and a novel, helping to inaugurate an age of a truly
                        _____
                           47
homespun American Modernism.

46. F. NO CHANGE
    G. this
    H. a new movement
    J. a thing

47. A. NO CHANGE
    B. which helped
    C. helped
    D. was helped

GO ON TO THE NEXT PAGE.

[2]

As other writers began to supplant him in the popular
imagination, Anderson tireless continued his literary
₄₈
experimentation until his death in 1941. In the contemporary

48. The best placement for the underlined word would be:
F. where it is now.
G. before the word *death*.
H. after the word *experimentation*.
J. before the word *literary*.

popular imagination, Anderson's influence often appears to be
diminishing. But it takes only a few pages of *Winesburg, Ohio*
₄₉
or many of his other short stories, articles, and novels to see
that Anderson is still very much with us today and that much
of what we understand about ourselves as Americans was made
clear to us only by the pen of the advertising man from Ohio.

49. Which of the following alternatives to the underlined portion would NOT be acceptable?
A. can seem to be
B. appeared to be
C. seems to be
D. can appear to be

[3]

Sherwood Anderson would be seen by a new generation
of American writers as the first author to take a real step until
₅₀
creating a type of literature that was in tune with something
previously only associated with Europe. Anderson was able to

50. F. NO CHANGE
G. at
H. toward
J. DELETE the underlined portion.

fuse his sense of the passing of the Industrial Age in America
₅₁
with a type of uniquely American expression that sought
to replace previous literary conventions with more local
expressions of fragmentation and alienation.

51. A. NO CHANGE
B. fuse;
C. fuse:
D. fuse,

[4]

With *Winesburg, Ohio*, Anderson inspired a younger group
₅₂
of writers, among whose ranks were Ernest Hemingway and
William Faulkner, to embrace their American experiences and
to express them in ways separate from those being expressed by

52. Which of the following alternatives to the underlined portion would be LEAST acceptable?
F. encouraged
G. motivated
H. forced
J. emboldened

European writers or American expatriates, as American writers
living abroad were known. When *Winesburg, Ohio* finally
₅₃

53. A. NO CHANGE
B. expatriates, as American writers living abroad, were known.
C. expatriates as American writers living abroad were known.
D. expatriates as American writers living abroad, were known.

GO ON TO THE NEXT PAGE.

appeared in 1919, its general reception was <u>positive, but limited</u>
₅₄

to those who were able to find copies of the book. <u>Anderson's</u>
₅₅
<u>later books, such as *Dark Laughter*, would go on to sell many</u>
₅₅
<u>more copies.</u>
₅₅

[5]

In the 1920s, Anderson wrote some direct responses to the
more explicit examples of literary Modernism in Europe. In

the 1930s, Anderson wrote *Beyond Desire* [56] But Anderson's
most important contributions in the 1920s and 1930s are best

felt indirectly through the works <u>of the various writers</u> he
₅₇
inspired. Anderson was among the first to explore the troubled
relationship between the city and the rural town, the direct

style to which we so often apply the <u>name, "American,"</u> and
₅₈
the idea that deeply intellectual concerns can be relevant to
everyday people as much as they can to academics. Even
today, Anderson's initial treatment of these themes remains
an important starting point for anyone interested in
American culture.

54. F. NO CHANGE
G. positive but limited,
H. positive; but limited
J. positive but limited

55. Given that all the choices are true, which one best supports
the point that although Anderson's book was difficult to
find, those who read it were very impressed?
A. NO CHANGE
B. Many critics still preferred the older European models
of writing.
C. *Winesburg, Ohio* remains one of Anderson's best-loved
books.
D. Those who did secure a copy of *Winesburg, Ohio* felt
that it inaugurated a new age in American literature.

56. Given that all the following are true, which one, if added
here, would provide the clearest and most effective indication that Anderson was doing things that had not been
done before in American literature?
F. , which addressed social questions that only social
scientists and propagandists dared touch.
G. , which was heavily influenced by the literature of the
Southern Populist movement.
H. , which has been named by many literary critics as a
highlight from Anderson's later work.
J. , which was not as highly revered as *Winesburg, Ohio.*

57. The best placement for the underlined phrase would be:
A. where it is now.
B. after the word *contributions.*
C. after the word *1930s.*
D. after the word *inspired* (ending the sentence with a
period).

58. F. NO CHANGE
G. name "American,"
H. name "American"
J. name, "American"

GO ON TO THE NEXT PAGE.

Questions 59 and 60 ask about the preceding passage as a whole.

59. For the sake of the logic and coherence of this essay, Paragraph 2 should be placed:

    A. where it is now.
    B. after Paragraph 3.
    C. after Paragraph 4.
    D. after Paragraph 5.

60. Suppose the writer's goal was to draft an essay that would show the influence of one American author on the work of future authors. Does this essay successfully accomplish this goal?

    F. Yes, because it describes an interesting group of authors and focuses on the literature of a particular country.
    G. Yes, because it gives a brief description of Sherwood Anderson's writing career and discusses his influence on writers whom his work inspired.
    H. No, because it limits the focus to the contrasts between American writing and European writing.
    J. No, because it refers only to events that took place in the twenties and thirties.

GO ON TO THE NEXT PAGE.

Passage V

Women at Work

World War II offered numerous employment opportunities for women in the United States. As the men headed to the war front, the work force <u>retracted and diminished</u> on the
₆₁

home front, and women <u>begun</u> to take over responsibilities
₆₂

traditionally assigned to men. <u>These</u> responsibilities included
₆₃
work previously deemed inappropriate for women.

The government realized that participation in the war <u>but</u>
₆₄
required the use of all national resources. American industrial facilities were turned into war production factories, and the government targeted the female population as an essential source of labor. Women worked in factories and shipyards as riveters, welders, and <u>machinists making</u> everything from
₆₅
uniforms to munitions to airplanes, they directly contributed

to the war effort. The number of women in the <u>workforce</u>
₆₆
increased from 12 million in 1940 to 18 million in 1944. By 1945, 36% of the laborers were women.

The increased presence of women in wartime workforces <u>were</u>
₆₇

61. A. NO CHANGE
B. retracted diminishingly
C. diminished
D. DELETE the underlined portion.

62. F. NO CHANGE
G. has began
H. would of begun
J. began

63. A. NO CHANGE
B. The traditionally male
C. Which
D. That

64. F. NO CHANGE
G. and it
H. although it
J. DELETE the underlined portion.

65. A. NO CHANGE
B. machinists, making
C. machinists. Making
D. machinists, who made

66. F. NO CHANGE
G. workforce, for example in factories and shipyards,
H. workforce, such as factories and shipyards,
J. factory and shipyard workforce

67. A. NO CHANGE
B. are
C. was
D. have been

GO ON TO THE NEXT PAGE.

not limited to factories and shipyards. [68] Thousands moved to Washington D.C. to fill government jobs exclusively held by men before the war. Some women engaged in farm labor, and others joined the military as field nurses. The shortage of men

also led to openings in non-traditional fields, such as day-care. Since many players had been drafted into the armed services, Major League Baseball parks around the country were on the verge of collapse when a group of Midwestern businessmen devised a brilliant solution to the player shortage.

The All-American Girls Professional Baseball League was created in 1943 and offered a unique blend of baseball and softball suitable for female players. Founder, Philip K. Wrigley and League president, Ken Sells promoted the new league with aggressive advertising campaigns that promoted the physical attractiveness of female athletes. Photographs displayed women players with pretty smiles on their faces and baseball mitts in their hands. Their silk shorts, fashionable knee-high socks,

68. At this point, the writer is considering adding the following true statement:

> The marriage rate increased significantly during the war, as did the rate of babies born to unmarried women.

Should the writer add this sentence here?

F. No, because it does not echo the style and tone that has already been established in the essay.
G. No, because it is not relevant to the essay's focus on the changing roles of women during World War II.
H. Yes, because it contributes to the essay's focus on women's roles in the home during World War II.
J. Yes, because it provides a contrast between women in the home and women in the workplace.

69. Given that all the choices are true, which one provides the most logical transition to the information presented in the rest of this essay?

A. NO CHANGE
B. the most notable of which was baseball.
C. which many women had to give up after the war.
D. shaking American society to the core.

70. **F.** NO CHANGE
G. Founder Philip K. Wrigley and League president
H. Founder Philip K. Wrigley, and, League president
J. Founder, Philip K. Wrigley, and League president,

71. Given that all the choices are true, which one most effectively helps the writer's purpose of helping readers visualize the players in the photographs?

A. NO CHANGE
B. at the plate during a live game.
C. clearly focused on playing well.
D. showing close camaraderie.

GO ON TO THE NEXT PAGE.

red lipstick, <u>having</u> flowing hair directly contrasted with the
72

competitive, masculine nature of the game. [73] These

photographs are indicative of the delicate balance between

feminine appeal and masculine labor that was expected

of all women throughout World War II. Although

its' success lasted only a decade, the All-American Girls
74

Professional Baseball League's role in expanding opportunities

for women during World War II and thereafter is everlasting. [75]

72. F. NO CHANGE
  G. their
  H. with
  J. and

73. If the writer were to delete the words *silk*, *fashionable*, and
  red from the preceding sentence, it would primarily lose:
  A. details that have already been presented in the vivid
    imagery of the previous sentence.
  B. a digression from the focus of this paragraph on the
    athletic talent of the players.
  C. description of what was written in the captions accompanying the photographs.
  D. details that highlight the femininity of the players in
    contrast to the masculinity of the game.

74. F. NO CHANGE
  G. it's
  H. their
  J. its

> Question 75 asks about the preceding passage as a
> whole.

75. Suppose the writer's goal was to write an essay that would
  illustrate the range of non-traditional activities women pursued during wartime. Does this essay achieve that goal?
  A. Yes, because it explains the impact of the
    All-American Girls Professional Baseball Team
    on public perception of women.
  B. Yes, because it gives several examples of women performing jobs during World War II that were typically
    filled by men.
  C. No, because it limits its focus to the type of work
    women engaged in during World War II.
  D. No, because it explains that women's importance
    in the workforce, especially in baseball, lasted only
    several years.

END OF TEST 1
STOP! DO NOT TURN THE PAGE UNTIL TOLD TO DO SO.

NO TEST MATERIAL ON THIS PAGE.

MATHEMATICS TEST

60 Minutes—60 Questions

DIRECTIONS: Solve each problem, choose the correct answer, and then darken the corresponding oval on your answer document.

Do not linger over problems that take too much time. Solve as many as you can; then return to the others in the time you have left for this test.

You are permitted to use a calculator on this test. You may use your calculator for any problems you choose, but some of the problems may best be done without using a calculator.

Note: Unless otherwise stated, all of the following should be assumed:

1. Illustrative figures are NOT necessarily drawn to scale.
2. Geometric figures lie in a plane.
3. The word *line* indicates a straight line.
4. The word *average* indicates arithmetic mean.

---

1. In the hiking trail shown below, X marks the trail's halfway point. If $\overline{YZ}$ measures 24 kilometers and is $\frac{1}{3}$ the length of $\overline{XZ}$, what is the total length, in kilometers, of the trail?

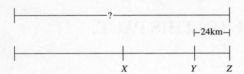

A. 144
B. 104
C. 96
D. 72
E. 48

DO YOUR FIGURING HERE.

2. What is the value of x when $\frac{4x}{5} + 7 = 6$?

F. $\frac{5}{4}$

G. $-\frac{4}{5}$

H. -1

J. $-\frac{5}{4}$

K. -5

GO ON TO THE NEXT PAGE.

3. Cyclist A averages 80 pedal revolutions per minute, and Cyclist B averages 61 pedal revolutions per minute. At these rates, how many more minutes does Cyclist B need than Cyclist A to make 9,760 pedal revolutions?

A. 19
B. 38
C. 122
D. 141
E. 160

4. The perimeter of a square is 36 inches. What is the area of the square, in square inches?

F. 6
G. 9
H. 18
J. 36
K. 81

5. For the rectangle shown in the standard (x,y) coordinate plane below, what are the coordinates of the unlabeled vertex?

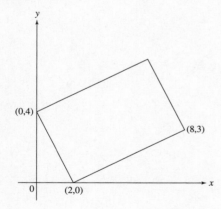

A. (4,5)

B. (4,7)

C. $\left(5, \frac{7}{2}\right)$

D. (6,7)

E. (10,4)

DO YOUR FIGURING HERE.

GO ON TO THE NEXT PAGE.

6. Carla has 5 times as many notebooks as her brother does. If they have 42 notebooks between them, how many notebooks does Carla have?

   F. 30
   G. 33
   H. 35
   J. 37
   K. 47

DO YOUR FIGURING HERE.

7. If G is in the interior of right angle $\angle DEF$, then which of the following could be the measure of $\angle GEF$?

   A.   85°
   B.   95°
   C. 105°
   D. 115°
   E. 125°

8. Susie has three T-shirts: one red, one blue, and one black. She also has three pairs of shorts: one red, one blue, and one black. How many different combinations are there for Susie to wear exactly one T-shirt and one pair of shorts?

   F.   3
   G.   6
   H.   8
   J.   9
   K. 27

9. 20% of 20 is equal to 50% of what number?

   A.   2
   B.   4
   C.   8
   D.   10
   E. 200

10. There are 45 musicians in an orchestra, and all play two instruments. Of these musicians, 36 play the piano, and 22 play the violin. What is the maximum possible number of orchestra members who play both the piano and the violin?

   F.   9
   G. 13
   H. 22
   J. 23
   K. 36

GO ON TO THE NEXT PAGE.

11. What is the largest value of m for which there exists a real value of n such that $m^2 = 196 - n^2$?

A. 14
B. 98
C. 182
D. 196
E. 392

DO YOUR FIGURING HERE.

12. Phil earned $800 at his summer job and saved all of his earnings. He wants to buy a deluxe drum kit that is regularly priced at $925 but is on sale for $\frac{1}{5}$ off. The drum kit is subject to 5% sales tax after all discounts are applied. If Phil buys the kit on sale and gives the sales clerk his entire summer earnings, how much change should he receive?

F. $23
G. $37
H. $40
J. $77
K. None; Phil still owes $171.25.

13. Which of the following numbers is an imaginary number?

A. $\sqrt{64}$

B. $\sqrt{11}$

C. $-\dfrac{4}{\sqrt{3}}$

D. $-\sqrt{-64}$

E. $-\sqrt{64}$

14. Which of the following correctly factors the expression $25x^4 - 16y^8$?

F. $(25 - 16)(x^2 - y^4)(x^2 + y^4)$
G. $(5x^2 - 4y^4)(5x^2 + 4y^4)$
H. $(25x^2 - y^4)(x^2 + 16y^4)$
J. $(5x^4 - 4y^8)(5x^4 + 4y^8)$
K. $(5x^4 - 8y^8)(5x^4 + 2y^8)$

GO ON TO THE NEXT PAGE.

15. The figure below shows a portion of a tile floor from which the shaded polygon will be cut in order to make a repair. Each square tile has sides that measure 1 foot. Every vertex of the shaded polygon is at the intersection of 2 tiles. What is the area, in square feet, of the shaded polygon?

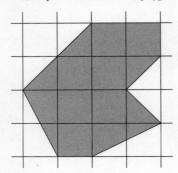

A. 9.5
B. 10.0
C. 10.5
D. 11.0
E. 11.5

16. The percent P of a population that has completed 4 years of college is given by the function $P(t) = -0.001t^2 + 0.4t$, where t represents time, in years. What percent of the population has completed four years of college after 20 years, to the nearest tenth?
F. 0.1
G. 7.6
H. 8.0
J. 8.4
K. 160.0

17. At Fatima's Fruits, a bag of eight grapefruits costs $4.40. At Ernie's Edibles, a bag of three grapefruits costs $1.86. How much cheaper, per grapefruit, is the cost at Fatima's Fruits than at Ernie's Edibles?
A. $0.07
B. $0.35
C. $0.59
D. $1.17
E. $2.54

18. Which of the following is equivalent to $(x^4 - 4)(x^4 + 4)$?
F. $2x^4$
G. $x^8 - 16$
H. $x^8 + 16$
J. $x^{16} - 16$
K. $x^8 - 8x^4 - 16$

DO YOUR FIGURING HERE.

GO ON TO THE NEXT PAGE.

19. Wade is making a tile mosaic. He begins the project by laying tile at a speed of 50 pieces per hour for 3.5 hours. He is then interrupted from his work for 60 minutes. He resumes working and lays tile at a speed of 35 pieces per hour, until he has laid 280 pieces of tile total. How many hours did Wade spend working on the mosaic after he started working again?

   A. 2.5
   B. 3
   C. 3.5
   D. 4
   E. 4.5

DO YOUR FIGURING HERE.

20. Point C (1,2) and point D (7,−10) lie in the standard coordinate plane. What are the coordinates of the midpoint of $\overline{CD}$?

   F. (1, 8)
   G. (3,−6)
   H. (4,−4)
   J. (4,−6)
   K. (7,−4)

21. Michael is planning to put fencing along the edge of his rectangular backyard, which is 22 yards by 16 yards. One long side of the backyard is along his house, so he will need to fence only 3 sides. How many yards of fencing will Michael need?

   A. 38
   B. 54
   C. 60
   D. 76
   E. 352

22. What is the y-intercept of the line given by the equation $7x - 3y = 21$?

   F. −7

   G. $-\dfrac{7}{3}$

   H. $\dfrac{7}{3}$

   J. 7

   K. 21

GO ON TO THE NEXT PAGE.

DO YOUR FIGURING HERE.

23. On April 8th, a flower at Blooming Acres Florist was 15.0 centimeters tall. On April 16th, the flower was 17.4 centimeters tall. If the flower grew at a constant rate, on what day was the flower 16.5 centimeters tall?

    A. April 11th
    B. April 12th
    C. April 13th
    D. April 14th
    E. April 15th

24. Which of the following expressions is equivalent to the expression given below?

    $(2x^3 - x - 1) - 3(x^4 + 2x^3 - 2x^2 - x + 3)$

    F. $x^{14} - 3$
    G. $-3x^{14}$
    H. $-3x^4 + 8x^3 - 6x^2 - 4x + 8$
    J. $-3x^4 + 4x^3 - 2x^2 - 2x - 3$
    K. $-3x^4 - 4x^3 + 6x^2 + 2x - 10$

25. The playground equipment shown below has a ladder that is 6 feet tall and a diagonal slide that is 7 feet long. If the ladder makes a right angle with the ground, approximately how many feet is the base of the slide from the base of the ladder?

    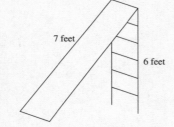

    7 feet   6 feet

    A. 2
    B. 4
    C. 6
    D. 8
    E. 10

26. In a data set of 5 points, the mean, median, and mode are each equal to 8. Which of the following could be the data set?

    F. {5, 7, 8, 8, 12}
    G. {7, 7, 8, 8, 12}
    H. {7, 8, 8, 8, 12}
    J. {7, 8, 8, 10, 12}
    K. {7, 8, 8, 12, 12}

GO ON TO THE NEXT PAGE.

DO YOUR FIGURING HERE.

27. In a certain sequence of numbers, each term after the 1st term is the result of adding 2 to the previous term and multiplying that sum by 3. If the 4th term in the sequence is 186, what is the 2nd term?

    A.   2
    B.   4
    C.   18
    D.   60
    E.   174

28. Which of the following values of x does NOT satisfy the inequality $|x - 3| \geq 12$?

    F.   −15
    G.   −12
    H.   −9
    J.   9
    K.   15

29. For all real numbers s, t, u, and v, such that $s + t + u = 29$ and $s < v$, which of the following statements is true?

    A. $s + t + v < 29$
    B. $t + u + v > 29$
    C. $s + t + v = 29$
    D. $s + u + v = 29$
    E. $s + t + v > 29$

30. In the figure below, rectangle $ABCD$ shares $\overline{CD}$ with $\triangle CDE$, diagonal $\overline{BD}$ of the rectangle extends in a straight line beyond D to E to create $\overline{DE}$, and the measure of $\angle CDE$ is 155°. What is the measure of $\angle CBD$?

    F.   25
    G.   55
    H.   65
    J.   90
    K.   155

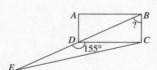

31. If a, b, and c are positive prime numbers, in the equation $a - b = c$, either b or c must represent which number?

    A.   13
    B.   11
    C.   7
    D.   5
    E.   2

GO ON TO THE NEXT PAGE.

32. Pierre competes in a triathlon, along a course as shown in the figure below. He begins swimming at starting point S and swims straight across the lake, gets on his bicycle at station A, bikes to station B, and then runs to finishing line F. The judges use a stopwatch to record his elapsed times of t_A, t_B, and t_F hours from point S to points A, B, and F, respectively. If the distance, in miles, between points S and A along the racecourse is denoted by SA, then what is Pierre's average speed for this race, in miles per hour?

DO YOUR FIGURING HERE.

F. $\dfrac{SA}{t_A}$

G. $\dfrac{SB}{t_B}$

H. $\dfrac{SF}{t_F}$

J. $\dfrac{SA}{t_F}$

K. $\dfrac{SF}{t_A}$

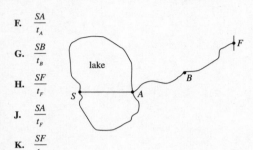

33. The triangle shown below has a hypotenuse with a length of 13 feet. The measure of $\angle A$ is 20° and the measure of $\angle B$ is 70°. Which of the following is closest to the length, in feet, of $\overline{BC}$?

(Note: sin 70° ≈ 0.9397
        cos 70° ≈ 0.3420
        tan 70° ≈ 2.747)

A. 4.4
B. 5.0
C. 12.0
D. 12.2
E. 35.7

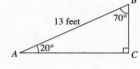

34. What is the value of $\dfrac{8}{y^2} - \dfrac{x^2}{y}$ when $x = -3$ and $y = -4$?

F. $-\dfrac{11}{4}$

G. $-\dfrac{7}{4}$

H. $\dfrac{7}{4}$

J. $\dfrac{11}{4}$

K. $\dfrac{56}{9}$

GO ON TO THE NEXT PAGE.

35. As shown in the figure below, with angles as marked, a ramp is being designed that will have a vertical height of 4 feet. Which of the following is closest to the horizontal length of the ramp, in feet?

DO YOUR FIGURING HERE.

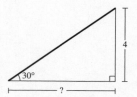

- **A.** 5
- **B.** 6
- **C.** 7
- **D.** 8
- **E.** 9

36. In the diagram below, $\triangle ABC$ is isosceles and $\triangle BCD$ is equilateral. $\overline{AB} = \overline{BC}$ and the measure of $\angle ABC$ is half the measure of $\angle BAC$. What is the measure of $\angle ABD$?

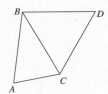

- **F.** 36°
- **G.** 60°
- **H.** 72°
- **J.** 96°
- **K.** 150°

GO ON TO THE NEXT PAGE.

Use the following information to answer questions 37–39.

DO YOUR FIGURING HERE.

The coordinates of the vertices of $\triangle MON$ are shown in the standard (x,y) coordinate plane below. Rectangle $MPQR$ is shown shaded. Point P lies on $\overline{MO}$, point Q lies on $\overline{ON}$, and point R lies on $\overline{MN}$.

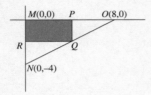

37. What is the slope of $\overline{ON}$?

   A. -2
   B. $-\dfrac{1}{2}$
   C. 0
   D. $\dfrac{1}{2}$
   E. 2

38. Which of the following is closest to the perimeter, in coordinate units, of $\triangle MON$?

   F.   12.0
   G.   16.9
   H.   18.0
   J.   20.9
   K.   92.0

39. What is the value of $\cos(\angle MNO)$?

   A. $\dfrac{4}{\sqrt{80}}$
   B. $\dfrac{8}{\sqrt{80}}$
   C. $\dfrac{1}{2}$
   D. 2
   E. $\dfrac{\sqrt{80}}{8}$

GO ON TO THE NEXT PAGE.

40. In a Spanish class there are m students, of which n did NOT pass the last exam. Which of the following is a general expression for the fraction of the class that did receive a passing grade?

F. $\dfrac{m-n}{m}$

G. $\dfrac{m}{n}$

H. $\dfrac{m-n}{n}$

J. $\dfrac{n-m}{n}$

K. $\dfrac{n-m}{m}$

DO YOUR FIGURING HERE.

41. The solution set of $5x + 9 \geq 2(3x + 4) + 7$ is shown by which of the following number line graphs?

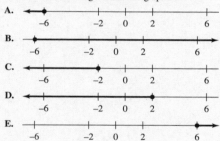

42. An artist wants to cover the entire outside of a rectangular box with mosaic tiles. The dimensions of the box shown below are given in centimeters. If each tile is exactly one square centimeter, and the artist lays the tiles with no space between them, how many tiles will he need?

F. 75
G. 96
H. 108
J. 126
K. 150

GO ON TO THE NEXT PAGE.

43. In the figure shown below, $\overline{BC}$ and $\overline{EF}$ are parallel and $\overline{AE} = \overline{FD}$. If $\angle ABC$ is 130° and $\angle BAE$ is 22°, what is the measure of $\angle AEF$?

- **A.** 50°
- **B.** 118°
- **C.** 152°
- **D.** 158°
- **E.** 164°

44. Given the figure below, what is the area of the trapezoid, in square inches?

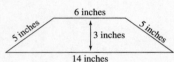

- **F.** 18
- **G.** 30
- **H.** 42
- **J.** 50
- **K.** 52

45. What is the solution set of $\sqrt[5]{x^2 + 4x} = 2$?

- **A.** {4}
- **B.** {8}
- **C.** {−4, 8}
- **D.** {−8, 4}
- **E.** {−2, ±2√2}

GO ON TO THE NEXT PAGE.

46. As shown in the figure below, a skateboard ramp leading from the top of a boulder is 10 feet long and forms a 32° angle with the level ground. Which of the following expressions represents the height, in feet, of the boulder?

DO YOUR FIGURING HERE.

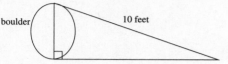

F. 10 tan 32°

G. $\dfrac{\sin 32°}{10}$

H. $\dfrac{10}{\cos 32°}$

J. 10 sin 32°

K. 10 cos 32°

47. The 4 integers j, j, k, and n have an average of 0. Which of the following equations *must* be true?

A. $k = n$
B. $k = -j$
C. $k + n = -2j$
D. $k + n = 0$
E. $k + n = j$

48. If $f(x) = \sqrt{x}$ and the composite function $f(g(x)) = \sqrt{4x^2 - 5}$, which of the following could be $g(x)$?

F. $\sqrt{4x^4 - 5}$

G. $\sqrt{16x^4 - 25}$

H. $2x^2 - 25$

J. $4x^2 - 5$

K. $16x^4 - 5$

GO ON TO THE NEXT PAGE.

Use the following information to answer questions 49–51.

In the qualifying rounds for a race, Rusty and Dale drive their cars around a 6,000-foot oval track. Rusty and Dale each drive 8 laps in the qualifying rounds in lanes of identical length.

49. On day one of the qualifying rounds, Rusty and Dale start from the same point, but their cars are reversed and each drives opposite ways. Rusty drives at a constant speed that is 8 feet per second faster than Dale's constant speed. Rusty passes Dale for the first time in 150 seconds. Rusty drives at a constant rate of how many feet per second?

   A. 16
   B. 20
   C. 24
   D. 32
   E. 40

50. On the second day of the qualifying rounds, Rusty averages 180 seconds per lap until he begins the last lap. He then goes into a lower gear. He averages 190 seconds per lap for this qualifying round. How many seconds does Rusty take to drive the final lap?

   F. 155
   G. 160
   H. 185
   J. 200
   K. 260

51. Dale drives 6 laps in 90 minutes. At what average rate, in feet per hour, does Dale drive these 6 laps?

   A.   400
   B.   5,400
   C. 10,000
   D. 24,000
   E. 48,000

52. Circle A has its center at point $(-5,2)$ with a radius of 2, and circle B is represented by the equation $(x + 4)^2 + (y - 2)^2 = 9$. Where is point $(-2,2)$ located?

   F. Inside circle A only
   G. Inside circle B only
   H. Inside both circle A and circle B
   J. Outside both circle A and circle B
   K. Cannot be determined from given information

GO ON TO THE NEXT PAGE.

53. A heart-shaped ornament is made from a square and two semicircles, each of whose diameter is a side of the square. The ornament is shown in the standard (x,y) coordinate plane below, where 1 coordinate unit represents 1 inch. The coordinates of six points on the border of the ornament are given. What is the perimeter, in inches, of the ornament?

DO YOUR FIGURING HERE.

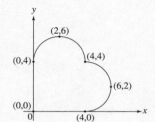

- **A.** $4 + 2\pi$
- **B.** $8 + 4\pi$
- **C.** $8 + 8\pi$
- **D.** $16 + 4\pi$
- **E.** $16 + 8\pi$

54. A function $f(x)$ is defined as even if and only if $f(x) = f(-x)$ for all real values of x. Which one of the following graphs represents an even function $f(x)$?

F.

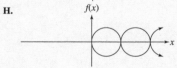

G.

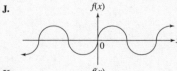

H.

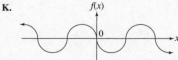

J.

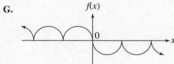

K.

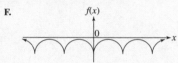

GO ON TO THE NEXT PAGE.

55. In the standard (x,y) coordinate plane, point A is located at $(w, w + 5)$ and point B is located at $(4w, w - 5)$. In coordinate units, what is the distance between A and B ?

A. $\sqrt{9w^2 + 2w + 10}$

B. $\sqrt{9w^2 + 100}$

C. $9w^2 + 100$

D. $|w|\sqrt{11}$

E. $|w|$

56. RST is a right triangle with side lengths of r, s, and t, as shown below. What is the value of $\cos^2 S + \cos^2 R$?

F. 1

G. $\sqrt{2}$

H. $\sqrt{3}$

J. $\dfrac{\sqrt{2}}{2}$

K. $\dfrac{1 + \sqrt{2}}{3}$

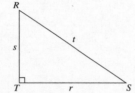

57. In isosceles triangle ABC below, the measures of $\angle BAC$ and $\angle BCA$ are equal and $\overline{DE} \parallel \overline{AC}$. The diagonals of trapezoid $DECA$ intersect at F. The lengths of $\overline{DF}$ and $\overline{EF}$ are 6 centimeters, the length of $\overline{DE}$ is 9 centimeters, and the length of $\overline{AC}$ is 27 centimeters. What is the length, in centimeters, of $\overline{FC}$?

A. 12
B. 15
C. 18
D. 33
E. 36

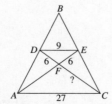

GO ON TO THE NEXT PAGE.

58. Which of the following represents the product of the matrices below?

$$\begin{bmatrix} 4 & -2 \\ 3 & -6 \end{bmatrix} \times \begin{bmatrix} 0 \\ 2 \end{bmatrix}$$

DO YOUR FIGURING HERE.

F. $\begin{bmatrix} -4 \\ -12 \end{bmatrix}$

G. $\begin{bmatrix} -12 \\ 0 \end{bmatrix}$

H. $\begin{bmatrix} -6 \end{bmatrix}$

J. $\begin{bmatrix} 6 & -12 \end{bmatrix}$

K. $\begin{bmatrix} -4 & -12 \end{bmatrix}$

59. If $\dfrac{(n+1)!}{(n-1)!} = 20$, then $n! = ?$

A. 6
B. 10
C. 12
D. 24
E. 120

60. What is the ratio of a circle's radius to its circumference?

F. $2\pi{:}1$
G. $2{:}1$
H. $\pi{:}1$
J. $1{:}\pi$
K. $1{:}2\pi$

END OF TEST 2
STOP! DO NOT TURN THE PAGE UNTIL TOLD TO DO SO.
DO NOT RETURN TO THE PREVIOUS TEST.

READING TEST
35 Minutes—40 Questions

DIRECTIONS: There are four passages in this test. Each passage is followed by several questions. After reading each passage, choose the best answer to each question and blacken the corresponding oval on your answer document. You may refer to the passages as often as necessary.

Passage I

PROSE FICTION: This passage is adapted from the short story "Ruby" by Tristan Ivory (©2007 by Tristan Ivory).

Ruby's Downhome Diner was an institution. If you only spent one night in Franklin, Texas, someone would inevitably direct you right off Highway 79 and Pink Oak Road to Ruby's Downhome Diner, Ruby's, or The Downhome; whatever
5 name the locals gave you, there was always something there that you would enjoy.

Ruby's was named after Ruby Sanders, my grandmother. She had opened the diner with money she saved from cleaning houses and with personal loans from friends. By the time
10 I was born, Ruby's did enough business to pay off all debts and obligations. It didn't take long before my grandmother was a person of considerable stature in and around Robertson County, just like the restaurant that bore her name.

Ever since I was knee-high, I spent each sweltering
15 summer with my grandmother. This, truth be told, meant that for all practical purposes I lived at Ruby's Downhome. Time familiarized me with all nuances in the diner: there were five steps and four ingredients that separated peach preserves from peach cobbler filling; Deputy Sheriff Walter Mayes
20 preferred his eggs, always cooked over-easy, to finish cooking on the top of his ham before it was transferred to his plate; Mr. Arnold delivered the milk and the buttermilk on Mondays, Thursdays, and Saturdays; and there were days when I would need to go to the general store to pick up whatever was in
25 short supply. By the time I entered high school, I could have run the diner from open to close if my Grandmother were absent, but she never was.

Perhaps the single greatest contributing factor to the success of Ruby's Diner was the omnipresent personality of
30 its namesake. Even the most hopelessly spun-around visitor who happened inside those doors would know who Ms. Ruby was. There were no sick days, vacations, or holidays. Between 5 A.M. and 9 P.M., you knew where Ruby Sanders could be found. If the diner were a sort of cell, then my grandmother was
35 its nucleus; without the nucleus, the cell would surely perish.

The people who worked at Ruby's were as dedicated as Ruby herself. There were the regulars: Del (short for Delmont) did double duty as a short-order cook and janitor,

while Marlene and Deborah waited tables. Extra help would
40 be hired from time to time depending on the season and individual need. No matter how long those extra helpers stayed, they and everyone else who worked at the Downhome were family, and no one ever fell out of touch.

Ruby's did the things you'd expect a diner to do, as
45 well as the things you wouldn't. You could stop in and get yourself a nice cool drink for the road. Or you could pull up a stool at the counter and grab a steaming hot bowl of red pepper chili with a slice of corn pone or a dish of chilled and creamy homemade ice cream. Or better still, you could
50 grab a booth and try any number of full-plate entrees made to order. But you could also order a wedding cake a week in advance, take a weekend course in food preparation, or, when the time came, have your wake catered with dignity and grace.

When I was very young, I would spend most of my time
55 exploring every inch of Ruby's until the entire layout was printed indelibly in my mind. I could walk blindfolded from the basement where the dry goods were kept, up to the kitchen with the walk-in refrigerator filled with perishables, over to the main restaurant with row after row of booths and counter and stools,
60 well-worn but always cleaned after each patron had finished, and finally to the front porch, with its old wooden swing. I can see my grandmother moving from her station near the door to the kitchen, over to the counter and tables, and then back to the front again. Even now, I can see Del speedily making a double
65 order of hash, Deborah picking up a generous tip, and Marlene topping off a customer's sweet tea. Every summer sunset from that porch seemed to be more magnificent than the last.

As I got older, I took on more responsibility. There were fewer sunsets to watch and more work to be done. It was hard
70 but never dull work. The company kept me coming back despite the increasing allure of summer football leagues and idle moments with friends or girls. After all, the woman who built Ruby's was strong enough to make me forget those things, if only for the summer. I didn't know that I would never return
75 after my sophomore year of college, and for that, I am glad—I could not have asked for a better end to my long history at Ruby's. It warms my heart when I think of the last memory of Ruby Sanders: tying her silver hair into a tight bun, hands vigorously wiping down tables with a rag, enjoying a story
80 and a laugh as we closed for the night.

GO ON TO THE NEXT PAGE.

1. The narrator's point of view can most correctly be described as that of an adult:

   A. remembering the events that brought a particular place into existence.
   B. analyzing how different his current life is from how things were when he was younger.
   C. thinking about the qualities of his grandmother and her restaurant that made her well-respected in the community.
   D. curious as to how many people's lives were positively impacted by his grandmother and her diner.

2. One of the main purposes of the first part of the passage (lines 1–27) is to:

   F. explain how Ruby got the money to pay for the diner and her eventual success in paying off her debts.
   G. state that the diner had taken its name from the narrator's grandmother although many of the locals called it by different names.
   H. explain how Ruby was able to become the most important person in Franklin and that her restaurant was the best place for visitors to the city.
   J. introduce the primary setting of the story and to describe a central character.

3. Based on the narrator's characterization, Ruby Sanders would best be described as:

   A. always at the diner, though she often preferred to be absent.
   B. the main force holding the diner and its employees together.
   C. carefree, particularly when it came to hearing humorous stories.
   D. the only woman the narrator had ever respected.

4. Information in the last paragraph most strongly suggests that the narrator felt his last summer at the diner to be:

   F. disappointing because he didn't know it would be his last.
   G. something he was forced to do when he would rather have been playing football.
   H. pleasant although he did not know it would be his last.
   J. exhausting because of all his new responsibilities.

5. According to the narrator, working at Ruby's Diner was:

   A. easy but tedious.
   B. difficult but enjoyable.
   C. hard and monotonous.
   D. unpredictable and overwhelming.

6. According to the narrator, his grandmother was like the diner in that she had:

   F. a position of high standing within the community at large.
   G. a desire to make all people feel comfortable no matter who they were.
   H. an ability to make money within the community.
   J. a refusal to settle for anything but the best.

7. The statement in lines 44–45 most strongly suggests that the Downhome Diner:

   A. served the community in ways beyond simple dining.
   B. was the most significant place within Robertson County.
   C. gave the people who worked there great importance in Robertson County.
   D. was a place where the waiting times were often unpredictable.

8. The narrator describes Ruby's Downhome Diner as providing all of the following EXCEPT:

   F. cooking classes.
   G. football leagues.
   H. wedding cakes.
   J. corn pone.

9. The passage indicates that one of the ways in which the narrator was familiar with Ruby's Downhome Diner was shown by his:

   A. ability to teach the cooking classes held on the premises.
   B. awareness of the habits of visitors to Robertson County.
   C. detailed memory of the layout of the kitchen and the restaurant.
   D. unwillingness to leave at the end of each summer before his return to school.

10. According to the narrator, which of the following most accurately represents the reason he was able to forget the summer activities outside while working at his grandmother's restaurant?

    F. His tips and wages helped to contribute to his college tuition.
    G. His grandmother's restaurant was chronically understaffed.
    H. It helped him to gain stature in and around the community.
    J. He admired his grandmother's strength.

GO ON TO THE NEXT PAGE.

Passage II

SOCIAL SCIENCE: This passage is adapted from the entry "Happiness" from The Psychologist's Scientific Encyclopedia (© 2004 by The Scientific Press of Illinois).

Lee D. Ross, a psychologist at Stanford University, has a friend who lost both her parents in the Holocaust. According to the woman, the awful events of the Holocaust taught her that it was inappropriate to be upset about trivial things in
5 life and important to enjoy human relationships. Even though the circumstances of her life were tragic, the woman was extremely happy, perhaps due to an innate sense of well-being.

According to psychologists, most of our self-reported level of happiness, a measure researchers call "subjective
10 well-being," seems to be genetically predetermined, rather than caused by experience. A study carried out by Auke Tellegen and David Lykken of the University of Minnesota compared the subjective well-being scores of both fraternal and identical twins, some of whom were raised together and
15 some of whom were separated and raised in different families. By comparing the scores of the twins, Tellegen and Lykken determined that most of the differences in people's levels of happiness are determined by differences in genetic makeup.

A genetic predisposition toward a certain level of hap-
20 piness means that regardless of what happens in a person's life, he or she will eventually adjust to the new circumstances and report the same level of subjective well-being as before. The tendency for people to maintain a consistent level of happiness despite their circumstances, known as "hedonic
25 adaptation," benefits those whose life-experiences are beset by adverse conditions, such as permanent disability or sudden loss of income. Because they return to a "genetic set point," they eventually feel just as happy as they did before the unfortunate event.

30 However, hedonic adaptation also affects the happiness of people who experience positive changes in their lives. For example, in one study conducted in the 1970s among lottery winners, it was found that a year after the winners received their money, they were no happier than non-winners.

35 Despite the quantity of research that supports hedonic adaptation, there is still some debate within the scientific community over how much people can change their baseline happiness. Kennon M. Sheldon, a psychologist at the University of Missouri-Columbia, explains that many research
40 psychologists hypothesized that certain behaviors, such as choosing particular goals in life, could affect long-term happiness. However, scientific literature suggests that these behaviors provide only a temporary increase in subjective well-being.

45 Sheldon worked alongside Sonja Lyubomirsky of the University of California at Riverside and David A. Schkade of the University of California at San Diego to determine exactly what is known about the science of happiness. They compiled the findings of existing scientific studies in the field
50 of happiness and determined that 50 percent of subjective well-being is predetermined by the genetic set point, while only about 10 percent is influenced by circumstances.

However, people are not completely at the mercy of their genes. Lyubomirsky notes that 40 percent of what contributes
55 to people's happiness is still unexplained, and she believes that much of this may be attributable to what she calls "intentional activity," which includes mental attitudes and behaviors that people can modify and improve. Conscious choices such as demonstrating kindness, fostering optimism, and expressing
60 gratitude may work to influence subjective well-being in much the same way that diet and exercise can affect a person's inherited predisposition toward heart disease. Lyubomirsky hopes to learn the specific mechanisms by which these conscious strategies counteract genetic forces. She and Sheldon are cur-
65 rently expanding their study of subjective well-being to large groups of subjects to be observed over extended periods of time. Using these longitudinal studies, the researchers hope to discover the inner workings of the correlations between behaviors and mood.

70 Lyubomirsky and Sheldon's studies have found that simply choosing "happy" activities may not be the most effective way to increase happiness. Lyubomirsky says that other factors, such as variation and timing of intentional activities, are crucial in influencing happiness. For example, one study
75 has shown that subjects who varied their acts of kindness from one day to the next experienced greater happiness than those who repeated the same kind act many times. Another study demonstrated that writing a list of things to be grateful for only once a week was more effective in improving levels of
80 happiness than keeping a gratitude journal every day.

The study of happiness is still a relatively new area of psychological research. Traditionally, much more psychological research focused on depression and other disorders associated with destructive mental health, leading some psychologists
85 to suspect that overall levels of subjective well-being are low. But now that more studies are focused on positive psychology, there is evidence to the contrary. Researchers have discovered not only that personal choices improve subjective well-being from a genetic set point, but also that this level is higher than
90 traditionally expected. According to surveys conducted by the University of Chicago, only about one in ten people claim to be "not too happy." Most Americans describe themselves as "pretty happy," and 30 percent as "very happy," even without using intentional activities specifically to improve
95 their well-being.

GO ON TO THE NEXT PAGE.

11. The passage's focus is primarily on the:

   A. search for the specific genes known to cause hedonic adaptation.
   B. scientific studies investigating various influences on happiness.
   C. attempts by experimental psychologists to develop cures for depression.
   D. conflicting opinions of psychologists regarding the influence of genes on happiness.

12. Based on the passage, the subjects in the studies by Tellegen and Lykken and the subjects in studies by Lyubomirsky and Sheldon were similar in that both groups were:

   F. part of large groups studied over an extended time.
   G. intentionally engaged in acts of kindness.
   H. asked to describe their own subjective well-being.
   J. either identical or fraternal twins.

13. Which of the following questions is NOT answered by the passage?

   A. To what extent is a person's level of happiness determined by his or her circumstances?
   B. According to Lyubomirsky and Sheldon's studies, what are some specific things people can do to improve their subjective well-being?
   C. Does the choice of specific life goals affect happiness over a lifetime?
   D. According to Tellegen and Lykken, were twins who were raised together happier than twins who were raised apart?

14. The passage most strongly suggests that the primary goal of Lyubomirsky and Sheldon's research is to:

   F. discover the specific mechanisms that may help people overcome the level of happiness determined by their genetic set point.
   G. contradict Tellegen and Lykken's findings that genes are the primary determinant in a person's overall level of happiness.
   H. find out whether keeping a gratitude journal or engaging in kind acts is more effective at improving happiness.
   J. determine which behaviors most completely eliminate hedonic adaptation.

15. Which of the following statements best summarizes the findings of the University of Chicago surveys on happiness?

   A. Earlier psychologists were mistaken to believe people are generally depressed and experience low levels of happiness.
   B. Depression and other destructive mood disorders are uncommon in America.
   C. People are happier if they do not try to improve their subjective well-being by writing in a gratitude journal.
   D. Most people report a level of happiness higher than was traditionally expected by psychologists and researchers.

16. According to the passage, all of the following are true of the Lykken and Tellegen study EXCEPT:

   F. The subjects were paired groups of twins.
   G. Subjects rated their happiness.
   H. The twins studied were all raised together.
   J. The study found happiness is genetic.

17. According to the passage, "hedonic adaptation" (lines 24–25) is a useful trait because it can help people to:

   A. restore levels of happiness that have been interrupted or altered by tragic events.
   B. forget that they have suffered a permanent disability or loss of income.
   C. adjust quickly to positive circumstances like winning the lottery and become happier.
   D. identify with immediate family members who share their genes and choose those who are more inclined to be happy.

18. If the author were to delete the first paragraph, the passage would primarily lose:

   F. the idea that events people experience are not the least important factor influencing their subjective well-being.
   G. a useful illustration of the idea that there may be little relationship between a person's circumstances and his or her level of happiness.
   H. a clear and complete articulation of the essay's main point regarding hedonic adaptation.
   J. all examples of adverse conditions people may overcome because of their genetic predisposition to happiness.

19. The main purpose of the final paragraph is to:

   A. conclude that psychological researchers make many errors and tend to focus on the negative.
   B. disprove the idea suggested by Ross's anecdote by showing that Americans are also happy.
   C. cite a specific study that gives a positive view of people's overall levels of happiness.
   D. undermine Lyubomirsky and Sheldon's studies indicating that people need to apply effort in order to become happier.

20. According to the passage, which of the following researchers have an ongoing collaboration?

   F. Tellegen and Lykken
   G. Sheldon and Schkade
   H. Sheldon and Lyubomirsky
   J. Schkade and Lykken

GO ON TO THE NEXT PAGE.

Passage III

HUMANITIES: Passage A is adapted from "Living Between Worlds: Searching for Identity" by Kenora Crowfeather (© 1998 by Birch Bark Press). Passage B is adapted from *American Indian Stories* by Zitkala-Sa (Gertrude Simmons Bonnin).

Passage A by Kenora Crowfeather

As I gaze at the picture of Zitkala-Sa that confronts me from the cover of her collected writings, *American Indian Stories*, I see a beautifully proud Sioux woman. Long, glossy black braids frame her serious and unflinching face, hang like
5 heavy silken cords in front of her traditional dress, and end somewhere out of the bottom of the frame, past her waist I imagine. It is hard to make myself believe that the woman in this picture was named Gertrude Simmons Bonnin; Zitkala-Sa (Red Bird) was her pen name.

10 Zitkala-Sa's life-long struggle with the clash between Native American culture and white men has intrigued me for the better part of two decades since I first began reading her essays. Returning home after a long trip and feeling un-settled is not unique to her experience, but the clash between
15 Native Americans and the "pale-faces" who misunderstood and exploited them adds fire to Zitkala-Sa's chronicles of her school years, which might otherwise have been written by any angst-filled teenager.

The daughter of a white man and a Sioux woman, Zitkala-
20 Sa spent the first years of her life firmly ensconced in Native American life with her mother on the Pine Ridge Reservation in South Dakota. She chose to leave home at age eight to go to a missionary school in Indiana. Her memoirs describe her unhappiness at school: her dismay at having her hair cut and
25 her moccasins taken away and her rage at the unjust rules and willful neglect on the part of the teachers. Yet when she returned home, she remained unsatisfied. She was able to wear her beloved moccasins again, but she felt friendless and misunderstood. She had discarded her school clothes and so
30 was ill-equipped to socialize with the young people on the reservation who had adopted that style of dress.

Her return to school and the white man's world for a time confused me, despite my understanding of her urge to leave. How could she have gone to work at an institution so
35 like her first, hated school? How could she have abandoned her mother and her heritage?

In the midst of my indignation, I forgot that Gertrude Bonnin was the daughter of a white man. Her mother, though she never learned English, married three different white men
40 over the course of her life. The clash between the two cultures began deep within Gertrude before she was even born. She was destined to feel like an outsider anywhere, and leaving home allowed her to embrace her Sioux identity. Pursuing education among white men was not, in the end, abandoning
45 her culture, but rather a step in her journey towards becoming an advocate for Native American rights.

Passage B by Zitkala-Sa (Gertrude Simmons Bonnin)

After my first three years of school, I roamed again in the Western country through four strange summers.

During this time I seemed to hang in the heart of chaos,
50 beyond the touch or voice of human aid. My brother, being almost ten years my senior, did not quite understand my feel-ings. My mother had never gone inside of a schoolhouse, and so she was not capable of comforting her daughter who could read and write. Even nature seemed to have no place for me.
55 I was neither a wee girl nor a tall one; neither a wild Indian nor a tame one. This deplorable situation was the effect of my brief course in the East, and the unsatisfactory "teenth" in a girl's years.

It was under these trying conditions that, one bright af-
60 ternoon, as I sat restless and unhappy in my mother's cabin, I caught the sound of the spirited step of my brother's pony on the road which passed by our dwelling.

I met him there with a hurried greeting, and, as I passed by, he looked a quiet "What?" into my eyes.

65 "No, my baby sister, I cannot take you with me to the party to-night," he replied. Though I was not far from fifteen, and I felt that before long I should enjoy all the privileges of my tall cousin, Dawée persisted in calling me his baby sister.

That moonlight night, I cried in my mother's presence
70 when I heard the jolly young people pass by our cottage. They were no more young braves in blankets and eagle plumes, nor Indian maids with prettily painted cheeks. They had gone three years to school in the East, and had become civilized. The young men wore the white man's coat and trousers, with
75 bright neckties. The girls wore tight muslin dresses, with ribbons at neck and waist. At these gatherings they talked English. I could speak English almost as well as my brother, but I was not properly dressed to be taken along. I had no hat, no ribbons, and no close-fitting gown. Since my return
80 from school I had thrown away my shoes, and wore again the soft moccasins.

While Dawée was busily preparing to go I controlled my tears. But when I heard him bounding away on his pony, I buried my face in my arms and cried hot tears.

GO ON TO THE NEXT PAGE.

Questions 21–23 ask about Passage A.

21. The author's attitude towards Zitkala-Sa can best be described as:

A. impatient because Zitkala-Sa's writings reveal her as a spoiled teenager.
B. admiring because Zitkala-Sa established herself as an advocate for Native Americans.
C. disapproving because Zitkala-Sa abandoned her mother and her culture.
D. confused because of Zitkala-Sa's difficulty choosing between conflicting cultures.

22. The author describes the clash of Native American and white cultures as:

F. the reason that Zitkala-Sa eventually abandoned her mother and adapted to a white lifestyle.
G. extra detail that is ultimately unimportant in Zitkala-Sa's chronicles of her school years.
H. the cause of Zitkala's unhappiness at school.
J. the dramatic material that makes Zitkala-Sa's writing compelling.

23. When Crowfeather claims "It is hard to make myself believe that the woman in this picture was named Gertrude Simmons Bonnin" (lines 7–8) she is most nearly referring to:

A. the apparent incongruity between a picture of a Sioux woman and a white woman's name.
B. the confusion created by Bonnin's use of a pen name.
C. her belief that the picture had been incorrectly identified and was not of Bonnin.
D. her preference for Bonnin's traditional Sioux name.

Questions 24–27 ask about Passage B.

24. The author "cried hot tears" (line 84) because:

F. her brother refused to take her to the party.
G. she missed the Indian maids who had gone away to school.
H. her mother was incapable of comforting her.
J. she wished she had a muslin dress with ribbons.

25. The passage most strongly suggests that when she returned home from school, Zitkala-Sa was:

A. content to be back home where she could wear moccasins again.
B. distraught to find that she wasn't happy at home.
C. eager to teach her mother to read and write.
D. upset that her brother still thought of her as a baby.

26. The narrator's statement in lines 55–56 most nearly describes:

F. her average height.
G. the awkwardness of her teenage years.
H. her sense of not belonging.
J. the rejection she felt from her family.

27. In line 73, the word "civilized" is used to describe:

A. the good manners the young people used at the party.
B. the change of living quarters on the reservation from teepees to houses.
C. the education the young people had received while away at school.
D. the young people's adoption of aspects of white culture.

Questions 28–30 ask about both passages.

28. Both passages emphasize Zitkala-Sa's:

F. refusal to fit in on the reservation after she returned home from school.
G. desire to become an advocate for sending Native Americans to school.
H. difficulty getting along with her mother as a teenager.
J. sense of not belonging either at home or in the world of white men.

29. In both passages, moccasins function as a symbol of:

A. the oppression of Native Americans by white men.
B. Zitkala-Sa's frustration at being caught between two cultures.
C. Native American culture.
D. comfortable and practical footwear.

30. The author of Passage A would most likely view the events described in Passage B as:

F. a struggle that ultimately led Zitkala-Sa to have a strong sense of identity.
G. an emotional outburst by Zitkala-Sa typical of a teen-age girl.
H. a time when Zitkala-Sa came to fully appreciate Sioux culture.
J. a period of conflict between Zitkala-Sa and her mother and brother.

GO ON TO THE NEXT PAGE.

Passage IV

NATURAL SCIENCE: This passage is adapted from the article "A Tree Frog Grows Up in Hawaii" by Ashley C. Tulliver (© 2005 by Ashley Tulliver).

As night falls on Hawaii's Big Island, a low, jarring sound begins. It is a faint murmur at first, but as the darkness deepens, the sound grows louder, rending the stillness of the evening. These deep cries, from male *E. coquí* frogs, are met with
5 lower, guttural croaks from their prospective mates; during this time, the sound for which the coquí is named (ko-KEE) fills the air. This sound has become the theme song of a growing environmental problem: invasive species' threat to ecological biodiversity.

10 Native to Puerto Rico, the small tree frogs—measuring about five millimeters long—probably arrived in Hawaii as passengers aboard potted plants imported from the Caribbean. Once coquíes explored their new environment, they found an abundance of food, including insects, tiny spiders, and mites.
15 In addition, they faced little ecological competition, as there are no other amphibians native to the islands, nor are there the snakes, tarantulas, or other Caribbean hunters that usually serve to keep the coquí population in check.

The way the coquí hatch also gives the coquí an advan-
20 tage in Hawaii's ecosystem. Frogs usually hatch into tadpoles, which require a consistent and substantial amount of water to survive. By contrast, the coquí emerges from the egg as a tiny but fully formed frog, which allows it to thrive in saturated moss, the dampened plastic that importers wrap around plants,
25 or even a drop of water on a plant leaf. Moreover, young co- quíes don't begin to emit their signature calls until they are about a year old; consequently, avian predators are unable to locate the tiny frogs by sound.

Perhaps the coquí's most noteworthy feature is its ex-
30 tremely loud calling song. To a listener one to two feet away, a single coquí can produce a mating call up to 100 decibels. The unusual volume of the frog's call is compounded by two other factors. First, coquíes congregate closely on relatively small parcels of land; one recent survey found 400 adult frogs
35 in one 20-by-20-meter plot. This degree of concentration amplifies the sound the frogs make. Second, coquíes tend to overlap their calls, with a single coquí seeking to fill gaps in other frogs' songs with its own effort to attract a mate. As a result, coquíes create a "wall of sound" that is even more
40 pronounced because Hawaii boasts few other night-calling species. For these reasons, human residents of Hawaii tend to regard coquíes as nuisances, polluting the air with their incessant noise.

Conservationists worry about other ramifications of the
45 coquí's invasion of the Hawaiian ecosystem. One problem is that while the coquí receives the bulk of residents' attention because of its nocturnal serenades, another, quieter genus of the frog—the greenhouse frog—represents an equal threat to the biodiversity of the island. As voracious insectivores,
50 coquíes and greenhouse frogs are threatening the survival of arthropods (invertebrate animals with jointed legs, including insects, scorpions, crustaceans, and spiders), whose popula- tions are already close to extirpation due to other foreign preda- tors. Ornithologists fear that depleting the insect population
55 could result in serious consequences for Hawaii's food web, especially considering that the birds native to the islands are also insectivores.

Symbiotic interactions between the coquí and other in- vasive species pose another ecological threat. The presence
60 of coquíes could permit the flourishing of other so-called "dissonant" species, such as non-native snakes that prey upon the frogs. Herpetologists have speculated that nematodes and other types of vertebrate parasites can be transported with coquíes and can infect indigenous fauna. Furthermore, many
65 ecologists believe the proliferation of these frogs will further homogenize the island's biota.

Debate persists about how best to reduce or even eradicate the population of coquíes and their cousins in Hawaii. Hand- capturing the tiny frogs is probably the most environmentally
70 sensitive way to remove them from their habitat, but their sheer number renders this approach inefficient. The maximum con- centration of pesticides that would not damage fauna or flora has not been potent enough to kill the frogs. Seeking a more creative solution, scientists have had some success treating the
75 frogs with caffeine citrate, a drug typically prescribed to treat breathing and metabolic abnormalities in humans. Caffeine citrate can penetrate the coquí's moist skin, and the drug's high acidity essentially poisons the animal and inactivates its nervous systems. From a biodiversity standpoint, this
80 technique has the added benefit of posing almost no danger to plants, which lack a nervous system, or to insects, which have an impenetrable, hard exoskeleton.

Even if new techniques finally exterminate the coquí, experts are skeptical that the invader's current effects on the
85 1,000 acres of Hawaii's ecosystem can be reversed. This patch of land is not expansive in comparison to Hawaii's total 4.1 million acres, yet it is an indication of potential widespread disaster: since the habitat and its native residents have thus far been able to adjust to the presence of coquíes, eliminating the
90 frogs could yield unintended and far-reaching consequences to the biodiversity of the habitat beyond arthropods. For now, scientists are likely to continue the delicate balancing act of limiting the coquí's population growth while preventing further damage to Hawaii's ecosystem.

GO ON TO THE NEXT PAGE.

31. Which of the following questions is NOT answered by this passage?

   A. On an annual basis, how often do coquí frogs mate and produce offspring?

   B. Which predators native to Puerto Rico are absent in the Hawaiian islands?

   C. What behaviorial factors influence the volume of the coquí's calls?

   D. How could the coquí potentially disrupt the food chain on the islands it inhabits?

32. It is most reasonable to infer from the passage that the lack of amphibian life in Hawaii:

   F. benefits coquíes, which don't have to compete for food and space.

   G. provides little opportunity for coquíes to form symbiotic relationships.

   H. forces coquíes to build their own nests in order to mate and breed.

   J. is a result of invasive species' attacks on the biodiversity of the islands.

33. Which of the following statements about the noise levels produced by the coquí is supported by the passage?

   A. The coquí males have lower, guttural croaks than do females of the species.

   B. Calls are louder when coquíes are defending their territory than when they are mating.

   C. The calls of coquí sound particularly loud because there are no gaps of silence.

   D. Coquí are noisier at dawn and dusk than at other times of day.

34. The primary purpose of the third paragraph (lines 19–28) is to:

   F. describe wet weather conditions in Hawaii necessary for the coquí to breed.

   G. provide a physical description of the coquí's habitat in Hawaii compared to that in Puerto Rico.

   H. explain the ecological and behavioral advantages that permit the coquí to thrive in Hawaii.

   J. give an overview of the amphibian life cycle, from the tadpole to frog stage.

35. Compared to the language of the first paragraph, the language of the sixth paragraph (lines 58–66) is more:

   A. opinionated.

   B. scientific.

   C. optimistic.

   D. casual.

36. As it is used in line 53, the word *extirpation* most nearly means:

   F. competition.

   G. extinction.

   H. overpopulation.

   J. pursuit.

37. Which of the following ideas is presented in the passage as theory and not fact?

   A. Coquí frogs cluster together in high concentrations, amplifying the sound they make.

   B. Store-bought poisons, in permissible doses, are not strong enough to kill the frogs.

   C. The exoskeleton of insects is a better defense against caffeine citrate than the skin of amphibians.

   D. A decrease in Hawaii's insect population causes a decrease in bird populations.

38. The passage states that coquíes often carry parasites called:

   F. nematodes.

   G. arthropods.

   H. scorpions.

   J. arachnids.

39. Which of the following statements best reflects the information provided in the passage about the relevance of the greenhouse frog to the discussion of the coquí?

   A. The greenhouse frog lives primarily indoors, whereas the coquí lives primarily in island rain forests.

   B. The greenhouse frog is less prominent than the coquí but can be equally damaging to the Hawaiian ecosystem.

   C. The greenhouse frog does not pose as dangerous a threat to the Hawaiian ecosystem as the coquí does.

   D. It is easier to locate and eliminate the coquí because the greenhouse frog does not produce loud mating calls.

40. The phrase "1,000 acres" (line 85) refers to which type of land in Hawaii?

   F. Caribbean ecosystem

   G. Bird sanctuary

   H. Rain forest

   J. Coquí habitat

END OF TEST 3.
STOP! DO NOT TURN THE PAGE UNTIL TOLD TO DO SO.
DO NOT RETURN TO A PREVIOUS TEST.

SCIENCE TEST
35 Minutes—40 Questions

DIRECTIONS: There are seven passages in the following section. Each passage is followed by several questions. After reading a passage, choose the best answer to each question and blacken the corresponding oval on your answer sheet. You may refer to the passages as often as necessary.

You are NOT permitted to use a calculator on this test.

Passage I

A group of students studied the frictional forces involved on stationary objects.

In a series of experiments, the students used rectangular shaped objects of various materials that all had identical masses. One end of a plastic board coated with a polymer film was fastened to a table surface by a hinge so the angle θ between the board and table could be changed, as shown in Figure 1.

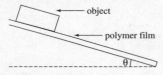

object

polymer film

θ

Figure 1

Objects were placed on the opposite end of the board, and the angle θ at which the object started to slide was recorded. The tangent of this angle represents the coefficient of static friction between the object and the polymer surface. This coefficient is proportional to the force required to move a stationary object. Higher coefficients mean that greater forces of friction must be overcome to initiate movement.

The dimensions of the objects gave them 3 distinct *faces* of unequal area as shown in Figure 2. Unless otherwise stated, the objects were placed on the ramp with Face A down.

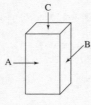

C

B

A

Figure 2

Experiment 1

Four objects made of different materials were placed on the ramp at a temperature of 25°C. The ramp was gradually raised and as soon as the object started to move, the angle θ of the ramp was recorded in Table 1.

Table 1	
Object material	θ (degrees)
Granite	12.1
Copper	16.8
Wood	22.0
Brick	31.1

Experiment 2

The procedure for Experiment 1 was repeated with the wooden object, varying which face was placed down on the ramp. Results were recorded in Table 2.

Table 2	
Face	θ (degrees)
A	22.0
B	22.0
C	22.0

GO ON TO THE NEXT PAGE.

Experiment 3

The procedure for Experiment 1 was repeated with the wooden object, varying the temperature of the polymer ramp. Results for 5 temperatures were recorded in Table 3.

Table 3	
Temperature (°C)	θ (degrees)
0	18.5
25	22.0
50	25.4
75	29.0
100	32.5

Experiment 4

The procedure for Experiment 1 was repeated with multiple wooden objects. For each trial, the objects were stacked on top of each other before raising the ramp. The angle θ where the stack started to slide was recorded in Table 4.

Table 4	
Number of objects	θ (degrees)
2	22.0
3	22.0
4	22.0

1. If the procedure used in Experiment 3 had been repeated at a temperature of 62.5°C, the angle required for the object to start moving down the ramp most likely would have been closest to which of the following?

   A. 27.2 degrees
   B. 29.2 degrees
   C. 30.3 degrees
   D. 31.4 degrees

2. Suppose the students had placed the 4 objects used in Experiment 1 on the ramp when it was flat and pushed each of the objects, such that the amount of force applied to each object gradually increased until it moved. Based on the results of Experiment 1, the object made of which material would most likely have taken the *greatest* amount of force to start moving?

   F. Brick
   G. Wood
   H. Copper
   J. Granite

3. Based on the results of Experiments 1 and 4, what was the effect, if any, of the weight of the object on the coefficient of static friction?

   A. The coefficient of static friction always increased as the object's weight increased.
   B. The coefficient of static friction always decreased as the object's weight increased.
   C. The coefficient of static friction increased and then decreased as the object's weight increased.
   D. The coefficient of static friction was not affected by the weight of the object.

4. In Experiment 1, the reason the students used objects made of different materials was most likely to vary the amount of frictional force between the:

   F. plastic board and the polymer surface.
   G. various objects and the polymer surface.
   H. objects made of different materials when brought into contact with each other.
   J. stacked objects, so that the objects would not fall over when the angle of the ramp was raised high enough to cause motion.

5. Which of the following ranks the different types of objects used, in order, from the material that presented the greatest resistance to movement to the material that presented the least resistance to movement?

   A. Granite, copper, wood, brick
   B. Copper, wood, granite, brick
   C. Granite, wood, brick, copper
   D. Brick, wood, copper, granite

6. The main purpose of Experiment 3 was to determine the effects of temperature on which of the following variables?

   F. Coefficient of static friction between wood and wood
   G. Coefficient of static friction between wood and polymer
   H. Mass of the wooden object
   J. Total frictional force of the polymer on all objects placed on the ramp

GO ON TO THE NEXT PAGE.

Passage II

Despite a global campaign since 1988 to eradicate *poliomyelitis* (polio), the virus that causes this disease continues to be endemic in four countries. This polio virus, which can exist as Type 1, Type 2, or Type 3, is most often transmitted through water that is contaminated by human waste. People can be immunized from this virus with a highly effective vaccine, which can be administered orally or by injection. Recent analyses of polio virus transmission have focused on the four polio-endemic countries: India, Pakistan, Afghanistan, and Nigeria.

Study 1

In 2004, a temporary ban on polio vaccines was instituted in Nigeria in response to concerns that they were contaminated. Researchers reviewed World Health Organization (WHO) records to determine the number of Type 1 polio virus infections that were reported in Nigeria in 2004 and tallied their findings by month (see Figure 1). The World Health Organization has noted that in polio-endemic countries, official records underestimate the number of people actually infected, because numerous infected individuals do not report their symptoms to clinics or rely on local therapists who are not surveyed. In a polio-endemic country, for every person who has reported an infection, as many as ten people may actually be infected in the local population.

Study 2

Although polio eradication efforts have been most consistent in the urban areas of polio-endemic countries, these areas also have a high risk for a reemergence of polio, especially when the large urban populations are exposed to water contaminated with wastes that harbor the polio virus. In 2007, researchers analyzed the number of people who reported infections with Type 3 polio virus in the five largest cities in India. These cities were Mumbai in western India, New Delhi and Kolkata in northern India, and Chennai and Hyderabad in southern India. The analysis was undertaken in the months of June and August. June 2007 was chosen as a representative month for the dry summer season in India, during which there was minimal rainfall. August 2007 was chosen as a representative month for the wet monsoon season in India, during which there was daily rainfall. The results of the findings are shown in Figure 2.

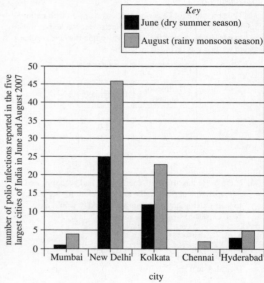

Figure 2

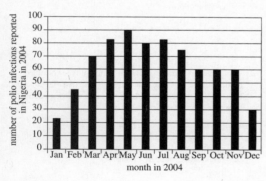

Figure 1

GO ON TO THE NEXT PAGE.

7. According to Figure 1, the greatest increase in the number of reported polio infections in Nigeria occurred between which two months?

    A. January and February
    B. February and March
    C. April and May
    D. November and December

8. It is estimated that for every person infected with the polio virus in an endemic country, there are 200 people at risk for contracting the virus. Given the results of Study 1, how many people would have been at risk for becoming infected with the polio virus in Nigeria in June 2004 ?

    F.   80
    G.   200
    H.   800
    J. 16,000

9. Given the information in Figure 2, which of the following might explain the difference in reported cases of polio in major Indian cities between June and August of 2007 ?

    A. Water is more likely to become contaminated with polio-infected human waste in periods of high rainfall.
    B. Water is less likely to become contaminated with polio-infected human waste in periods of high rainfall.
    C. The polio virus infects more people in India during the summer and monsoon seasons than during the autumn and winter seasons.
    D. Those diagnosed with the polio virus in June are able to recover by August.

10. Which of the following hypotheses was most likely tested in Study 2 ?

    F. The number of reported cases of polio infections varies significantly between Nigeria and India.
    G. Most cases of polio infections are not reported to medical authorities in India.
    H. Polio infections affect more people in certain regions in India than in other regions.
    J. The number of reported cases of polio infections in India is greatest during the summer and least during the winter.

11. Polio-endemic countries are located in warm climates that harbor many mosquitoes. Would the presence of mosquitoes directly affect the transmission of the polio virus?

    A. Yes, because the polio virus is primarily transmitted through mosquitoes.
    B. Yes, because the polio virus is primarily transmitted through human waste.
    C. No, because the polio virus is primarily transmitted through mosquitoes.
    D. No, because the polio virus is primarily transmitted through human waste.

12. The comparison of reported polio infections in India in 2007, as shown in Figure 2, indicates that relative to the number of people in Kolkata infected with polio in June, the number of people infected with polio in Kolkata in August was approximately:

    F. half as much.
    G. the same.
    H. twice as much.
    J. ten times as much.

GO ON TO THE NEXT PAGE.

Passage III

Osmotic pressure (Π) is the amount of pressure, in atm, required to maintain equilibrium of a solvent across a semipermeable membrane. At a constant temperature, osmotic pressure is dependent only on a solute's ability to dissociate or ionize in the solvent (van 't Hoff factor, i) and the concentration of solute particles. The osmotic pressure is determined by the equation:

$$\Pi = iMRT$$

M represents the concentration (in molarity, M), R is the ideal gas constant (0.0821 L atm mol^{-1} K^{-1}), and T (300 K) is the temperature in Kelvin (K). The value of R is assumed to be a constant for all osmotic pressure calculations.

The dissociation of a solute depends on its unique chemical properties. The van 't Hoff factors for some common substances are displayed in Table 1. Higher van 't Hoff factors correlate with greater dissociation or ionization. The effect of the van 't Hoff factor on the osmotic pressure may be seen in Figure 1.

Table 1	
Substance	van 't Hoff factor *
sucrose	1.0
NaCl	1.9
MgCl$_2$	2.7
FeCl$_3$	3.4
*Values at 300 K	

Key
— sucrose
- - - NaCl
······· MgCl$_2$
–·–·– FeCl$_3$

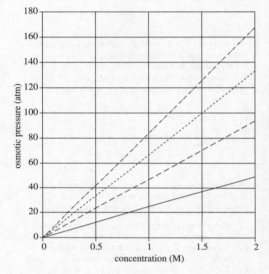

Figure 1

GO ON TO THE NEXT PAGE.

13. According to Figure 1, which of the following solutions would exhibit the *least* osmotic pressure?

    A. 1.0 M $FeCl_3$ solution
    B. 1.0 M $MgCl_2$ solution
    C. 2.0 M NaCl solution
    D. 2.0 M sucrose solution

14. If 1.0 M solutions of various solutes were prepared, which of the following solutions would have the highest level of ionization?

    F. Sucrose
    G. NaCl
    H. $MgCl_2$
    J. $FeCl_3$

15. Which of the following solutions would exhibit the closest osmotic pressure to that of a 1.5 M NaCl solution at 300 K, if the gas constant is 0.0821 L atm/ mol⁻¹ K⁻¹ ?

    A. 1.0 M NaCl solution ($i = 1.9$)
    B. 2.0 M NaCl solution ($i = 1.9$)
    C. 2.9 M sucrose solution ($i = 1.0$)
    D. 3.5 M sucrose solution ($i = 1.0$)

16. Based on Figure 1, as the concentration of solute decreases, the pressure required to hold solvent concentration across a membrane at equilibrium will:

    F. increase only.
    G. decrease only.
    H. remain constant.
    J. increase, then remain constant.

17. A scientist recently discovered a compound that ionizes readily in solution ($i = 3.8$) and results in low osmotic pressures. Are the findings of this scientist consistent with Figure 1 ?

    A. Yes, because $FeCl_3$ causes higher osmotic pressure than sucrose.
    B. No, because sucrose causes higher osmotic pressure than $FeCl_3$.
    C. Yes, because $FeCl_3$ causes lower osmotic pressure than sucrose.
    D. No, because sucrose causes lower osmotic pressure than $FeCl_3$.

GO ON TO THE NEXT PAGE.

Passage IV

Soil salinity is the concentration of potentially harmful salts dissolved in the groundwater that fills soil pores. Salinity is determined by measuring a soil's *electrical conductivity (EC)* and *exchangeable sodium percentage (ESP)*. High EC indicates a high concentration of dissolved salt particles; ESP indicates the proportion of electrical conductivity that is due to dissolved sodium ions.

Soil samples were collected from five different distances west of a particular river. Figure 1 shows the electrical conductivity of the soil samples at four different depth ranges measured in milli-Siemens per centimeter (mS/cm).

Figure 2 shows the exchangeable sodium percentage of the five sites at different depths.

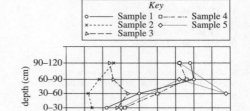

Figure 2

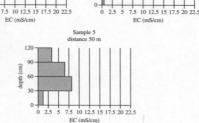

Figure 1

18. Figure 2 indicates that, compared with the soil tested in Sample 1, the soil tested in Sample 4 contains:

F. a higher percentage of sodium ions throughout.
G. a lower percentage of sodium ions throughout.
H. a higher percentage of sodium ions at shallower depths only.
J. a lower percentage of sodium ions at shallower depths only.

19. According to Figure 2, in the soil collected in Sample 3 at a depth of 30–60 cm, approximately what percent of the soil conductivity is due to sodium ions?

A. 14%
B. 17%
C. 24%
D. 44%

20. Based on Figures 1 and 2, the electrical conductivity due to sodium ions in the sample collected 40 m west of the river was:

F. greatest at a depth of 90–120 cm.
G. greatest at a depth of 0–30 cm.
H. least at a depth of 30–60 cm.
J. least at a depth of 0–30 cm.

GO ON TO THE NEXT PAGE.

21. Based on Figure 2, which of the following figures best represents the exchangeable sodium percentage for the five soil samples collected at a depth of 90–120 cm ?

A.
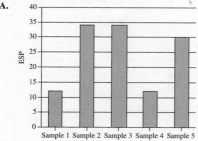

B.
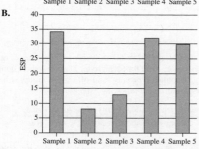

C.
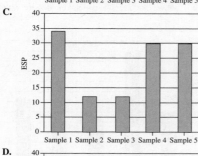

D.
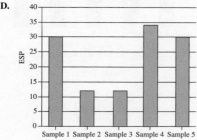

22. A student claimed that as soil moves away from a major water source, such as a river, the salinity of the soil increases. Is this claim supported by Figures 1 and 2 ?

F. No; the electrical conductivity and exchangeable sodium percentage both decreased from Sample 1 to Sample 5.

G. No; there was no consistent trend for electrical conductivity and exchangeable sodium percentage.

H. Yes; the electrical conductivity and exchangeable sodium percentage both increased from Sample 1 to Sample 5.

J. Yes; the electrical conductivity increased and exchangeable sodium percentage decreased from Sample 1 to Sample 5.

GO ON TO THE NEXT PAGE.

Passage V

A group of researchers performed the following study in order to investigate declines in primarily carnivorous polar bear populations in the Arctic over a 10-year period.

Study

The researchers obtained previously collected data from several areas previously identified as polar bear habitats. From this data, the researchers selected sixty 5 km × 5 km blocks that do not overlap with one another. The blocks were selected to fall into six groups, each with a different set of conditions selected in order to conform to criteria for listing animals as threatened species. Previous research has indicated that Arctic sea ice and available food are among the factors which may affect polar bear populations.

Table 1 identifies each of the groups utilized in the study. Conditions other than the ones listed were considered to be normal.

Table 1	
Group	Conditions
1	These areas had significantly decreased populations of marine mammals consumed by polar bears.
2	These areas had significantly increased populations of seaweed commonly consumed by marine mammals.
3	These areas had been subject to excess thawing of Arctic sea ice.
4	These areas were subject to the same conditions as Groups 1 and 3.
5	These areas were subject to the same conditions as Groups 2 and 3.
6	Unaffected polar bear habitat.

Data for each of the plots was collected, and the population density of polar bears was calculated in terms of adult polar bears/km². Table 2 shows the population density of the blocks in Group 6.

Table 2	
Area label	Population density of Group 6 areas (polar bears/km²)
A	0.93
B	2.10
C	0.21
D	0.72
E	0.88
F	0.72
G	0.91
H	0.53
I	1.12
J	0.74

The data collected was analyzed to find the *average population density ratio* for each group. The researchers defined the average population density ratio of a given group as being equal to the result of the following expression:

$$\frac{\text{average population density of the group's areas}}{\text{average population density of Group 6 areas}}$$

Figure 1 shows the average population density ratio of Groups 1–5.

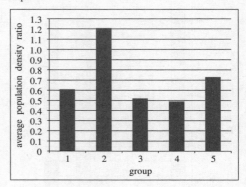

Figure 1

GO ON TO THE NEXT PAGE.

23. Which of the following statements provides the best explanation for why the researchers collected data for Group 6
in their study?

   A. Group 6 provided data indicating the types of predators that most threaten polar bears in their natural
   habitat.
   B. Group 6 provided a standard by which the other
   groups could be compared in order to determine how
   each set of conditions affected polar bear populations.
   C. Group 6 provided a means by which the researchers
   could carefully identify and select the conditions for
   the remaining five groups.
   D. Group 6 provided a means of determining the greatest
   number of polar bears that would be likely to survive
   in an area of 25 km².

24. Which one of the following is a question that most likely
explains why Group 2 areas were included in the study?

   F. Does an increase in the food source of their prey affect
   the population density of polar bears?
   G. If additional masses of seaweed were to be introduced to the Arctic, would polar bears be increasingly
   omnivorous?
   H. If additional masses of seaweed were to be introduced
   to the Arctic, would prey population density increase?
   J. Does an increase in the number of prey animals living
   in the same area as polar bears affect the amount of
   Arctic ice?

25. Which of the following correctly ranks Groups 1–5 from
the group where the conditions are *most* conducive to polar
bear population density in the study to the group where the
conditions are *least* conducive?

   A. Group 1, Group 2, Group 3, Group 4, Group 5
   B. Group 4, Group 3, Group 1, Group 5, Group 2
   C. Group 2, Group 5, Group 1, Group 3, Group 4
   D. Group 2, Group 1, Group 5, Group 3, Group 4

26. Which of the following is most likely an organism that
the researchers identified as exhibiting a significantly
decreased population when defining Group 1 ?

   F. Snowy owl
   G. Seal
   H. Salmon
   J. Polar bear

27. *Synergy* between two effects is said to exist when their
combined effect is greater than the sum of each effect
considered separately. The study appears to be designed
such that the researchers can investigate possible synergy
in which of the following two groups?

   A. Groups 1 and 2
   B. Groups 1 and 4
   C. Groups 4 and 5
   D. Groups 1 and 3

28. Before performing their analysis of the data, the researchers developed four different hypotheses. Each one of the
four hypotheses below is supported by the results of the
study EXCEPT:

   F. Declining prey populations have had some effect on
   polar bear populations.
   G. The melting of Arctic sea ice has a greater effect on
   polar bear populations than declining prey populations.
   H. Declining prey populations have a greater effect on
   polar bear populations than the melting of Arctic sea
   ice.
   J. The melting of Arctic sea ice has had some effect on
   polar bear populations.

GO ON TO THE NEXT PAGE.

Passage VI

Methane (CH_4) is an important energy source and a powerful greenhouse gas. CH_4 levels in the atmosphere are increasing, largely as a result of increasing livestock populations and energy emissions. Two scientists debate possible consequences of rising levels of atmospheric methane.

Scientist 1

Increasing CH_4 levels are a serious concern because, in the atmosphere, CH_4 can be converted into *formaldehyde* (H_2CO). H_2CO is a dangerous chemical, banned in some countries and used as an embalming fluid in others.

When *ozone* (O_3) is struck by solar radiation (light) in the presence of water, *hydroxyl radicals* ($\cdot OH$) are created (Reaction 1):

(1) $$light + O_3 + H_2O \rightarrow 2 \cdot OH + O_2$$

When $\cdot OH$ comes into contact with CH_4, another radical, $\cdot CH_3$, is formed (Reaction 2):

(2) $$\cdot OH + CH_4 \rightarrow \cdot CH_3 + H_2O$$

In the presence of oxygen (O_2) and nitric oxide (NO), the highly reactive $\cdot CH_3$ is converted into H_2CO (Reaction 3):

(3) $$\cdot CH_3 + NO + 2O_2 \rightarrow H_2CO + NO_2 + HO_2$$

The product HO_2 is unstable and reacts with NO, yielding more $\cdot OH$ (Reaction 4):

(4) $$HO_2 + NO \rightarrow NO_2 + \cdot OH$$

Together, Reactions 2–4 are called a *chain reaction* because the OH formed in Reaction 4 can react with another CH_4 molecule in Reaction 2:

(2) $$\cdot OH + CH_4 \rightarrow \cdot CH_3 + H_2O$$

(3) $$\cdot CH_3 + NO + 2O_2 \rightarrow H_2CO + NO_2 + HO_2$$

(4) $$HO_2 + NO \rightarrow NO_2 + \cdot OH$$

As a result, one $\cdot OH$ can convert a great deal of CH_4. At current CH_4 levels, this chain reaction is the primary fate of atmospheric $\cdot OH$, making the formation of H_2CO an urgent concern.

Scientist 2

H_2CO is a dangerous chemical, but atmospheric formaldehyde levels will not increase dramatically due to methane emissions. *Carbon monoxide* (CO) generation may be the greater concern. Hydroxyl radicals can break down methane, leading to the formation of H_2CO and nitric oxide, as in Reactions 1–4; in the presence of light, however, H_2CO quickly decomposes to CO and *hydrogen*, H_2 (Reaction 5):

(5) $$H_2CO \rightarrow H_2 + CO$$

Furthermore, the OH generated by Reactions 1 and 4 will react rapidly with any H_2CO in the atmosphere to produce CO and water: (Reaction 6)

(6) $$H_2CO + 2 \cdot OH \rightarrow CO + 2H_2O$$

In addition to reducing the amount of H_2CO by breaking down the H_2CO molecule, this reaction removes OH from the atmosphere, inhibiting the chain reaction of Reactions 2–4.

29. Which of the following substances do the two scientists agree must be present in order for $\cdot CH_3$ to be generated by atmospheric methane?

A. H_3O^+
B. NO_2
C. HNO_3
D. O_3

GO ON TO THE NEXT PAGE.

30. Which of the following graphs reflects Scientist 1's hypothesis of how levels of H_2CO in the atmosphere will change as more CH_4 is released into the atmosphere?

F.

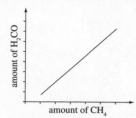

G.

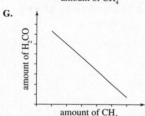

H.

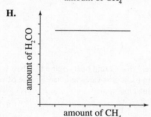

J.

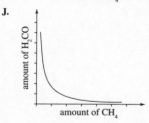

31. A student suggested that the molecular mass of either product in Reaction 5 would be greater than the molecular mass of the reactant in Reaction 5. Is he correct?

A. No; H_2CO is composed not of molecules, but of atoms.
B. Yes; the mass of a molecule of H_2CO is greater than the mass of either reactant.
C. No; the mass of a molecule of H_2CO is greater than the mass of either product.
D. Yes; the mass of a molecule of CO is greater than the mass of a molecule of H_2.

32. In certain parts of the atmosphere, the amount of O_3 is decreasing. As O_3 levels decrease, which of the following would Scientist 1 *most strongly agree with* regarding the levels of $\cdot CH_3$ and H_2CO in the atmosphere?

F. The amount of $\cdot CH_3$ would increase and the amount of H_2CO would decrease.
G. The amount of $\cdot CH_3$ would decrease and the level of H_2CO would remain constant.
H. The amounts of $\cdot CH_3$ and H_2CO would both decrease.
J. The amounts of $\cdot CH_3$ and H_2CO would both increase.

33. Of the following statements, with which would Scientist 2 *most strongly disagree*?

A. O_3 is involved in the generation of H_2CO in the atmosphere.
B. $\cdot OH$ is contributing to the formation of carbon monoxide in the atmosphere.
C. Solar radiation contributes to the break down of CH_4.
D. As CH_4 emissions increase, levels of H_2CO will rise dramatically.

34. After examining Scientist 1's hypothesis, Scientist 2 claimed that Reaction 3 would lead to increased levels of carbon monoxide. By which of the following explanations would Scientist 2 most likely support this argument?

F. Reaction 3 reduces the amount of NO present, inhibiting Reaction 4.
G. Reaction 3 produces H_2CO, which can react in Reaction 5 and Reaction 6.
H. Reaction 3 produces HO_2, which can react with H_2CO to produce CO.
J. Reaction 3 reduces the amount of O_2 present, making it more difficult for CO to form.

35. Further investigation has shown that Reaction 6 occurs on a large scale. Which of the following statements explains how the new evidence *most* weakens the argument of Scientist 1 ?

A. The OH produced in Reaction 4 reacts with CH_4.
B. The OH produced in Reaction 4 reacts with H_2CO.
C. The H_2O produced in Reaction 6 reacts with light and O_3.
D. The OH produced in Reaction 6 reacts with H_2CO.

GO ON TO THE NEXT PAGE.

Passage VII

A *Carnot heat engine* is an engine which runs by compressing and expanding a gas and transferring heat.

Figures 1 and 2 show the changes in pressure, *P*, and volume, *V*, that occur as two Carnot heat engines, A and B, run. For every gas, $PV = \Omega T$, where Ω is a constant and *T* represents the time.

The cycle begins as the gas is at its highest temperature and pressure. First, the gas expands, so volume increases while pressure decreases. As the gas expands, it can do work, such as pushing a piston. After the gas has run out of thermal energy and can no longer do work it is at its lowest temperature and pressure and the gas begins to be compressed, for instance a piston falling back down on the gas. As the gas is compressed, pressure increases while volume decreases and temperature begins to rise. In every Carnot heat engine, the gas ends at the same pressure, temperature, and volume as it began, thus completing a cycle.

Carnot Heat Engine B

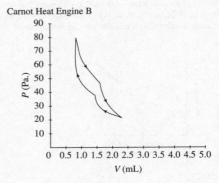

Figure 2

Carnot Heat Engine A

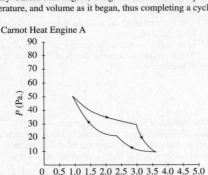

Figure 1

36. According to Figure 2, for Carnot heat engine B, when *V* was decreasing from its largest value and had a value of 1.5 mL, *P* had a value closest to:

F.　10 Pa.
G.　30 Pa.
H.　50 Pa.
J.　70 Pa.

GO ON TO THE NEXT PAGE.

37. For a new Carnot heat engine, F, a partial graph of *V* versus *P* is obtained.

If Carnot heat engine F behaves like Carnot heat engines A and B, the remainder of the graph of *V* versus *P* for Carnot heat engine F will look most like which of the following?

A.

C.

B.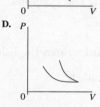

D.

38. For Carnot heat engine A, the minimum value of *P* was obtained at a *V* closest to:

F. 0.5 mL.
G. 2.0 mL.
H. 3.5 mL.
J. 5.0 mL.

39. Consider the largest value of *V* and the smallest value of *V* on the graph in Figure 2. How are these values related?

A. The smallest value of *V* is −1 times the largest value of *V*.
B. The smallest value of *V* is 1/3 times the largest value of *V*.
C. The smallest value of *V* is 1 times the largest value of *V*.
D. The smallest value of *V* is 2 times the largest value of *V*.

40. The *reversible isothermal expansion* step of a Carnot heat engine cycle takes place when *P* is decreased from its highest value and *V* is increased from its lowest value. According to Figure 1, the *reversible isothermal expansion* step for Carnot heat engine A begins when *V* is closest to:

F. 1.0 mL.
G. 2.25 mL.
H. 3.0 mL.
J. 3.5 mL.

END OF TEST 4
STOP! DO NOT RETURN TO ANY OTHER TEST.

Directions

This is a test of your writing skills. You will have forty (40) minutes to read the prompt, plan your response, and write an essay in English. Before you begin working, read all material in this test booklet carefully to understand exactly what you are being asked to do.

You will write your answer on the lined pages in the answer document provided. Your writing on those pages will be scored. You may use the unlined pages in this test booklet to plan your essay. Your work on these pages will not be scored.

Your essay will be evaluated based on the evidence it provides of your ability to:

- clearly state your own perspective on a complex issue and analyze the relationship between your perspective and at least one other perspective
- develop and support your ideas with reasoning and examples
- organize your ideas clearly and logically
- communicate your ideas effectively in standard written English

Lay your pencil down immediately when time is called.

DO NOT OPEN THIS BOOK UNTIL YOU ARE TOLD TO DO SO.

Composition paper for the essay can be found beginning on page 69.

Cell Phones While Driving

In only a short time, the use of cell phones, or "smartphones," has significantly increased. In direct relation, problems with their use at certain times have also risen. While driving, people use the smartphone for various activities such as texting, searching the Internet, or mapping a route with GPS. Certain studies suggest that operating a vehicle while using a cell phone is almost as severe, if not the same, as driving while intoxicated. Certain parts of the world have banned talking on the phone while driving, whereas regulations in the United States currently vary from state to state.

Read and carefully consider these perspectives. Each suggests a particular way of thinking about the conflict between driving with a cell phone and both public and personal safety.

Perspective One	**Perspective Two**	**Perspective Three**
Teenage drivers are more likely to use phones in cars. Teens are already the highest-risk drivers, so a cell-phone ban would decrease reckless driving at a proportionately higher rate among the most dangerous group.	There will always be distractions. Anything—other passengers, commotion outside, news interruptions on the radio—might distract a driver. Rather than ban cell phones, spend time teaching drivers how to better handle interferences.	Holding a cell phone while driving is dangerous. One hand is not on the steering wheel, which can significantly hinder the reaction time one needs to deal with an occurrence. In the case of an emergency, having one hand unavailable will slow the driver's reaction time and increase the chance of an accident.

Essay Task

Write a unified, coherent essay in which you evaluate multiple perspectives on the usage of cell phones while driving. In your essay, be sure to:

- clearly state your own perspective on the issue and analyze the relationship between your perspective and at least one other perspective
- develop and support your ideas with reasoning and examples
- organize your ideas clearly and logically
- communicate your ideas effectively in standard written English

Your perspective may be in full agreement with any of the others, in partial agreement, or wholly different. Whatever the case, support your ideas with logical reasoning and detailed, persuasive examples.

ACT Diagnostic Test Form

USE A SOFT LEAD NO. 2 PENCIL ONLY.
(Do NOT use a mechanical pencil, ink, ballpoint, correction fluid, or felt-tip pen.)

E-MAIL: _____

PHONE NO.: _____
(Print)

SCHOOL: _____

CLASS OF: _____

IMPORTANT: Please fill in these boxes exactly as shown on the back cover of your tests book.

2. TEST FORM

_____

3. TEST CODE

⓪	⓪	⓪	⓪
①	①	①	①
②	②	②	②
③	③	③	③
④	④	④	④
⑤	⑤	⑤	⑤
⑥	⑥	⑥	⑥
⑦	⑦	⑦	⑦
⑧	⑧	⑧	⑧
⑨	⑨	⑨	⑨

ALL examinees must complete Blocks A, B, C, and D – please print.

A — NAME, MAILING ADDRESS, AND TELEPHONE (Please print.)

Last Name   First Name   MI (Middle Initial)

House Number & Street (Apt. No.); or PO Box & No.; or RR & No.

City   State/Province   ZIP/Postal Code

Area Code   Number   Country

B — MATCH NAME
(First 5 letters of last name)

Ⓐ Ⓑ Ⓒ Ⓓ Ⓔ Ⓕ Ⓖ Ⓗ Ⓘ Ⓚ Ⓛ Ⓜ Ⓝ Ⓞ Ⓟ Ⓠ Ⓡ Ⓢ Ⓣ Ⓤ Ⓥ Ⓦ Ⓧ Ⓨ Ⓩ

C — MATCH NUMBER

| ① | ② | ③ | ④ | ⑤ | ⑥ | ⑦ | ⑧ | ⑨ | ⓪ |

D — DATE OF BIRTH

Month	Day	Year
○ January		
○ February		
○ March	① ①	① ①
○ April	② ②	② ②
○ May	③ ③	③ ③
○ June	④	④
○ July	⑤	⑤
○ August	⑥	⑥
○ September	⑦	⑦
○ October	⑧	⑧
○ November	⑨	⑨
○ December	⓪	⓪

Marking Directions: Mark only **one** oval for each question. Fill in response completely. Erase errors cleanly without smudging.

Correct mark: ○ ● ○ ○

Do NOT use these *incorrect* or *bad* marks.

Incorrect marks: ⊘ ⊗ ⊖ ●
Overlapping mark: ○ ○ ◑◐
Cross-out mark: ○ ⊗ ○ ○
Smudged erasure ○ ○ ◐ ○
Mark is too light: ◐ ○ ○ ○

BOOKLET NUMBER

①	①	①	①	①	①
②	②	②	②	②	②
③	③	③	③	③	③
④	④	④	④	④	④
⑤	⑤	⑤	⑤	⑤	⑤
⑥	⑥	⑥	⑥	⑥	⑥
⑦	⑦	⑦	⑦	⑦	⑦
⑧	⑧	⑧	⑧	⑧	⑧
⑨	⑨	⑨	⑨	⑨	⑨
⓪	⓪	⓪	⓪	⓪	⓪

FORM

Print your 3-character **Test Form** in the boxes above and fill in the corresponding oval at the right

BE SURE TO FILL IN THE CORRECT FORM OVAL.

PRE ○

THIS PAGE INTENTIONALLY LEFT BLANK

The Princeton Review
Diagnostic ACT Form

TEST 1: ENGLISH

1 Ⓐ Ⓑ Ⓒ Ⓓ	14 Ⓕ Ⓖ Ⓗ Ⓙ	27 Ⓐ Ⓑ Ⓒ Ⓓ	40 Ⓕ Ⓖ Ⓗ Ⓙ	53 Ⓐ Ⓑ Ⓒ Ⓓ	66 Ⓕ Ⓖ Ⓗ Ⓙ
2 Ⓕ Ⓖ Ⓗ Ⓙ	15 Ⓐ Ⓑ Ⓒ Ⓓ	28 Ⓕ Ⓖ Ⓗ Ⓙ	41 Ⓐ Ⓑ Ⓒ Ⓓ	54 Ⓕ Ⓖ Ⓗ Ⓙ	67 Ⓐ Ⓑ Ⓒ Ⓓ
3 Ⓐ Ⓑ Ⓒ Ⓓ	16 Ⓕ Ⓖ Ⓗ Ⓙ	29 Ⓐ Ⓑ Ⓒ Ⓓ	42 Ⓕ Ⓖ Ⓗ Ⓙ	55 Ⓐ Ⓑ Ⓒ Ⓓ	68 Ⓕ Ⓖ Ⓗ Ⓙ
4 Ⓕ Ⓖ Ⓗ Ⓙ	17 Ⓐ Ⓑ Ⓒ Ⓓ	30 Ⓕ Ⓖ Ⓗ Ⓙ	43 Ⓐ Ⓑ Ⓒ Ⓓ	56 Ⓕ Ⓖ Ⓗ Ⓙ	69 Ⓐ Ⓑ Ⓒ Ⓓ
5 Ⓐ Ⓑ Ⓒ Ⓓ	18 Ⓕ Ⓖ Ⓗ Ⓙ	31 Ⓐ Ⓑ Ⓒ Ⓓ	44 Ⓕ Ⓖ Ⓗ Ⓙ	57 Ⓐ Ⓑ Ⓒ Ⓓ	70 Ⓕ Ⓖ Ⓗ Ⓙ
6 Ⓕ Ⓖ Ⓗ Ⓙ	19 Ⓐ Ⓑ Ⓒ Ⓓ	32 Ⓕ Ⓖ Ⓗ Ⓙ	45 Ⓐ Ⓑ Ⓒ Ⓓ	58 Ⓕ Ⓖ Ⓗ Ⓙ	71 Ⓐ Ⓑ Ⓒ Ⓓ
7 Ⓐ Ⓑ Ⓒ Ⓓ	20 Ⓕ Ⓖ Ⓗ Ⓙ	33 Ⓐ Ⓑ Ⓒ Ⓓ	46 Ⓕ Ⓖ Ⓗ Ⓙ	59 Ⓐ Ⓑ Ⓒ Ⓓ	72 Ⓕ Ⓖ Ⓗ Ⓙ
8 Ⓕ Ⓖ Ⓗ Ⓙ	21 Ⓐ Ⓑ Ⓒ Ⓓ	34 Ⓕ Ⓖ Ⓗ Ⓙ	47 Ⓐ Ⓑ Ⓒ Ⓓ	60 Ⓕ Ⓖ Ⓗ Ⓙ	73 Ⓐ Ⓑ Ⓒ Ⓓ
9 Ⓐ Ⓑ Ⓒ Ⓓ	22 Ⓕ Ⓖ Ⓗ Ⓙ	35 Ⓐ Ⓑ Ⓒ Ⓓ	48 Ⓕ Ⓖ Ⓗ Ⓙ	61 Ⓐ Ⓑ Ⓒ Ⓓ	74 Ⓕ Ⓖ Ⓗ Ⓙ
10 Ⓕ Ⓖ Ⓗ Ⓙ	23 Ⓐ Ⓑ Ⓒ Ⓓ	36 Ⓕ Ⓖ Ⓗ Ⓙ	49 Ⓐ Ⓑ Ⓒ Ⓓ	62 Ⓕ Ⓖ Ⓗ Ⓙ	75 Ⓐ Ⓑ Ⓒ Ⓓ
11 Ⓐ Ⓑ Ⓒ Ⓓ	24 Ⓕ Ⓖ Ⓗ Ⓙ	37 Ⓐ Ⓑ Ⓒ Ⓓ	50 Ⓕ Ⓖ Ⓗ Ⓙ	63 Ⓐ Ⓑ Ⓒ Ⓓ	
12 Ⓕ Ⓖ Ⓗ Ⓙ	25 Ⓐ Ⓑ Ⓒ Ⓓ	38 Ⓕ Ⓖ Ⓗ Ⓙ	51 Ⓐ Ⓑ Ⓒ Ⓓ	64 Ⓕ Ⓖ Ⓗ Ⓙ	
13 Ⓐ Ⓑ Ⓒ Ⓓ	26 Ⓕ Ⓖ Ⓗ Ⓙ	39 Ⓐ Ⓑ Ⓒ Ⓓ	52 Ⓕ Ⓖ Ⓗ Ⓙ	65 Ⓐ Ⓑ Ⓒ Ⓓ	

TEST 2: MATHEMATICS

1 Ⓐ Ⓑ Ⓒ Ⓓ Ⓔ	11 Ⓐ Ⓑ Ⓒ Ⓓ Ⓔ	21 Ⓐ Ⓑ Ⓒ Ⓓ Ⓔ	31 Ⓐ Ⓑ Ⓒ Ⓓ Ⓔ	41 Ⓐ Ⓑ Ⓒ Ⓓ Ⓔ	51 Ⓐ Ⓑ Ⓒ Ⓓ Ⓔ
2 Ⓕ Ⓖ Ⓗ Ⓙ Ⓚ	12 Ⓕ Ⓖ Ⓗ Ⓙ Ⓚ	22 Ⓕ Ⓖ Ⓗ Ⓙ Ⓚ	32 Ⓕ Ⓖ Ⓗ Ⓙ Ⓚ	42 Ⓕ Ⓖ Ⓗ Ⓙ Ⓚ	52 Ⓕ Ⓖ Ⓗ Ⓙ Ⓚ
3 Ⓐ Ⓑ Ⓒ Ⓓ Ⓔ	13 Ⓐ Ⓑ Ⓒ Ⓓ Ⓔ	23 Ⓐ Ⓑ Ⓒ Ⓓ Ⓔ	33 Ⓐ Ⓑ Ⓒ Ⓓ Ⓔ	43 Ⓐ Ⓑ Ⓒ Ⓓ Ⓔ	53 Ⓐ Ⓑ Ⓒ Ⓓ Ⓔ
4 Ⓕ Ⓖ Ⓗ Ⓙ Ⓚ	14 Ⓕ Ⓖ Ⓗ Ⓙ Ⓚ	24 Ⓕ Ⓖ Ⓗ Ⓙ Ⓚ	34 Ⓕ Ⓖ Ⓗ Ⓙ Ⓚ	44 Ⓕ Ⓖ Ⓗ Ⓙ Ⓚ	54 Ⓕ Ⓖ Ⓗ Ⓙ Ⓚ
5 Ⓐ Ⓑ Ⓒ Ⓓ Ⓔ	15 Ⓐ Ⓑ Ⓒ Ⓓ Ⓔ	25 Ⓐ Ⓑ Ⓒ Ⓓ Ⓔ	35 Ⓐ Ⓑ Ⓒ Ⓓ Ⓔ	45 Ⓐ Ⓑ Ⓒ Ⓓ Ⓔ	55 Ⓐ Ⓑ Ⓒ Ⓓ Ⓔ
6 Ⓕ Ⓖ Ⓗ Ⓙ Ⓚ	16 Ⓕ Ⓖ Ⓗ Ⓙ Ⓚ	26 Ⓕ Ⓖ Ⓗ Ⓙ Ⓚ	36 Ⓕ Ⓖ Ⓗ Ⓙ Ⓚ	46 Ⓕ Ⓖ Ⓗ Ⓙ Ⓚ	56 Ⓕ Ⓖ Ⓗ Ⓙ Ⓚ
7 Ⓐ Ⓑ Ⓒ Ⓓ Ⓔ	17 Ⓐ Ⓑ Ⓒ Ⓓ Ⓔ	27 Ⓐ Ⓑ Ⓒ Ⓓ Ⓔ	37 Ⓐ Ⓑ Ⓒ Ⓓ Ⓔ	47 Ⓐ Ⓑ Ⓒ Ⓓ Ⓔ	57 Ⓐ Ⓑ Ⓒ Ⓓ Ⓔ
8 Ⓕ Ⓖ Ⓗ Ⓙ Ⓚ	18 Ⓕ Ⓖ Ⓗ Ⓙ Ⓚ	28 Ⓕ Ⓖ Ⓗ Ⓙ Ⓚ	38 Ⓕ Ⓖ Ⓗ Ⓙ Ⓚ	48 Ⓕ Ⓖ Ⓗ Ⓙ Ⓚ	58 Ⓕ Ⓖ Ⓗ Ⓙ Ⓚ
9 Ⓐ Ⓑ Ⓒ Ⓓ Ⓔ	19 Ⓐ Ⓑ Ⓒ Ⓓ Ⓔ	29 Ⓐ Ⓑ Ⓒ Ⓓ Ⓔ	39 Ⓐ Ⓑ Ⓒ Ⓓ Ⓔ	49 Ⓐ Ⓑ Ⓒ Ⓓ Ⓔ	59 Ⓐ Ⓑ Ⓒ Ⓓ Ⓔ
10 Ⓕ Ⓖ Ⓗ Ⓙ Ⓚ	20 Ⓕ Ⓖ Ⓗ Ⓙ Ⓚ	30 Ⓕ Ⓖ Ⓗ Ⓙ Ⓚ	40 Ⓕ Ⓖ Ⓗ Ⓙ Ⓚ	50 Ⓕ Ⓖ Ⓗ Ⓙ Ⓚ	60 Ⓕ Ⓖ Ⓗ Ⓙ Ⓚ

The Princeton Review
Diagnostic ACT Form

TEST 3: READING

1 Ⓐ Ⓑ Ⓒ Ⓓ	8 Ⓕ Ⓖ Ⓗ Ⓙ	15 Ⓐ Ⓑ Ⓒ Ⓓ	22 Ⓕ Ⓖ Ⓗ Ⓙ	29 Ⓐ Ⓑ Ⓒ Ⓓ	36 Ⓕ Ⓖ Ⓗ Ⓙ
2 Ⓕ Ⓖ Ⓗ Ⓙ	9 Ⓐ Ⓑ Ⓒ Ⓓ	16 Ⓕ Ⓖ Ⓗ Ⓙ	23 Ⓐ Ⓑ Ⓒ Ⓓ	30 Ⓕ Ⓖ Ⓗ Ⓙ	37 Ⓐ Ⓑ Ⓒ Ⓓ
3 Ⓐ Ⓑ Ⓒ Ⓓ	10 Ⓕ Ⓖ Ⓗ Ⓙ	17 Ⓐ Ⓑ Ⓒ Ⓓ	24 Ⓕ Ⓖ Ⓗ Ⓙ	31 Ⓐ Ⓑ Ⓒ Ⓓ	38 Ⓕ Ⓖ Ⓗ Ⓙ
4 Ⓕ Ⓖ Ⓗ Ⓙ	11 Ⓐ Ⓑ Ⓒ Ⓓ	18 Ⓕ Ⓖ Ⓗ Ⓙ	25 Ⓐ Ⓑ Ⓒ Ⓓ	32 Ⓕ Ⓖ Ⓗ Ⓙ	39 Ⓐ Ⓑ Ⓒ Ⓓ
5 Ⓐ Ⓑ Ⓒ Ⓓ	12 Ⓕ Ⓖ Ⓗ Ⓙ	19 Ⓐ Ⓑ Ⓒ Ⓓ	26 Ⓕ Ⓖ Ⓗ Ⓙ	33 Ⓐ Ⓑ Ⓒ Ⓓ	40 Ⓕ Ⓖ Ⓗ Ⓙ
6 Ⓕ Ⓖ Ⓗ Ⓙ	13 Ⓐ Ⓑ Ⓒ Ⓓ	20 Ⓕ Ⓖ Ⓗ Ⓙ	27 Ⓐ Ⓑ Ⓒ Ⓓ	34 Ⓕ Ⓖ Ⓗ Ⓙ	
7 Ⓐ Ⓑ Ⓒ Ⓓ	14 Ⓕ Ⓖ Ⓗ Ⓙ	21 Ⓐ Ⓑ Ⓒ Ⓓ	28 Ⓕ Ⓖ Ⓗ Ⓙ	35 Ⓐ Ⓑ Ⓒ Ⓓ	

TEST 4: SCIENCE

1 Ⓐ Ⓑ Ⓒ Ⓓ	8 Ⓕ Ⓖ Ⓗ Ⓙ	15 Ⓐ Ⓑ Ⓒ Ⓓ	22 Ⓕ Ⓖ Ⓗ Ⓙ	29 Ⓐ Ⓑ Ⓒ Ⓓ	36 Ⓕ Ⓖ Ⓗ Ⓙ
2 Ⓕ Ⓖ Ⓗ Ⓙ	9 Ⓐ Ⓑ Ⓒ Ⓓ	16 Ⓕ Ⓖ Ⓗ Ⓙ	23 Ⓐ Ⓑ Ⓒ Ⓓ	30 Ⓕ Ⓖ Ⓗ Ⓙ	37 Ⓐ Ⓑ Ⓒ Ⓓ
3 Ⓐ Ⓑ Ⓒ Ⓓ	10 Ⓕ Ⓖ Ⓗ Ⓙ	17 Ⓐ Ⓑ Ⓒ Ⓓ	24 Ⓕ Ⓖ Ⓗ Ⓙ	31 Ⓐ Ⓑ Ⓒ Ⓓ	38 Ⓕ Ⓖ Ⓗ Ⓙ
4 Ⓕ Ⓖ Ⓗ Ⓙ	11 Ⓐ Ⓑ Ⓒ Ⓓ	18 Ⓕ Ⓖ Ⓗ Ⓙ	25 Ⓐ Ⓑ Ⓒ Ⓓ	32 Ⓕ Ⓖ Ⓗ Ⓙ	39 Ⓐ Ⓑ Ⓒ Ⓓ
5 Ⓐ Ⓑ Ⓒ Ⓓ	12 Ⓕ Ⓖ Ⓗ Ⓙ	19 Ⓐ Ⓑ Ⓒ Ⓓ	26 Ⓕ Ⓖ Ⓗ Ⓙ	33 Ⓐ Ⓑ Ⓒ Ⓓ	40 Ⓕ Ⓖ Ⓗ Ⓙ
6 Ⓕ Ⓖ Ⓗ Ⓙ	13 Ⓐ Ⓑ Ⓒ Ⓓ	20 Ⓕ Ⓖ Ⓗ Ⓙ	27 Ⓐ Ⓑ Ⓒ Ⓓ	34 Ⓕ Ⓖ Ⓗ Ⓙ	
7 Ⓐ Ⓑ Ⓒ Ⓓ	14 Ⓕ Ⓖ Ⓗ Ⓙ	21 Ⓐ Ⓑ Ⓒ Ⓓ	28 Ⓕ Ⓖ Ⓗ Ⓙ	35 Ⓐ Ⓑ Ⓒ Ⓓ	

The Princeton Review
Diagnostic ACT Form

ESSAY

Begin your essay on this side. If necessary, continue on the opposite side.

Continue on the opposite side if necessary.

The Princeton Review
Diagnostic ACT Form

Continued from previous page.

PLEASE PRINT
YOUR INITIALS

First	Middle	Last

The Princeton Review
Diagnostic ACT Form

Continued from previous page.

The Princeton Review
Diagnostic ACT Form

Continued from previous page.

Chapter 3
Test 1: Answers and Explanations

TEST 1 ENGLISH ANSWERS

1.	D		48.	J
2.	F		49.	B
3.	B		50.	H
4.	H		51.	A
5.	C		52.	H
6.	J		53.	A
7.	D		54.	J
8.	J		55.	D
9.	A		56.	F
10.	F		57.	A
11.	B		58.	G
12.	G		59.	D
13.	C		60.	G
14.	H		61.	C
15.	B		62.	J
16.	F		63.	A
17.	D		64.	J
18.	J		65.	C
19.	B		66.	F
20.	H		67.	C
21.	A		68.	G
22.	J		69.	B
23.	B		70.	G
24.	J		71.	A
25.	B		72.	J
26.	F		73.	D
27.	D		74.	J
28.	F		75.	B
29.	D			
30.	F			
31.	D			
32.	G			
33.	D		**TEST 1 MATH ANSWERS**	
34.	H		1.	A
35.	C		2.	J
36.	J		3.	B
37.	A		4.	K
38.	G		5.	D
39.	C		6.	H
40.	F		7.	A
41.	B		8.	J
42.	F		9.	C
43.	D		10.	H
44.	G		11.	A
45.	D		12.	F
46.	H		13.	D
47.	C		14.	G

15.	D	1.	C	
16.	G	2.	J	
17.	A	3.	B	
18.	G	4.	H	
19.	B	5.	B	
20.	H	6.	F	
21.	B	7.	A	
22.	F	8.	G	
23.	C	9.	C	
24.	K	10.	J	
25.	B	11.	B	
26.	F	12.	H	
27.	C	13.	D	
28.	J	14.	F	
29.	B	15.	D	
30.	H	16.	H	
31.	E	17.	A	
32.	H	18.	G	
33.	A	19.	C	
34.	J	20.	H	
35.	C	21.	B	
36.	J	22.	J	
37.	D	23.	A	
38.	J	24.	F	
39.	A	25.	B	
40.	F	26.	H	
41.	A	27.	D	
42.	K	28.	J	
43.	C	29.	C	
44.	G	30.	F	
45.	D	31.	A	
46.	J	32.	F	
47.	C	33.	C	
48.	J	34.	H	
49.	C	35.	B	
50.	K	36.	G	
51.	D	37.	D	
52.	G	38.	F	
53.	B	39.	B	
54.	F	40.	J	
55.	B			
56.	F			
57.	C			
58.	F			
59.	D			
60.	K			

TEST 1 SCIENCE ANSWERS

1. A
2. F
3. D
4. G
5. D
6. G
7. B
8. J
9. A
10. H
11. D
12. H
13. D
14. J
15. C
16. G
17. D
18. H
19. B
20. J
21. C
22. G
23. B
24. F
25. C
26. G
27. D
28. H
29. D
30. F
31. C
32. H
33. D
34. G
35. B
36. G
37. C
38. H
39. B
40. F

SCORING YOUR PRACTICE EXAM

Step A

Count the number of correct answers for each section and record the number in the space provided for your raw score on the Score Conversion Worksheet below.

Step B

Using the Score Conversion Chart on the next page, convert your raw scores on each section to scaled scores. Then compute your composite ACT score by averaging the four subject scores. Add them up and divide by four. Don't worry about the essay score; it is not included in your composite score.

Score Conversion Worksheet		
Section	Raw Score	Scaled Score
1	_____/75	_____
2	_____/60	_____
3	_____/40	_____
4	_____/40	_____

SCORE CONVERSION CHART

Scaled Score	Raw Score			
	English	Mathematics	Reading	Science
36	75	60	39–40	40
35	74	59	38	39
34	72–73	58	37	38
33	71	57	36	—
32	70	55–56	35	37
31	69	53–54	34	36
30	67–68	52	33	—
29	65–66	50–51	32	35
28	62–64	46–49	30–31	33–34
27	59–61	43–45	28–29	31–32
26	57–58	41–42	27	30
25	55–56	39–40	26	29
24	52–54	37–38	25	28
23	50–51	35–36	24	27–26
22	49	33–34	23	25
21	48	31–32	21–22	24
20	45–47	29–30	20	23
19	43–44	27–28	19	22
18	40–42	24–26	18	20–21
17	38–39	21–23	17	18–19
16	35–37	18–20	16	16–17
15	32–34	16–17	15	15
14	29–31	13–15	14	13–14
13	27–28	11–12	12–13	12
12	24–26	9–10	11	11
11	21–23	7–8	9–10	10
10	18–20	6	8	9
9	15–17	5	7	7–8
8	13–14	4	—	6
7	11–12	—	6	5
6	9–10	3	5	—
5	7–8	2	4	4
4	5–6	—	3	3
3	3–4	1	2	2
2	2	—	1	1
1	0	0	0	0

TEST 1 ENGLISH EXPLANATIONS

Passage I

1. **D** The phrase *left by the delivery man* is an unnecessary detail added to the sentence and should be off-set by two commas, making (D) the best answer. The semicolon in (A) and (C) creates a fragment in the second half of the sentence.

2. **F** The sentence uses *scrawled* as an adjective to describe the words, not as a verb, so you can eliminate (G). Choice (H) uses the wrong form of *scrawl*, and (J) is the wrong idiomatic expression.

3. **B** The phrase *my heart skipping a beat (or two)* is incomplete and cannot be linked to the complete phrase with *and,* eliminating (A) and (C). *When* changes the meaning of the sentence, making (B) the best answer.

4. **H** The two halves of this sentence are both complete, eliminating (J). Since the second half already uses the pronoun *it* to refer to the box, *that* and *which* are unnecessary, making (H) the best answer.

5. **C** Since the question asks you to make a contrast, you can eliminate (B) and (D). Choice (C) better describes the people for whom the record holds value than (A).

6. **J** The verb should be in past perfect tense to show that he made his living as a musician before marrying, making (J) the only possible answer. Choices (F), (G), and (H) all use *would*, which is the conditional tense of will.

7. **D** The phrase *performing in music hall and local festivals* is incomplete and must be linked to the previous thought, eliminating (A) and (B). By using *which* to link the ideas, (C) makes it sound as if the grandfather performs the band, rather than the band performing.

8. **J** The best answer is (J) because it is the most concise of the choices. It is unnecessary to the meaning of the sentence to mention who produced the album.

9. **A** The phrase after the dash is adding further details to how rare the record truly is, making (A) the best answer. Choice (B) is a contrasting transition, and (C) and (D) use transition words that confuse the meaning of the sentence.

10. **F** The verb should be in past perfect tense because it is describing how long one copy had existed before the writer received the record in the mail, eliminating (H) and (J). Choice (G) uses the incorrect expression.

11. **B** The words *beg* and *plead* are synonyms, so it is redundant to use both. Choice (B) is the most concise answer.

12. **G** Since the question asks you to discuss the significance to the writer's upbringing, you can eliminate (F) and (H). Choice (G) is more personal to the writer than (J), making it the best answer.

13. **C** Choice (C) is the only answer that clearly expresses the writer's intended meaning. Choices (A), (B), and (D) all misplace phrases throughout the sentence, confusing who and what are being described.

14. **H** The punctuation should separate two complete ideas, eliminating (F) and (J). Choice (G) is an unnecessary transition word, because *however* is already used in the following sentence.

15. **B** The phrase *that he was still with me* is an incomplete thought and should be linked to the previous complete thought, eliminating (D). Since the sentence explains what the author feels reassured of, punctuation between *me* and *that* creates an unnecessary pause, making (B) the best answer.

Passage II

16. **F** This question requires that you determine whether an apostrophe or additional punctuation mark is required. No apostrophe is needed because the word *lives* is not possessing anything, so eliminate (H) and (J). No pause is required between the words *lives* and *completely*, so eliminate (G), which interrupts the sentence unnecessarily. The sentence is correct as written, so the best choice is (F).

17. **D** The question asks for a line that indicates some similarity between the narrator and his friends. Choice (A) discusses only the narrator; (B) and (C) contain information that is much too general to discuss only the narrator and his friends. Only (D) has all the appropriate elements, particularly as presented in the words *palpable likeness*.

18. **J** This question requires that you determine whether an apostrophe or additional punctuation mark is required. No apostrophe is needed because there is no indication that owners are possessing anything (hint: don't get thrown off by the phrase *restaurant's owners* in which the word appears), so you can eliminate (H). Only (J) has the appropriate comma placement to situate *chat with the restaurant's owners* within a list (the other items in this list are *sit, drink a cup of coffee,* and *figure out which new and exciting place we'd be driving to next*). A semicolon is inappropriate here because the semicolon is a punctuation mark used to separate two complete ideas, and the context indicates that it is not used to separate the items in this list.

19. **B** The sentence as written contains the phrase *looking forward to it in anticipation*, which is redundant, so you can eliminate (A). Choices (C) and (D) contain the same error. Only (B) preserves the meaning in a concise, non-redundant way. In addition, the word *it* in (A) and (C) is ambiguous.

20. **H** This question asks whether the writer's proposed addition would be appropriately placed at the end of this paragraph. If you're not sure whether to answer Yes or No, look at the reasons. Choice (F) must be eliminated because the proposed addition is too general and is consequently not relevant to other, more personal information in the passage. Choice (G) must be eliminated because it is too general and gives no indication why the narrator should choose a *specific* diner. Choice (J) suggests that the primary focus of the paragraph up to this point has been *driving*, which it has not; rather, the primary focus of the paragraph is the stop at the diner and the things the narrator and his friends did there. Accordingly, only (H) appropriately recognizes the personal tone of the paragraph and correctly advises not to include the proposed addition.

21. **A** The first place you should look in this question is to whether *that* or *whom* is an appropriate first word. *Whom* is the objective form of who, which is used to refer only to people. The word here refers back to *something*, not a person, so eliminate (B) and (C). Choice (D) changes the meaning of the sentence to suggest that something is doing the ordering, rather than being ordered. The sentence is correct as written, so NO CHANGE is required.

22. **J** This question asks you to determine which word would be most appropriately modified by the phrase *from childhood*. To place the phrase after any of the words in (F), (G), or (H) is to break the flow of the sentence and to make the meaning of the sentence unclear. Only (J) establishes the proper link between the underlined and non-underlined portions of the sentence in the phrase *remembered from childhood*.

23. **B** In an earlier part of the sentence, the narrator refers to the food in the city as *too expensive*. Only (B) supports and modifies this idea. Read the question closely: While the other choices may be true, the best answer will be one that supports and modifies a specific part of the passage.

24. **J** In EXCEPT/LEAST/NOT questions, the underlined portion of the sentence is correct. Compare your answer choices. What do words like *as* and *when* do to the first part of the sentence? They make it an introductory idea and an incomplete thought. When the first part of the sentence is incomplete, the comma after the word *could* sets this first part off from the complete idea after it. By contrast, if the first part of the sentence is made complete as it is in (J), this creates a comma splice, wherein two complete ideas are insufficiently separated by a comma.

25. **B** Identify the subject of the verb. Although the word *restaurants* is closest to the verb, it is not the subject; rather, the subject is the word *place*, a singular subject that requires a singular verb. Since (A), (C), and (D) all contain plural verbs, eliminate them. Only (B) remains, and the verb *was* does agree in number with the word *place*.

26. **F** Look for an idea that will signal the transition between the paragraph above, which is a recollection of the trips, and the paragraph below, which fast forwards to the present and discusses the narrator's life now. Only (F) contains this transition. Choice (G) deals only with the narrator's friends, who are not mentioned in the last paragraph. Choice (H) deals only with the past, and (J) deals only with the narrator's life after graduation. Only (F) has both the past and present components it needs to transition from one paragraph to the next.

27. **D** This question asks you to determine whether you need a transition between the first and second sentences of this last paragraph. Choices (A) and (C) suggest a disagreement between the two ideas where none exists. Choice (B) suggests a cause-and-effect relationship between the two sentences where none exists. Only (D) makes sense in the context, where no transition is needed.

28. **F** In EXCEPT/LEAST/NOT questions, the underlined portion of the sentence is correct. To answer this question, you need to determine which prepositions work idiomatically with the verb *drive*. Choice (G) contains the same preposition, *about*, used in the underlined portion, and although not a particularly common usage, *drive about* is idiomatically correct. The same goes for the more familiar *drive around*, as it is used in (H) and (J). Accordingly, only (F) does not work in the context of the sentence because it is incorrect usage to say *drive among the town*.

29. **D** All the answer choices mean roughly the same thing; each just presents a different way to say it. In situations such as this one, the most concise answer that preserves the meaning is the best. Accordingly, (A), (B), and (C) are all too wordy in comparison with (D).

30. **F** This question too asks you to determine which choice presents the most concise alternative that preserves the meaning of the sentence. Eliminate (G) and (J) because each presents an awkward, wordy alternative to the original. Choice (H) is as concise as (F), but note the context: Your answer will need to be parallel to other verbs in the sentence. In this case, only *came back* is parallel with the tense and tone of *drove by*, making the best answer (F).

Passage III

31. **D** In EXCEPT/LEAST/NOT questions, the underlined portion of the sentence is correct. The original sentence uses *even though* to introduce two contrasting ideas. Choices (A), (B), and (C) are all contrasting transition words and are acceptable. Choice (D) indicates that the ideas are similar and, therefore, is not an acceptable alternative.

32. **G** The best connecting statement should continue the previous idea that Siena has both ancient and modern elements, eliminating (F) and (J). The following sentence begins with *Another remnant*, which means the inserted sentence should already list specific examples and makes (G) better than (H).

33. **D** It is redundant to describe the horse race as *biannual* and as *held twice a year*, eliminating (A) and (B). Choice (D) is better than (C) because it is more concise.

34. **H** The phrase *dreaded right-angle turns* describes an obstacle racers must face as they complete each lap, therefore it must immediately follow *laps* to clarify meaning. Choices (F), (G), and (J) do not provide logical sentences because the phrase does not describe *horses*, *track*, or *plaza*.

35. **C** Choice (C) correctly agrees with the present tense of the other verb in the sentence. Choices (A), (B), and (D) do not agree in tense and alter the meaning of the sentence.

36. **J** *Because* introduces an incomplete thought, so (F) creates a sentence fragment. Choice (G) suggests contrasting rather than similar ideas. Choice (H) is incorrect because the preceding sentence has already mentioned *financial* commitments, so voluntary taxation cannot be considered an additional act by members.

37. **A** The previous sentence illustrates the enormous cost to hire a jockey, which contrasts with the idea that it is a small price to pay, so the best transition word is (A). Choices (B), (C), and (D) all indicate a similar relationship, which is not consistent with the passage.

38. **G** The phrase *even more so than getting married* is an unnecessary description within the sentence and should be offset by either two commas or dashes, eliminating (F). Since the non-underlined portion uses a dash before *even*, the best answer is (G) not (H). Choice (J) creates a sentence fragment, since a semicolon can separate only complete ideas.

39. **C** The word *throughout* begins an incomplete idea, and the phrase cannot stand on its own as a sentence, eliminating (A). Choice (C) connects the incomplete phrase to the complete idea before it with the smoothest transition. The comma in (D) creates an unnecessary pause. Since a semicolon is generally used to separate two complete sentences, (B) is also incorrect.

40. **F** The word *Contrade* ends a complete thought, and *Contrada* begins a second complete thought, so you need a period, making (F) the best answer. Choices (G), (H), and (J) all create run-on sentences because they do not separate complete ideas.

41. **B** The phrase *from baptisms to food festivals* is an unnecessary description within the sentence and should be offset by either two commas or dashes, eliminating (A). Since the non-underlined portion uses a comma after festivals, the best answer is (B) not (D). Choice (C) incorrectly uses a colon, which can be used only after a complete idea.

42. **F** The correct pronoun is *who* because *members* is the subject for the verb *become*. Choices (G) and (H) use possessive rather than subject case, and (J) is object case and does not indicate which noun become describes.

43. **D** The second half of the sentence is an incomplete idea and must be linked to the complete thought, eliminating (A), (B), and (C).

44. **G** The passage is written in the present tense, eliminating (F) and (H). Since the parties are *thrown* by the locals, you need the passive form for the verb (also called the past participle) not the past tense verb *threw*.

45. **D** The best location for Paragraph 3 is before Paragraph 5, (D), because Paragraph 4 introduces and defines the *contrada* discussed in the first sentence of Paragraph 3. There is also a logical sequence from winning the *Palio* at the end of Paragraph 3 to the celebration in the beginning of Paragraph 5.

Passage IV

46. **H** As written, the pronoun *it* in the underlined portion has no clear referent. Choices (G) and (J) do not fix the problem. Only (H) replaces the ambiguous pronoun with a clear referent.

47. **C** The sentence as written is a fragment. Choice (B) is also a fragment. Choices (C) and (D) both fix the sentence fragment, but (D) changes the meaning of the sentence.

48. **J** The sentence as written is incorrect because the adjective *tireless* cannot modify the verb *continued*. Choices (G) and (H) do not make sense in the given context. Only (J) links the word *tireless* with its appropriate noun, *literary experimentation*.

49. **B** In EXCEPT/LEAST/NOT questions, the underlined portion of the sentence is correct. Since the verbs *to seem* and *to appear* are synonyms, look for differences among the answer choices. Note that the original sentence and (A), (C), and (D) all contain the present tense, appropriately matched to the word *contemporary* used earlier in this sentence. Only (B) changes the tense to past, making (B) the LEAST acceptable substitution.

50. **H** The sentence as written is idiomatically incorrect. The prepositions *until* and *at*, as in (G), are incorrectly linked to the phrase *take a real step*. Only the word *toward* completes this phrase appropriately to create *take a real step toward*. Deleting the underlined portion, as in (J), makes the sentence unclear and changes its meaning.

51. **A** Choices (B), (C), and (D) all incorrectly separate the verb *fuse* from its objects. NO CHANGE is required here because no punctuation is necessary between the verb and its objects.

52. **H** In EXCEPT/LEAST/NOT questions, the underlined portion of the sentence is correct. Note the similarities between the words. *Encouraged*, *motivated*, and *emboldened*, in (F), (G), and (J), are all synonyms for the verb *inspired*. Only the word *forced* in (H) changes the meaning of the sentence and is thus the LEAST acceptable substitution.

53. **A** Since the phrase *as American writers living abroad were known* is a descriptive phrase that plays no essential role in determining the meaning of the sentence, it must be set off by a comma as it is in the sentence as written. Choices (B) and (D) introduce new punctuation that loses the clarity of the original sentence. Choice (C) suggests that the phrase is a portion necessary to preserve the meaning of the sentence and should not be set off from the rest. This is incorrect because *as American writers living abroad were known* is merely a phrase that clarifies and defines the word before it, *expatriates*.

54. **J** For two ideas to be separated by a comma and a coordinating conjunction such as *but*, the ideas on either side of this punctuation and conjunction must be complete. The sentence as written is incorrect because the phrase *limited to those who were able to find copies of the book* is not a complete idea. Choice (H) is incorrect because a semicolon is also a punctuation mark that requires that the two ideas on either side of it be complete. Choice (G) creates an unnecessary pause in the sentence. Accordingly, only (J), which removes all punctuation marks, maintains the proper flow of the sentence and correctly treats *positive but limited to those who were able to find copies of the book* as a modifying phrase for the word *reception*.

55. **D** The sentence as written discusses the reception of a different book, not the one discussed in the previous sentence. Choice (C) refers to the current reputation of the book, and (B) is too general to be said to refer to only the specific book mentioned in this paragraph. Only (D) contains the reaction of critics to the appropriate work and the idea that the book was difficult to obtain.

56. **F** This question asks you to identify which answer best indicates that the novel *Beyond Desire* had presented something new in American literature. Choice (G) suggests that this book had other influences and does not say whether Anderson was the first to incorporate these influences. Choices (H) and (J) discuss the reactions of critics and readers to the book, not the book itself.

57. **A** Choice (B) is idiomatically incorrect—the preposition used with the word *contributions* in this context should be *to*, rather than *from*. Choices (C) and (D) are unclear in creating the phrases *the 1930s of the various writers* and *he influenced of the various writers*, respectively. Only (A) properly links the noun and the proper prepositional phrase in *works of the various writers*.

58. **G** To keep the sentence as written is to suggest the word *American* is not an essential piece of the sentence, but without this information, the words *the name* are undefined and unclear. Choices (H) and (J) omit the necessary comma before the conjunction *and*, which, in this case, is separating the items in a list: *the troubled relationship, the direct style*, and *the idea* are the main nouns used in this list. Only (G) indicates the importance of the word *American* to the meaning of the sentence and sets this portion of the sentence in a list appropriately.

59. **D** Pay close attention to the years discussed in each of these paragraphs. Paragraph 2 discusses Anderson's death in *1941* and his influence *today*. It should be logically placed after the paragraph discussing the time period most directly before that. Paragraph 5 is appropriate here because it discusses the 1920s and the 1930s, the periods closest to 1941 in this passage.

60. **G** Pay close attention to the reasons given in each of these answer choices. Choice (F) is too general and does not accurately reflect the content of the passage. Choice (H) erroneously says that the passage is primarily about a difference between two large groups when in fact it is about only a single author and his influence on a group of other authors. Choice (J) suggests that the passage only discusses the 1920s and the 1930s when the years 1919 and 1941 are mentioned explicitly.

Passage V

61. **C** Choice (C) is the clearest and most concise option. The verbs *retracted* and *diminished* essentially mean the same thing, thus (A) and (B) are redundant. Choice (D) is incorrect, because without a verb the sentence is incomplete.

62. **J** The passage is written in past tense, eliminating (G) and (H). The correct past tense form of *to begin* is *began*, making (J) the best answer. The form *begun* is used after a helping verb.

63. **A** *These responsibilities* refer to the previous sentence, which describes the responsibilities to be *traditionally assigned to men*. Choice (B), therefore, is redundant. Choice (C) creates a sentence fragment. Choice (D) does not agree in number with the plural *responsibilities*.

64. **J** Choice (J) eliminates the word *but*, fixing the sentence fragment that is created by the pronoun *that*. Choices (F), (G), and (H) incorrectly add conjunctions that create incomplete sentences.

65. **C** The two words *machinists* and *making* should be separated by a period because the sentence has two complete ideas, making (C) the best answer. Choices (A) and (D) create run-on sentences. A comma cannot separate two complete ideas, eliminating (B).

66. **F** The previous sentence already mentions factories and shipyards, making (G) and (H) redundant. Choice (J) changes the meaning of the sentence; therefore, the best answer is (F).

67. **C** Choice (C) provides the correct verb, *was*, that agrees with the singular subject of the sentence, *presence*. Choices (A), (B), and (D) all incorrectly use a plural verb.

68. **G** Choice (G) is correct because the addition distracts the reader from the topic at hand, which is the changing role of women in the workforce during World War II. Choice (F) is wrong because although it suggests not adding the information, its reasoning is incorrect. The proposed sentence is consistent in style and tone with the rest of the essay. Choices (H) and (J) incorrectly recommend adding a sentence that is irrelevant to the essay.

69. **B** The rest of the essay is about the women's baseball league; therefore, the best transition is (B). Choices (A) and (C) do not reflect the focus of the essay, and (D) is too extreme.

70. **G** *Philip K. Wrigley* is necessary to clarify who the *Founder* is and should not be off-set by commas, eliminating (J). Choices (F) and (H) have unnecessary pauses due to too many commas; therefore, (G) is the clearest answer.

71. **A** Choice (A) describes a specific visual with *pretty smiles* and *baseball mitts in their hands*. Choices (B), (C), and (D) are incorrect because the added information does not qualify as descriptive detail that helps the reader visualize the photographs.

72. **J** The sentence lists different feminine characteristics but does not make clear where the list ends, usually indicated by *and* before the last item. Therefore, the best answer is (J). Choices (F) and (G) don't list the items in parallel form. Choice (H) uses the wrong linkage for a list of things.

73. **D** The following sentence states that the photographs of the female players exemplify the *balance between feminine appeal and masculine labor* of women during WWII, making (D) the best explanation. Choice (A) is incorrect because the previous sentence suggests the physical attractiveness of the players but does not give specific details about what they look like. Choice (B) is incorrect because women's athleticism is not the focus of the paragraph. Choice (C) is incorrect because the captions of the photographs are never discussed.

74. **J** Choice (J) is the correct answer because the correct form of the possessive pronoun is *its*. The correct possessive form of the pronoun does not use apostrophes, eliminating (F) and (G). Choice (H) uses the plural pronoun *their*, which incorrectly replaces the singular antecedent *All-American Girls Professional Baseball League*.

75. **B** The essay directly describes various jobs that women held during World War II, all of which were roles traditionally filled by men, eliminating (C) and (D). Choice (A)'s reasoning only addresses the *All-American Girl's Baseball League*, which is the focus of Paragraph 4 but not the essay as a whole.

TEST 1 MATH EXPLANATIONS

1. **A** Since $\overline{YZ}$ is $\frac{1}{3}$ the length of $\overline{XZ}$, $\overline{XZ}$ will be 3 × 24 = 72 kilometers. Since X is the halfway point of the trail, the trail's entire length will be twice $\overline{XZ}$, or 72 × 2 = 144 kilometers.

2. **J** To find the value of x, first subtract 7 from both sides to get $\frac{4x}{5} = -1$. Next, multiply both sides by 5 to get $4x = -5$. Finally, divide both sides by 4 to give you (J). Choice (F) neglects the negative sign. Choice (G) is the reciprocal of the correct answer. Choices (H) and (K) are partial answers.

3. **B** Determine how many minutes it takes each cyclist to make 9,760 pedal revolutions. Cyclist A takes 9,760 rev ÷ 80 rev/min = 122 minutes. Cyclist B takes 9,760 rev ÷ 61 rev/min = 160 minutes. So, Cyclist B takes 160 – 122 = 38 more minutes than Cyclist A. Notice that (C) and (E) are partial answers. Choice (D) is the sum of each cyclist's rate, and (A) is the difference of their rates.

4. **K** The perimeter of a square is $4s$, so one side of this square is $\frac{36}{4}$ = 9 inches. The area of the square is $s^2 = 9^2 = 81$. Choice (F) is the length of one side if the square had an *area* of 36. Choice (G) is the length of one side rather than the area. Choice (H) is the result of 9 + 9. Choice (J) is the result of 6^2, rather than 9^2.

5. **D** From the figure, you can see that the y-coordinate must be greater than 4, eliminating (C), and the x-coordinate must be less than 8, eliminating (E). Since the figure is a rectangle, opposite sides must be parallel and thus have the same slope. The slope from (2,0) to (8,3) is 3 units up and 6 units right. Now calculate the fourth vertex from the point (0,4): (0 + 6, 4 + 3), which gives you (6,7). Choices (A) and (B) have an x-coordinate of 4, which is halfway between 0 and 8.

6. **H** If Carla's brother has x notebooks, Carla has $5x$ notebooks, so $5x + x = 42$. Since $x = 7$ and Carla has $5x$ notebooks, she has 5(7) = 35. Alternatively, use the answer choices to solve this problem: divide the answer choices by 5 to calculate the number of notebooks Carla's brother has and determine when Carla (the answer) and Carla's brother (the answer ÷ 5) add up to 42. A calculation error of $x = 6$ leads to (F). Choices (J) and (K) add and subtract numbers from the problem without answering the question asked.

7. **A** A right angle has a measure of 90°; therefore, any angle contained within a right angle must be smaller than 90°, leaving only (A).

8. **J** Count the number of different ways Susie can choose her one T-shirt and her one pair of shorts. She has 3 options for her T-shirt and 3 options for her pair of shorts. She can combine any of the T-shirts with any of the pairs of shorts, so there are 3 × 3, or 9, combinations. Choices (F) and (G) do not account for all possible combinations. Choice (H) is 2^3 rather than 3^2.

9. **C** Use the words in the problem to create an equation: *percent* means "divide by 100," *of* means "multiply," and *what number* means "use a variable." The resulting equation is $\frac{20}{100} \times 20 = \frac{50}{100} \times y$. Solve to find that $y = 8$. Be careful of (B), which is 20% of 20, and (D), which is 50% of 20.

10. **H** The number of piano players exceeds the number of violin players; thus, the number of musicians who play both instruments cannot exceed the number who play violin, eliminating (J) and (K). Since all 22 musicians who play the violin could also play the piano, (H) gives the maximum possible number.

11. **A** In order to make m^2 (and therefore m) as large as possible, make n^2 as small as possible. The square of any real number can't be negative, so the smallest that n^2 can be is 0. This makes $m^2 = 196$, so m equals either -14 or 14. Choices (B), (C), (D), and (E) are based on multiplication, division, or subtraction, not on taking a square root.

12. **F** To solve this problem, break it down into manageable pieces. $\frac{1}{5} \times \$925 = \$185$, so the sale price of the drum kit is $\$925 - \$185 = \$740$. Since the sales tax is $.05 \times \$740 = \$37$, the total owed is $\$740 + \$37 = \$777$. Phil receives back the amount he gave the sales clerk minus the amount he owes: $\$800 - \$777 = \$23$. Choice (G) is the amount of tax paid. Choices (H) and (J) resemble numbers from steps within the problem, and (K) calculates the taxed price without applying the sale discount.

13. **D** Taking the square root of a negative number yields an imaginary number. Choice (C) is tricky—this number is not *rationalized*, but that does not mean it is not a *real number*.

14. **G** The general quadratic expression $a^2 - b^2$ equals $(a - b)(a + b)$. In this question, take the square root of $25x^4$ and the square root of $16y^8$; thus $a = 5x^2$ and $b = 4y^4$. Choice (F) correctly factors the variables but not the coefficients, introducing an incorrect factor of the coefficients. Choices (H) and (K) incorrectly factor the coefficients. Choice (J) incorrectly factors the variables.

15. **D** Use the formula *Shaded Area = Total Area − Unshaded Area*. In this case, the *Total Area* is the area of the square, which is $4^2 = 16$. To find the *Unshaded Area*, add up the areas of the 4 unshaded triangles. Starting at the lower left of the figure and going clockwise, those areas are: $\frac{1}{2}(1 \times 2) + \frac{1}{2}(2 \times 2) + \frac{1}{2}(2 \times 1) + \frac{1}{2}(1 \times 2) = 5$. So, the *Shaded Area* = $16 - 5 = 11$.

16. **G** To find the percent, P, substitute 20 for t to calculate $-0.001(20)^2 + 0.4(20) = 7.6$. Choice (F) is the rounded value of 0.076%, which is not equivalent to 7.6%. Choices (H) and (J) may be the result of not paying attention to the order of operations (PEMDAS) or distribution of the negative sign. Choice (K) results if t^2 and t are switched.

17. **A** Find the cost per grapefruit at each store by dividing the cost of each bag by the number of grapefruits in each bag. The cost per grapefruit at Fatima's is $\$4.40 \div 8 = \$0.55$, while the cost per grapefruit at Ernie's is $\$1.86 \div 3 = \$0.62$. Find the difference: $\$0.62 - \$0.55 = \$0.07$. Choice (B) comes from multiplying $0.07 by the difference in the number of grapefruits ($8 - 3 = 5$). Choice (C) comes from averaging $0.55 and $0.62. Choice (D) comes from adding $0.55 and $0.62. Choice (E) is the difference in costs of the two bags.

18. **G** In order to multiply factors, FOIL (First, Outer, Inner, Last). Remember to *add* exponents when multiplying numbers with the same base and watch the signs carefully: $x^8 + 4x^4 - 4x^4 - 16 = x^8 - 16$. Choice (F) adds rather than multiplies the factors. Choice (J) multiplies the exponents instead of adding them. Choices (H) and (K) confuse the signs.

19. **B** First, calculate the number of tile pieces laid in the first period of work: $\dfrac{50 \text{ pieces}}{1 \text{ hour}} \times 3.5$ hours = 175 pieces. Next, you'll need to figure out how many tile pieces still need to be laid down. Subtract 280 pieces – 175 pieces = 105 pieces. Calculate the number of hours he spends in the second work session by dividing $\dfrac{105 \text{ pieces}}{35 \text{ pieces per hour}}$ = 3 hours. If you chose (D), be careful—you may have included the 60 minutes during which Wade is interrupted, but the question is looking for the time it took Wade to complete his work *after he started working again*.

20. **H** To find the midpoint of a line, take the average of the *x*-coordinates, $\dfrac{x_1 + x_2}{2}$, and the average of the *y*-coordinates of the endpoints, $\dfrac{y_1 + y_2}{2}$. Choices (F), (G), and (K) incorrectly average the *x*-coordinates. Choice (J) incorrectly averages the *y*-coordinates.

21. **B** Draw a picture to see what is happening. Add the lengths of the two short sides of the backyard and one long side: 16 + 16 + 22 = 54. Choice (C) is the sum of two long sides and one short side. Choice (D) is the perimeter of the backyard but the problem says the fencing is needed only on 3 sides. Choice (E) is the area of the backyard.

22. **F** One way to solve this problem is to rewrite the equation in the slope-intercept form, $y = mx + b$, by subtracting 7*x* and dividing by –3 on both sides. The resulting equation is $y = \dfrac{7}{3}x - 7$, where –7 is the value of *b*, the *y*-intercept. Another way to solve this problem is to remember that the *y*-intercept occurs at $x = 0$ and calculate $7(0) - 3y = 21$. Choice (H) is the slope of the line, and the other choices do not modify the equation correctly.

23. **C** Find the flower's growth rate by dividing the total growth by the number of days. This is the same thing as finding the slope: $\dfrac{17.4 - 15.0}{16 - 8} = \dfrac{2.4}{8} = 0.3$ cm per day. You want to know when the flower was 16.5 cm tall, which means it has grown 16.5 – 15.0 = 1.5 cm: 1.5 cm ÷ 0.3 cm/day = 5 days after April 8th, which is April 13th.

24. **K** To subtract, first distribute –3 to each term in the second parentheses. The result is $2x^3 - x - 1 - 3x^4 - 6x^3 + 6x^2 + 3x - 9$. Combine like terms to get $-3x^4 - 4x^3 + 6x^2 + 2x - 10$. Choices (H) and (J) incorrectly distribute the –3. Choices (F) and (G) incorrectly combine terms and exponents.

25. **B**   As mentioned in the question, the slide makes a right triangle with the ground. Use the Pythagorean Theorem ($a^2 + b^2 = c^2$) to solve $7^2 = 6^2 + x^2$. Therefore, $49 = 36 + x^2$, $x^2 = 13$, $x \approx 3.61$, which rounds to 4. Choice (A) is too small, and (C) is too large.

26. **F**   Look for a set in which the mean (average), median ("middle" value), and mode (number that appears most often) all equal 8. All five answer choices have a median of 8, but (G) and (K) can be eliminated because their modes are not 8. Then eliminate (H) and (J) by calculating their means—8.6 and 9, respectively. That leaves (F) as the correct answer.

27. **C**   The easiest approach to this problem is to test out the answer choices. For (C), if the 2nd term is 18, then the 3rd term is $(18 + 2) \times 3 = 60$, and the 4th term is $(60 + 2) \times 3 = 186$. Alternatively, work backward: if the 4th term is 186, then the 3rd term is $(186 \div 3) - 2 = 60$, and the 2nd term is $(60 \div 3) - 2 = 18$. Be sure to read the problem carefully. Choices (B) and (D) are the 1st and 3rd terms of the sequence, respectively.

28. **J**   The easiest approach to this problem is to test all the answer choices. $|9 - 3| \geq 12$ is false; thus the correct answer is (J). Alternatively, solve algebraically by solving the equation where $(x - 3) \geq 12$ and $-(x - 3) \geq 12$. The other choices solve the inequality with the wrong direction of signs, or confusion of positive/negative values within the absolute value.

29. **B**   Given that v is larger than s, then $t + u + v$ must be larger than $s + t + u$, since $t + u$ are equal in both expressions. Because $s + t + u = 29$, $t + u + v$ must be larger than 29. Choices (A), (C), (D), and (E) are not necessarily true, because no information is given about the relationships of t, u, and v. Another way to approach this question is to plug in numbers for the variables: for example, let $s = 20$, $t = 5$, $u = 4$, and $v = 21$. Using these numbers, (A), (C), and (D) are false. Now plug in different numbers: $s = 5$, $t = 4$, $u = 20$, and $v = 6$. Choice (B) is still true ($30 > 29$), but (E) is now false ($15 > 29$).

30. **H**   Eliminate (J) and (K) immediately, as $\angle CBD$ is clearly less than 90° in the figure. Since $\overline{BE}$ is a straight line, $\angle CDE + \angle BDC = 180°$, $\angle BDC = 180° - 155° = 25°$. $\overline{AB}$ and $\overline{CD}$ are opposite sides of a rectangle, so the line segments are parallel. Extend line segments $\overline{AB}$, $\overline{CD}$, and $\overline{BE}$ to reveal that the two parallel lines are crossed by a transversal, which means $\angle BDC$ and $\angle ABD$ are congruent. Thus, $\angle ABD = 25°$. $\angle ABD$ and $\angle CBD$ make up one of the right angles of rectangle $ABCD$; thus $\angle CBD = 90° - 25° = 65°$. Choices (F), (J), and (K) are all angles within the figure, but do not answer the question.

31. **E**   Test the prime numbers from the answer choices in the equation. Since all the numbers in the equation $a - b = c$ must be positive prime numbers, the only possible result for c can be 2 (e.g., $13 - 11 = 7 - 5 = 2$). The only exceptions to $c = 2$ are $5 - 2 = 3$, $13 - 2 = 11$, and $7 - 2 = 5$. Even so, the only number common to all of these equations is 2, (E).

32. **H**   Determine Pierre's average speed, in miles per hour, by dividing his total mileage by his total time. The total number of miles he covers is the distance from starting point S to finish line F, which is SF. Eliminate (F), (G), and (J) because they don't include the entire length of the racecourse. The total elapsed time from point S to point F is t_F. Eliminate (K) because it doesn't use the elapsed time clocked at the end of the race.

33. **A** Given the hypotenuse of the triangle, use SOHCAHTOA to find the adjacent side of $\angle ABC$: $\dfrac{\overline{BC}}{13}$ = cos (70°). So, $\overline{BC}$ = 13 cos (70°) $\approx$ 4.4. Choices (D) and (E) are the result of using either the sine or the tangent functions. Choices (B) and (C) may be the result of assuming that the figure is a 5:12:13 right triangle.

34. **J** When $x = -3$ and $y = -4$, then $\dfrac{8}{(-4)^2} - \dfrac{(-3)^2}{(-4)} = \dfrac{1}{2} - (-\dfrac{9}{4}) = \dfrac{11}{4}$. Choices (F) and (G) confuse the signs. Choice (K) switches x and y.

35. **C** The ramp forms a 30°-60°-90° triangle with side lengths in a ratio of 1:$\sqrt{3}$:2. Since the shortest leg measures 4, the other leg of the triangle will be $\sqrt{3}$ times the short side: $4\sqrt{3} = 6.92 \approx 7$. Choice (D) gives the length of the ramp itself, not the horizontal length.

36. **J** $\triangle BCD$ is equilateral, so $\angle CBD$ is 60°. $\angle ABD$ must be larger than 60°, eliminating (F) and (G). Choice (J) would mean $\angle ABC$ is 96° − 60° = 36°. Since $\angle ABC$ is half the measure of $\angle BAC$ and $\angle BAC = \angle BCA$, each base angle of the isosceles triangle would be (180° − 36°) ÷ 2 = 72°, which works within $\triangle ABC$: 36° + 72° + 72° = 180. Choice (K) mistakenly calculates $\angle ABC$ to be twice, rather than half, the measure of $\angle BAC$.

37. **D** Use the standard slope formula with points (8,0) and (0,−4): $m = \dfrac{y_2 - y_1}{x_2 - x_1} = \dfrac{(-4) - (0)}{(0) - (8)} = \dfrac{-4}{-8} = \dfrac{1}{2}$. If you selected (E), you may have flipped the x and the y when you calculated the slope. If you selected (B), you may have confused some of the negative signs.

38. **J** Find the hypotenuse with the Pythagorean Theorem: $a^2 + b^2 = c^2$. With the values given in the figure, this becomes $(8)^2 + (4)^2 = c^2$, and $c^2 = 80$, so $c \approx 8.9$. Accordingly, the sides of this triangle have lengths of 4, 8, and 8.9. To find the perimeter, add these sides together to get 20.9.

39. **A** The formula for cosine is as follows: $\cos\theta = \dfrac{adjacent}{hypotenuse}$. Since you are dealing with $\angle MNO$, the adjacent side will be 4, and the hypotenuse (the same whether dealing with sine or cosine) is $\sqrt{80}$. Accordingly, the cosine is $\dfrac{4}{\sqrt{80}}$. Choice (B) gives the sine of $\angle MNO$, and (D) gives the tangent.

40. **F** The fraction is equal to $\dfrac{\# \text{ of students who passed}}{\text{total \# of students}}$. If there are m students in the class, m must be the denominator, so eliminate (G), (H), and (J). The number of students who received a passing grade is calculated by subtracting the number who didn't pass the last exam, n, from the total number of students, m. Choice (K) would give a negative fraction, which is not possible.

41. **A** To solve the inequality, distribute the 2 on the right side of the inequality: $5x + 9 \geq 6x + 8 + 7$. Then combine like terms to get: $-x \geq 6$. Remember to flip the sign when dividing by −1 for x to give you the range $x \leq -6$. Choice (B) forgets to flip the sign. Choices (C) and (D) are the result if you forget to distribute 2 to the 4 in the first step. Choice (E) results if you missed a negative sign.

42. **K** The tiles must equal the surface area of the box, which is the sum of the areas of all 6 faces. There are three sets of faces: front/back, top/bottom, and the two sides: $2(4 \times 9) + 2(3 \times 9) + 2(3 \times 4)$ = 72 + 54 + 24 = 150. Because each tile covers 1 cm², the artist must have 150 cm² ÷ 1 cm² = 150, (K). Choice (F) finds the area of only three faces, and (G) and (J) account for only two of the three pairs of faces. Choice (H) finds the volume of the box.

43. **C** Draw in $\overline{AD}$, which is parallel to both $\overline{BC}$ and $\overline{EF}$, to find $\angle BAD$. The interior angles of two parallel lines add up to 180°, so you can subtract $\angle ABC$ (130°) from 180° to yield $\angle BAD = 50°$. Subtract $\angle BAE$ from the larger angle $\angle BAD$ to get $\angle EAD = 50° - 22° = 28°$. Since $\angle AEF$ and $\angle EAD$ are also interior angles of two parallel lines, subtract: $180° - \angle EAD = 180° - 28° = 152°$ = $\angle AEF$. You could also extend $\overline{AE}$ to $\overline{BC}$ and find the third angle of the triangle. The same rule will apply—the third angle of this triangle will be equal to $\angle AEF$ because $\overline{BC}$ and $\overline{EF}$ are parallel.

44. **G** To find the area of a trapezoid, multiply the height by the average of the bases. The bases are 6 and 14, so their average is 10. Therefore, $3 \times 10 = 30$, (G). Don't confuse the height of the trapezoid with the length of one of the slanted sides, which would give you (J). Choices (F) and (H) are the results when you multiply the length of only one of the bases by the height. You can also solve this problem by breaking the trapezoid apart into one central rectangle and right triangles on either side.

45. **D** First, raise both sides of the equation to the fifth power to get rid of the fifth root: $\left(\sqrt[5]{x^2 + 4x} \right)^5 = 2^5$ becomes $x^2 + 4x = 32$. Then, subtract 32 from both sides to get a standard quadratic form: $x^2 + 4x - 32 = 0$. Factor the quadratic to get $(x + 8)(x - 4) = 0$. So, $x = -8$ or $x = 4$. Alternatively, plug in until you find all the numbers that satisfy the equation. Choice (A) gives only one of the possible values for x. Choice (C) reverses the signs. Be careful of (E)—that's the result of only squaring the 2 and then using the quadratic formula!

46. **J** Given the length of the *hypotenuse* (the ramp) and needing the height *opposite* the angle of 32°, use SOHCAHTOA: $\sin A = \dfrac{\text{opposite}}{\text{hypotenuse}}$. By process of elimination, get rid of (F), (H), and (K). If $\sin 32° = \dfrac{\text{height}}{10}$, the height h is 10 sin 32°.

47. **C** Since average is $\dfrac{\text{sum}}{\text{\# of terms}}$, the sum of $j + j + k + n$ must equal 0 to make the average equal 0. Combining like terms gives you $2j + k + n = 0$. Subtracting $2j$ from both sides, you get $k + n = -2j$. Choices (A) and (B) are not necessarily true (for example, if $j = -3$, k could equal 4 and n could equal 2). Choices (D) and (E) are only true when j is equal to 0.

48.   J   In the composite function $f(g(x))$, the value of $g(x)$ is the input x value in $f(x)$; therefore, $f(x)$ is taking the square root of $g(x)$. When $g(x) = 4x^2 - 5$, its square root is $\sqrt{4x^2 - 5}$. Choices (G) and (K) make errors in taking the square root of $4x^2 - 5$. Choices (F) and (G) reverse the composite and use $g(f(x))$.

49.   C   Start with the rate formula: $d = rt$. In this problem, $t = 150$ s, and you'll want to set up equations

for as much as you can. If r_r is Rusty's rate and d_r is Rusty's distance, the equation will be $d_r = r_r t$.

When the two cars meet, their combined distances will equal the length of the entire track, 6,000 m.

Therefore, you can use the relationships given in the problem to set up an equation as follows:

6000 ft $= r_r t + (r_r - 8 \text{ ft/s})(t)$. Since t is constant at 150 s throughout this problem, substitute it into the

equation to get 6000 ft $= (150 \text{ s})(r_r) + (150 \text{ s})(r_r - 8)$. The (150 s) is common to both terms so you can

factor it out and divide both sides by 150 s to get this: $\dfrac{6{,}000 \text{ ft}}{150 \text{ s}} = r_r + r_r - 8$ and 40 ft/s $= 2r_r - 8$ ft/s.

Manipulate the equation to isolate and find $r_r = \dfrac{48 \text{ ft/s}}{2} = 24$ ft/s. Note that (A) is Dale's rate!

50.   K   Since Rusty drives the first 7 laps at an average time of 180 s, multiply these values together to find that he drives the first 7 laps in a total time of 1,260 s. Complete the same operation for the second set of numbers: since Rusty drives 8 laps at an average time of 190 s, multiply these values together to find that he drives all 8 laps in a total time of 1,520 s. Now take these two totals and find the difference between them for the time of the last lap: 1,520 s − 1,260 s = 260 s. Be careful not to hastily choose (H)—this is the average of 180 and 190, but it doesn't take into account that Rusty drives 7 laps at an average of 180 s and only one lap at an average of 190 s.

51.   D   Dale drives 6 laps, each of which is 6,000 ft, for a total of 36,000 ft in 90 minutes. The question asks for this value in feet per hour, so convert the 90 minutes to 1.5 hours. 36,000 ft ÷ 1.5 hrs = 24,000 ft/hr. If you selected (A), you may have forgotten to change the 90 minutes to 1.5 hours.

52. **G** The equation of a circle is $(x - h)^2 + (y - k)^2 = r^2$, where (h, k) is the center of the circle and r is the radius. Thus, circle B has its center at $(-4,2)$ with a radius of 3. If you draw a diagram, you'll find that point $(-2,2)$ lies outside circle A and inside circle B.

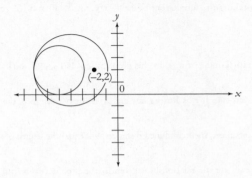

53. **B** The perimeter is the distance of the shape's outline. There are two straight lines: from $(0,0)$ to $(0,4)$ and from $(0,0)$ to $(4,0)$, each with a length of 4. The straight lines total 8, eliminating (A), (D), and (E). The curved parts are two semicircles and two semicircles make one complete circle, so find the circumference of one circle with radius 2: $C = 2\pi r = 2\pi(2) = 4\pi$. Eliminate (C) and pick (B). If you picked (D), you may have found the area instead of the perimeter.

54. **F** An even function is defined in the question as a function for which the value of $f(x) = f(-x)$. This means that $f(x)$ has the same value for both x and $-x$. If you fold the graph of an even function along the $f(x)$ axis, the two sides of the graph will be mirror reflections of each other. Choices (G), (J), and (K) are odd functions, in which $f(-x) = -f(x)$ for all values of x. Odd functions rotate 180° about the point $(0,0)$. Choice (H) is not a function, because it does not pass the vertical line test; the same x value yields two values for $f(x)$.

55. **B** Use the distance formula: $d = \sqrt{(x_2 - x_1)^2 + (y_2 - y_1)^2}$. This results in $d = \sqrt{(4w - w)^2 + (w - 5 - (w + 5))^2} = \sqrt{9w^2 + 100}$.

56. **F** In a right triangle with angle A, $\cos A = \dfrac{\text{length of adjacent side}}{\text{length of hypotenuse}}$. In this triangle, $\cos S = \dfrac{r}{t}$ and $\cos R = \dfrac{s}{t}$. So $\cos^2 S + \cos^2 R = \dfrac{r^2}{t^2} + \dfrac{s^2}{t^2}$, or $\dfrac{r^2 + s^2}{t^2}$. Since $\triangle RST$ is a right triangle, use the Pythagorean Theorem to determine that $r^2 + s^2 = t^2$. You're left with $\cos^2 S + \cos^2 R = \dfrac{t^2}{t^2} = 1$.

57. **C** Trapezoid *DECA* is isosceles because $\triangle ABC$ is isosceles and, since $\overline{DE} \parallel \overline{AC}$, line segments $\overline{AD}$ and $\overline{CE}$ have equal lengths. Since the trapezoid is isosceles, the diagonals are congruent. Thus, $\triangle DFE$ and $\triangle AFC$ are similar. Set up a proportion to find the missing side: $\dfrac{9}{6} = \dfrac{27}{\overline{FC}}$. So, $\overline{FC} = 18$. Choice (A) is the short side of $\triangle DFE$ multiplied by 2. Choice (B) is $9 + 6$. Choice (D) is $27 + 6$ and (E) is $27 + 9$. Remember that hard problems typically require more work than just adding together some of the numbers from the problem!

58. **F** The dimensions of a matrix product are determined by the number of rows in the first matrix and the number of columns in the second matrix, in this case 2×1. Thus, (H), (J), and (K) have the wrong dimensions. To find the product value, multiply rows by columns and add the products of one row-column: $(4 \times 0) + (-2 \times 2) = -4$ and $(3 \times 0) + (-6 \times 2) = -12$.

59. **D** An ! symbol denotes a factorial, which is the product of decreasing consecutive integers starting from the integer in front of the ! sign. (For example, $5! = 5 \times 4 \times 3 \times 2 \times 1 = 120$.) You can simplify this expression if you separate the two largest factors in the numerator; in other words, write $(n + 1)!$ as $(n + 1) \times (n) \times (n - 1)!$ Canceling $(n - 1)!$ from numerator and denominator leaves you with $(n + 1)(n)$. So $(n + 1)(n) = 20$, which means that $n + 1 = 5$ and $n = 4$. Finally, the question asks for $n! = 4! = 4 \times 3 \times 2 \times 1 = 24$. Choice (A) is $3!$ Choice (B) is half of 20. Choice (C) is half of 24. Choice (E) is $5!$

60. **K** To simplify this abstract problem, substitute a value in for the circle's radius. If the radius is 3, the circumference is $2\pi r = 2(\pi)(3) = 6\pi$. $\dfrac{radius}{circumference} = \dfrac{3}{6\pi} = \dfrac{1}{2\pi}$. Choice (F) gives the ratio of the circumference to the radius. Choices (H) and (J) work with the diameter instead of the radius, and (G) finds the ratio of the diameter to the radius.

TEST 1 READING EXPLANATIONS

Passage I

1. **C** Choice (C) points to the portion of the passage in which the narrator says that his grandmother had gained considerable stature in Robertson County and, more importantly, refers to information concerning the story's principal character. The main topic of the passage is Ruby and her diner, so you can safely assume there will be a connection between the main topic and the correct answer. Choice (A) focuses on information that occurs only in the beginning of the story and (B) and (D) are too general and not directly supported by information in the passage.

2. **J** The second paragraph begins by introducing the character of Ruby Sanders, the narrator's grandmother. This indicates that the paragraph will explain who she is and why she is important. Choices (F) and (G) point out topics in the beginning of the passage, but they do not serve to cover the character of Ruby. Finally, (H) is an overstatement, so we have to dismiss it as a viable in light of (J).

3. **B** Only (B) contains an answer that refers correctly to a part of the text—*If the diner were a sort of cell, then my grandmother was its nucleus; without the nucleus, the cell would surely perish.* The other answer choices contain words from the passage as well, but the things stated in those answer choices are either untrue or not supported by the passage.

4. **H** Choice (H) should be selected in this instance because the question asks you to make an inference, and inferences must always be supported by the facts within the area in question. The end of the paragraph directly states that the narrator was glad that he didn't know that he wouldn't return to the diner after his last summer there. Choices (F), (G), and (J) force us to make unfounded assumptions as to how the narrator would feel.

5. **B** Locate where the author talks about working at the diner (paragraph 8). The narrator mentions that the work was *hard but never dull*. Therefore, you should select (B). Although each of the others contains individual characteristics that may be true, both characteristics listed in the correct answer must be true.

6. **F** Note the sentence at the end of the second paragraph: *It didn't take long before my grandmother was a person of considerable stature in and around Robertson County, just like the restaurant that bore her name.* From this sentence, you can easily infer that both Ruby and her restaurant were popular in and around the community. If you chose one of the other answers, be careful—these refer to either Ruby or the restaurant, but never to both.

7. **A** The lines in question provide the introduction to this paragraph, which details the ways in which Ruby's was significant to the community in ways other than as a restaurant—(A). Choice (B) is not supported in the text, and (D) gives a too literal interpretation of the lines referred to in the passage and misreads the word *expect*. Choice (C) is deceptive—the passage does suggest that Ruby herself had risen to prominence, but it does not mention anyone else in this regard.

8. **G** The author speaks of (F), (H), and (J) in the sixth paragraph. He mentions football leagues in the last paragraph, but as something he had to forego to continue to work at the restaurant.

Accordingly, the passage mentions all of the things as being available at the diner EXCEPT the football leagues, (G).

9. **C** In the seventh paragraph, the author vividly describes the physical details of the restaurant. In this paragraph, he gives a detailed description of the grounds, down to the furniture and the locations of some minor items. Choices (A), (B), and (D) use words from the passage, but the information in these choices is not supported.

10. **J** In the last paragraph, the narrator says, *After all, the woman who built Ruby's was strong enough to make me forget those things, if only for the summer.* It can therefore be inferred that the narrator is impressed by his grandmother's strength. None of the other answer choices are supported by evidence in the passage.

Passage II

11. **B** The passage is about studies on several different factors that contribute to happiness. According to the second paragraph, Tellegen and Lykken state that genes play a part in happiness, but no specific genes have been found that cause hedonic adaptation, eliminating (A). Although an account of Lyubomirsky and Sheldon's studies indicates that there may be ways to improve happiness levels (lines 70–80), there is no discussion of the cure for depression mentioned in (C). No scientist in the passage disagrees that genes have an influence on happiness levels, eliminating (D).

12. **H** All the studies in the passage involve subjects telling researchers how happy they are, which is the same as *subjective well-being* as defined in lines 8–11. Only Lyubomirsky and Sheldon's study made specific note of studying their subjects' levels of happiness *over time* (lines 64–67), eliminating (F), or involved subjects engaging in *acts of kindness* (line 75), eliminating (G). Only Tellegen and Lykken's study mentioned using *identical twins* (lines 13–14), eliminating (J).

13. **D** Tellegen and Lykken's study of twins that had been *separated and raised in different families* (line 15) does not indicate whether separated twins were less happy. The question presented by (A) can be answered by the statistic on line 52, which says *10 percent is influenced by circumstances.* Descriptions of Lyubomirsky and Sheldon's studies suggest that people who *varied their acts of kindness* (line 75) and who wrote *a list of things to be grateful for* (line 78) can improve their subjective well-being, which answers the question posed in (B). In lines 43–44, Sheldon explains that scientific literature suggests that behaviors such as choosing the right goals *provide only a temporary increase in subjective well-being,* answering the question in (C).

14. **F** Lyubomirsky hopes to show how *conscious strategies counteract genetic forces* (lines 63–64)—in other words, to help people to overcome their genetic predispositions. You can eliminate (J) because the passage never indicates that hedonic adaptation can be eliminated entirely. Sheldon and Lyubomirsky also agree that *50 percent of subjective well-being is predetermined by the genetic set point* (lines 50–51), which confirms, rather than contradicts, Tellegen and Lykken's study, eliminating (G). Determining which intentional act is more effective is not the primary purpose of their research, eliminating (H).

15. **D** The statistics cited in the last sentence of the passage best support (D). Though the passage indicates that some psychologists' emphasis caused them to *suspect that overall levels of subjective well-being are low* (line 85), this does not summarize the University of Chicago studies, so eliminate (A). Though Americans are mostly happy people, this does not mean that depression is *uncommon*, as (B) states. You can also eliminate (C), because it suggests that happiness levels are actually harmed by attempts to improve them.

16. **H** The Lykken and Tellegen study is discussed in paragraph two. Choice (H) is correct, as the passage clearly states that only some of the twins were raised together, not all of them. The paragraph states that the members of the study were both fraternal and identical twins and that researchers compared the scores of the twins, making (F) true. Choice (G) is true because the study compared the twins' subjective well-being, which is described as our self-reported level of happiness in the first sentence. Choice (J) is found in the final sentence of the paragraph, which states that most of the difference in people's levels of happiness are determined by differences in genetic makeup.

17. **A** Hedonic adaptation is useful because it benefits people who experience adverse conditions in their lives (lines 25–26). Although these adverse conditions may include *permanent disability or sudden loss of income* (lines 26–27), hedonic adaptation does not cause people to *forget* about these problems, as indicated in (B). It is not useful to adjust to the higher level of happiness caused by *winning the lottery*, eliminating (C). Hedonic adaptation helps people to adjust their levels of happiness back to their own genetic set point, not to identify better with family members, eliminating (D).

18. **G** If you deleted the first paragraph, you wouldn't get a detailed story about a particular person whose life shows that happiness and life events, in this case the Holocaust, are not necessarily correlated, as in (G). The passage mentions in the third paragraph that circumstances are not a large contributor to happiness, so eliminate (F). The first paragraph includes an example that is relevant to establishing the main idea of the passage, eliminating (H). Lines 26–27 mention *permanent disability or sudden loss of income* as specific examples of adverse conditions people may experience, so you can eliminate (J).

19. **C** The topic sentence of the last paragraph suggests that its purpose is to focus on people's generally positive assessment of their own happiness. The researchers mentioned in the paragraph had an incorrect suspicion, which is different from making *many errors*, so you can eliminate (A). Choice (B) can be eliminated because Ross's anecdote in the first paragraph is not meant to suggest that Americans are unhappy. Lyubomirsky and Sheldon's findings that certain behaviors may improve happiness are still valid even if people are already generally happy, eliminating (D).

20. **H** Lines 64–65 state that Lyubomirsky and Sheldon *are currently expanding their study*. Though it is possible that the researchers mentioned in (F), (G), and (J) may still collaborate, the passage never explicitly gives this information, making (H) the best answer.

Passage III

21. **B** The author never describes Zitkala-Sa as spoiled, so (A) can be eliminated. Additionally, the author specifically states that Zitkala-Sa was *not, in the end, abandoning her culture*, which eliminates (C). And while the author was previously confused over Zitkala-Sa's cultural difficulties, she now recognizes the importance of Zitkala-Sa's cultural journey. Therefore, you can eliminate (D). This leaves (B), which is supported by the concluding line of the passage in which the author describes how Zitkala-Sa began her *journey towards becoming an advocate for Native American rights*.

22. **J** Throughout the passage, the author describes how the clash between white and Native American cultures informs and enriches Zitkala-Sa's writing, an idea best expressed by (J). Choices (F) and (H) can be eliminated because Zitkala-Sa ultimately embraces her Sioux identity. And far from being an extraneous detail, this cultural clash is what *adds fire to Zitkala-Sa's chronicles of her school years*, eliminating (G).

23. **A** The author describes the photograph of a woman in Native American dress and then states *It is hard to make myself believe that the woman in this picture was named Gertrude Simmons Bonnin*. This suggests that the author sees a discrepancy between the image and the name, an idea expressed in (A). There is no evidence that the author was confused by Bonnin's use of a pen name, as stated in (B), or that she thought the photo had been misidentified, as stated in (C). Additionally, the author does not state a preference for either name, eliminating (D).

24. **F** Zitkala-Sa describes how her brother told her *"No, my baby sister, I cannot take you with me to the party to-night"* and how she cried hot tears at his departure. These lines support the reason expressed in (F). Choice (H), though true, is not the stated reason for Zitkala-Sa's tears. And while Zitakala does mention the Indian maids in (G) and the Muslim dress in (J), she does not describe missing the former or wishing for the latter.

25. **B** Zitkala-Sa describes her time at home as one in which she hung *in the heart of chaos, beyond the touch or voice of human aid*. Choice (B) is the only choice that describes this complete unhappiness. Although she could wear her moccasins, Zitkala-Sa was not content, as stated in (A). She also makes no reference to teaching her mother to read or write, eliminating (C). And although her brother's view of her might have contributed to her unhappiness, it was by no means the only factor, eliminating (D).

26. **H** In the sentence just before the referenced lines, Zitkala-Sa describes how *Even nature seemed to have no place for me*. The referenced lines then explain the different ways in which she didn't belong, making (H) the most appropriate answer. Zitkala-Sa's height is used to describe a way in which she doesn't belong and so is not the central focus of the lines, eliminating (F). There is no evidence that Zitkala-Sa's family rejects her, eliminating (J). And while the awkwardness of Zitkala-Sa's teen years are referenced later in the paragraph, this idea is not the focus of these lines, eliminating (G).

27. **D** The word "civilized" is used to describe Indian students who go away to school in the East. Zitkala-Sa describes how these students have adopted aspects of white culture: *The young men wore the white man's coat and trousers, with bright neckties*. Choice (D) most effectively summarizes this transformation. There is no evidence in the passage for (A) or (B), and the type of education the students received is never directly discussed, eliminating (C).

28. **J**   Both passages emphasize Zitkala-Sa's sense of not belonging either at home or in the white man's world, which supports (J). At no point in either passage does Zitkala-Sa advocate for sending Native Americans to school, eliminating (G). Additionally, both passages describe her inability to fit in as something she struggles against, rather than a choice she actively makes, eliminating (F). And Zitkala-Sa's difficulties with her mother, as stated in (H), are only discussed in Passage B.

29. **C**   Both passages describe how Zitkala-Sa is happy to be able to wear her moccasins again once she returns to the reservation. In this way, moccasins function as a symbol of her Native American heritage, as expressed in (C). Choice (A) argues the opposite idea and so can be eliminated. Her moccasins' comfortableness is only referenced in Passage B, eliminating (D). In both passages, Zitkala-Sa views her moccasins as a positive part of living at the reservation, so (B) is not the correct interpretation.

30. **F**   The author of Passage A describes how Zitkala-Sa's struggles eventually led to her to *embrace her Sioux identity*. This idea is best summarized in (F). The author describes how Zitkala-Sa's complex heritage sets her apart from other teenage girls, so (G) can be eliminated. The author also makes it clear that Zitkala-Sa's journey toward self-acceptance was a long one, eliminating (H). And while Passage B references the conflicts in (J), they are not discussed in Passage A.

Passage IV

31. **A**   Although the passage mentions that the frogs' calls concern mating behavior, it doesn't specify how often they mate, so (A) is the best answer. Choice (B) is addressed in line 17, (C) is answered in lines 29–43, and (D) is answered in lines 54–57.

32. **F**   Lines 15–16 state that the coquí faces almost no ecological competition because there are no other native amphibians; thus, (F) is the best answer. Choice (G) is contradicted in lines 58–62.

33. **C**   Paragraph 4 (lines 29–43) states that the *volume of the frog's call is compounded by two other factors*, one of which is the *wall of sound* produced by overlapping calls, making (C) the best answer. Choice (A) is contradicted by lines 4–5. Choices (B) and (D) refer to facts that aren't supported by the passage.

34. **H**   This paragraph states that the coquí thrives because it doesn't need as much water as it would if it were born a tadpole. The end of the paragraph also implies that the coquí faces little predatory threat before it has matured. The paragraph does describe the environmental conditions in Hawaii, but description of the habitat isn't the primary purpose of the paragraph, eliminating (F) and (G). Choice (J) is not the primary purpose of the paragraph, nor does it accurately describe the coquí.

35. **B**   The first paragraph is a descriptive, evocative passage that attempts to capture the sound of the frog calls in the night. By contrast, the sixth paragraph explains specifically how scientists believe these frogs could endanger the local environment, so (B) is the best description of the change in the language's tone. Nothing in the passage suggests the *author's* opinion, so (A) doesn't fit. The sixth paragraph talks about the frogs as a potential threat, so you wouldn't select (C) or (D) as the best option.

36. **G** Earlier in the sentence, the coquí populations are described as *threatening the survival of arthropods*, which indicates that the arthropod population is struggling, eliminating (H) and (J). The word *pursuit* doesn't fit as well as *extinction*, making (G) the best answer.

37. **D** The last sentence of the fifth paragraph (lines 54–57) begins with the phrase *Ornithologists fear*, which means that the potential outcome hasn't happened yet. Choice (A) is stated as factual information in lines 33–34, (B) in lines 71–73, and (C) in lines 81–82.

38. **F** The passage states that *nematodes and other types of vertebrate parasites could be transported with coquíes and infect indigenous fauna*, making (F) the best answer. Choices (G) and (H) refer to the frogs' food sources, not parasites; *arachnids* in (J) aren't mentioned specifically in the passage, although they are a member of the arthropod class.

39. **B** The fifth paragraph states that *another quieter genus of the frog—the greenhouse frog—represents an equal threat to the biodiversity of the island*, which is best summarized by (B). Choice (C) incorrectly states that the greenhouse frog is less, rather than equally, dangerous. It is true that the greenhouse frog is relatively quiet, but that characteristic isn't necessarily what makes the frog hard to eliminate, eliminating (D). Although the name *greenhouse frog* points to an indoor habitat, the passage doesn't support that assumption, so you can rule out (A).

40. **J** The last paragraph mentions *1,000 acres* in the first sentence and continues in the next sentence to describe the land as the habitat in which the coquí has adopted as its home in Hawaii, making (J) the best answer. There is no evidence in the passage to support (F), (G), or (H).

TEST 1 SCIENCE EXPLANATIONS

Passage I

1. **A**   The data in Table 3 indicate that for every increase of 25°C, there is a corresponding increase in θ of approximately 3.5 degrees. A temperature of 62.5°C falls halfway between 50°C and 75°C, so the corresponding angle should fall halfway between 25.4 and 29.0 degrees. Only (A) has a value anywhere within this range.

2. **F**   According to Table 1, the object made of brick required the largest ramp angle θ before any movement took place. Therefore, it is the most resistant to movement. Raising the angle of the ramp accomplishes the same thing as applying increasing force to the object to eventually overcome friction.

3. **D**   In Experiments 1 and 4, the angle θ where the wooden object starts to move stays the same, no matter how many objects are stacked on top of each other. Since any change to this angle will signal a change to the coefficient of static friction, you can confidently say that if the angle doesn't change, the coefficient of friction will not change.

4. **G**   The interaction of interest is between the various objects and the polymer coating of the ramp. The polymer coating is what comes into contact with the objects, while the underlying plastic board is not participating, eliminating (F). Objects of different material are not brought into contact during the experiment, eliminating (H). Objects are not stacked until Experiment 4, eliminating (J).

5. **D**   The object with the largest angle θ is the object that is most resistant to movement. According to Table 1, this is brick. Only (D) ranks brick as the most resistant to movement, eliminating all other answer choices.

6. **G**   The data in Table 3 indicate that when temperature increases, the corresponding θ increases. The passage states that the *tangent of this angle represents the coefficient of static friction between the object and the polymer surface.* The experiment is not exploring the interaction between wood and wood, eliminating (F). The mass of the object is constant, eliminating (H). Only wooden objects are used in Experiment 3, eliminating (J).

Passage II

7. **B**   The transition from April to May shows a small increase in the number of reported polio infections, and the transition from November to December shows a decrease, so neither (C) nor (D) would be the correct answer. There are large increases in the number of reported cases from January to February and from February to March, but upon close inspection, the transition from February to March is larger. Therefore, (B) is the best answer.

8. **J**   In June 2004, 80 cases of polio infection were reported, so $80 \times 200 = 16,000$ people would have been at risk for contraction of the infection.

9. **A** In all the Indian cities, there are more reported cases of polio virus infections in August than in June. Choices (B) and (D) are consistent with *decreases*, not increases, in the reported polio cases. The study described by Figure 2 only covers the dry summer and rainy monsoon season, not the autumn or winter, so the explanation given in (C) is unsupported. Choice (A) is the best answer because the month of August is expected to have more rainfall, and therefore is more likely to feature water contamination.

10. **H** Figure 2 presents findings that are applicable only to India, not Nigeria, so (F) is incorrect. The findings only present information on reported infections during June and August 2007, not on unreported infections (choice (G) is wrong) nor on winter months (choice (J) is wrong). The findings do, however, show a stark contrast between the small number of reported cases in the cities in western and southern India (Mumbai, Chennai, and Hyderabad) and the large number of cases in the northern cities (New Delhi and Kolkata), making (H) the best answer.

11. **D** The passage states that the polio virus is most often transmitted through water contaminated with human waste and makes no mention of the role (or the lack thereof) that other life forms play in the transmission of the virus. The answer that summarizes this is (D).

12. **H** In June 2007, there were between 10 and 15 reported polio infections in Kolkata, while in August 2007, there were between 20 and 25 reported polio infections. This is an approximate doubling of the number of reported infections, so (H) is the best answer.

Passage III

13. **D** The solution with the *least osmotic pressure* will have the smallest value from Figure 1. The pressure for (A) is 85 atm; (B) is 70 atm; (C) is 90 atm; (D) is 50 atm. Therefore, a 2.0 M sucrose solution has the least osmotic pressure.

14. **J** The introduction states that *higher van 't Hoff factors correlate with greater dissociation or ionization*. According to Table 1, $FeCl_3$ exhibits the greatest van 't Hoff factor, which means the highest degree of ionization.

15. **C** Examine the equation given in the introduction: $\Pi = iMRT$. Since the values of R and T remain constant among all the answer choices as seen in the question, osmotic pressure is determined by the product of M and i. The product of concentration of solute particles and van 't Hoff factor for a 1.5 M NaCl solution is $1.5 \times 1.9 = 2.85$. The product for the solution in (A) is $1.0 \times 1.9 = 1.9$; (B) is $2.0 \times 1.9 = 3.8$; (C) is $2.9 \times 1.0 = 2.9$; (D) is $3.5 \times 1.0 = 3.5$. Choice (C) has the closest product to 2.85.

16. **G** The pressure required to maintain solvent equilibrium across a membrane is the solution's osmotic pressure, as discussed in the introduction. Figure 1 shows a linear relationship between solute concentration and osmotic, eliminating (H) and (J). As concentration of solute decreases, the osmotic pressure will also decrease, eliminating (F).

17. **D** Comparing different solutes in Figure 1 at a given concentration greater than $M = 0$, you will determine that $FeCl_3$ always has greater osmotic pressure than sucrose, eliminating (B) and (C). The trend in Figure 1 predicts that a substance with $i = 3.8$ would have a greater osmotic pressure than $FeCl_3$, which does *not* support the scientist's findings.

Passage IV

18. **H** Examine the relationship between the line for Sample 1 and the line for Sample 4. Between the 30–60-cm depth range and the 60–90-cm depth range, the line for Sample 1 crosses over to become higher than the line for Sample 4. Choices (F) and (G) suggest that the lines would never cross over, while (J) incorrectly states that Sample 4's shallower sodium concentrations were lower than Sample 1's.

19. **B** On the line for Sample 3 in Figure 2, the second data point most closely matches 17%. Choice (A) would describe the earliest data point for Sample 3, from a soil depth of 0–30 cm; (C) and (D) describe Samples 4 and 5 at this depth, respectively.

20. **J** Only Figure 1 references EC, so find 40 m in Figure 1. Sample 4 occurs at 40 m. Now, use POE: the greatest EC occurs between 60 and 90 cm, so eliminate (F) and (G). The lowest EC occurs at 0–30 cm; the answer is (J).

21. **C** This question is essentially asking you to convert one set of data points on a line graph into a bar graph. Choice (C) does this correctly, while (A) inverts the values, making small values large and large values small. Choice (B) measures the wrong data point—it would be accurate for a sample depth of 60–90 cm, not 90–120 cm. Choice (D) is very close, but mixes up the values for Sample 4 and Sample 1.

22. **G** Compare all five samples in Figure 1 using a common depth such as 30–60 cm. In Sample 1, the EC is approximately 1 mS/cm; 20 mS/cm in Sample 2; 1 mS/cm in Sample 3; 0.5 mS/cm in Sample 4; 8 mS/cm in Sample 5. Thus, there is no consistent trend in the electrical conductivity, which means salinity does not increase with consistency with distance from the river, eliminating choices (H) and (J). The explanation in (F) is also not supported by the passage.

Passage V

23. **B** Examine the conditions associated with each group in Table 1. Group 6 is the only group that does not include data from an area affected by habitat loss or declines in prey population. It therefore allows the researchers to compare areas affected by these factors to one unaffected by them. Choices (A), (C), and (D) suggest that Group 6 provides information to the researchers that is not included in the passage.

24. **F** Examine the conditions associated with Group 2. These areas have additional seaweed that is consumed by marine mammals, the likely prey of the primarily carnivorous polar bear. Choice (G) implies that polar bears may prefer to eat seaweed, but there is nothing in the passage to support this statement. Choice (H) is eliminated because the study does not directly measure the population density of prey animals. Choice (J) would require additional information that links the population of prey animals to Arctic sea ice.

25. **C** A greater average population density ratio for a certain group indicates that more polar bears are living in areas that are a part of that group. Choice (C) correctly lists the groups by average population density ratio as given in Figure 1.

26. **G** Group 1 exhibits declines in the number of marine mammals consumed by polar bears. Choices (F) and (H) are not mammals so they are eliminated. Choice (J) is eliminated because the population of polar bears is the outcome being studied as a result of some other environmental change, and there is nothing in the passage to suggest that polar bears consume other polar bears. Only (G) describes a marine mammal that is likely consumed by a polar bear.

27. **D** You can use the process of elimination with the definitions in Table 1 to find the correct answer for this problem. Choice (A) includes Groups 1 and 2; these are likely to cause effects in opposite directions, not the same direction. Choices (B) and (C) each include Group 4; as Group 4 is simply a combination of Groups 1 and 3, the researchers are never directly comparing the effects of Group 4 conditions to any other conditions. Choice (D) lists Groups 1 and 3, both groups where there have been conditions likely to make it difficult for polar bears to survive. This is confirmed by data in Figure 1.

28. **H** Choices (F) and (J) are both true. As seen in Figure 1, average polar bear population ratios for both Groups 1 and 3 are not equal to 1. If they were equal to 1, this would indicate that there is no difference between those areas with the conditions listed and those without. Choice (H) reverses the relationship between Groups 1 and 3 in Figure 1, which means it is not supported. Choice (G) states the relationship from (H) correctly, which means (G) is supported and therefore not the correct answer.

Passage VI

29. **D** Scientist 2 says "*the •OH generated by Reactions 1 and 4 will react rapidly with any H_2CO*," indicating that she does agree those reactions occur; the dispute is what formaldehyde decomposes to after Reaction 3. So according to both scientists, O_3 leads to the formation of •OH (Reaction 1), and OH leads to the formation of •CH_3 (Reaction 2).

30. **F** As methane (CH_4) levels increase, CH_3 levels will increase (Reaction 2). As •CH_3 levels increase, H_2CO levels will increase (Reaction 3). Therefore, the correct graph should show low levels of H_2CO when methane levels are low, and high levels of H_2CO when methane levels are high. Choice (F) is the only graph that reflects this direct relationship.

31. **C** Remember: reactants on the left; products on the right. From that you can eliminate (B) and (D). For (A), it is true that H_2CO is composed of atoms (it *is* a molecule); however, composition is not mentioned in the question. Since there are no other reactants, the mass of H_2CO (the reactant) must be exactly the mass of the products (H_2 and CO). Therefore, the molecular mass of each of the products must be less than that of H_2CO.

32. **H** According to Scientist 1, the first step in the production of formaldehyde requires ozone (O_3). Follow the reactions: if O_3 levels decrease, •OH levels would decrease (Reaction 1), leading to a decrease in •CH_3 levels (Reaction 2), which in turn would lead to a decrease in H_2CO levels (Reaction 3). Thus, both •CH_3 and H_2CO levels would decrease.

33. **D** Scientist 2 says Reactions 1–4 do occur, which supports (A) and (C). Choice (B) is Scientist 2's central argument: that the •OH produced by Reactions 1 and 4 can react with H_2CO to form CO (Reaction 6). While Scientist 2 does say that some H_2CO may form from CH_4 and O_3, she says that "H_2CO quickly decomposes" and that the chain reaction of Reactions 2–4 is inhibited. Thus, she would *not* expect an increase in CH_4 levels to cause levels of H_2CO to rise dramatically.

34. **G** If Reaction 4 were inhibited, the amount of H_2CO generated would be reduced, and therefore, according to Scientist 2, the amount of CO generated would be reduced, not increased, so (F) is incorrect. $\cdot OH$ can react with H_2CO to form CO, but there is no evidence of HO_2 reacting with H_2CO, as in (H). O_2 is not involved in the generation of CO, so (J) cannot be correct. Choice (G) is Scientist 2's hypothesis: The H_2CO generated in Reaction 3 will react in Reactions 5 and 6 to produce CO.

35. **B** Reaction 6 shows $\cdot OH$ reacting with H_2CO in the atmosphere, which weakens Scientist 1's hypothesis in 2 ways: It reduces the level of H_2CO, which Scientist 1 says is *increasing* in the atmosphere, and consumes $\cdot OH$, inhibiting the chain reaction (Reactions 2–4), which is central to Scientist 1's hypothesis. Thus, (B) is the best explanation. The $\cdot OH$ produced in Reaction 4 reacts with CH_4 (in Reaction 2), which agrees with Scientist 1's argument, so (A) is incorrect. The H_2O produced in Reaction 6 may react with light and O_3, as in Reaction 1, but this does not weaken Scientist 1's argument, so (C) is incorrect. For (D), $\cdot OH$ is not produced in Reaction 6, as it is a reactant.

Passage VII

36. **G** To solve this problem, you must be sure to read the question carefully: You are looking at the section of the graph where V is *decreasing* from its largest value. First, find the largest value of V; this is the point on the curve that is furthest to the right, since V increases left to right. Once you are looking in the right place, you just draw a line up from 1.5 mL on the V-axis to where it meets the curve, then draw a line over to the P-axis to get your answer: 30 Pa, (G).

37. **C** From the passage and Figures 1 and 2, you know that both ends of the second half of the curve must meet the ends of the first half to complete the cycle, so P must be higher on the left side than on the right side. Choices (A) and (B) cannot be correct because P is higher on the right side than on the left side. Choice (D) is simply the wrong shape to complete the cycle, so it cannot be correct. Choice (C) has P higher on the left side than on the right side, so it must be correct.

38. **H** Looking at Figure 1, all you need to do is find the lowest point on the curve, then draw a line down to the V-axis. Choice (H), 3.5 mL, is the closest answer.

39. **B** To solve this question, you must first locate the approximate lowest and highest values of V on Figure 2. The lowest value is about 0.75 mL and the highest value is about 2.25 mL, so the lowest value is about 1/3 times the highest value, (B). Another way to solve this problem is to check the answer choices against the graph. Choice (A) cannot be correct because there are no negative numbers on the graph. Choice (C) doesn't really make sense because if the lowest value were 1 times the highest value, it would have to be the same number as the highest value, and then there wouldn't be a highest or lowest. Choice (D) doesn't make sense either because if the lowest value were 2 times the highest value, the lowest value would have to be higher than the highest value. Choice (B) is the only choice that could work because it is the only choice which is not negative and would make the lowest value actually lower than the highest value.

40. **F** Watch out for all the tricky wording. Here's what the question is asking: What is the value of V when P is at its highest value? Find the highest value of P, and then find the value of V: 1.0 mL, (F).

WRITING TEST

Essay Checklist

- ❏ Clearly state your own perspective

- ❏ Reference the ideas of all 3 perspectives

- ❏ Use examples to explain your point of view

- ❏ Have 2–3 body paragraphs with 5–7 sentences each

- ❏ Have an introduction and a conclusion paragraph

- ❏ Write neatly

- ❏ Use a formal tone and mature level of vocabulary

- ❏ Avoid spelling and grammar errors

Chapter 4
Test 2

Please turn to page 173 to find the bubble sheet for this test.

ENGLISH TEST
45 Minutes—70 Questions

DIRECTIONS: In the five passages that follow, certain words and phrases are underlined and numbered. In the right-hand column, you will find alternatives for each underlined part. In most cases, you are to choose the one that best expresses the idea, makes the statement appropriate for standard written English, or is worded most consistently with the style and tone of the passage as a whole. If you think the original version is best, choose "NO CHANGE." In some cases, you will find in the right-hand column a question about the underlined part. You are to choose the best answer to the question.

You will also find questions about a section of the passage or the passage as a whole. These questions do not refer to an underlined portion of the passage but rather are identified by a number or numbers in a box.

For each question, choose the alternative you consider best and blacken the corresponding oval on your answer document. Read each passage through once before you begin to answer the questions that accompany it. For many of the questions, you must read several sentences beyond the question to determine the answer. Be sure that you have read far enough ahead each time you choose an alternative.

Passage I

> The following paragraphs may or may not be in the most logical order. Each paragraph is numbered in brackets, and question 14 will ask you to choose where Paragraph 5 should most logically be placed.

A Window into History

[1]

One very long summer during high school, my mom volunteered me to help Grandpa research our family tree. Great, I thought, imagining hours spent pawing through dusty, rotting boxes and listening to boring stories about people I didn't know. "You'll be surprised," my mom promised. "Family histories can be very interesting."

[2]

In truth, Grandpa didn't want to limit my work to just research. Hoping to also preserve our family memories. He'd discovered a computer program that helps digitally scan old

pictures, and letters to preserve their contents before they crumble from old age. Grandpa wanted me to help him connect

1. Given that all the choices are true, which one best conveys the author's initial expectations and effectively leads into her mother's comments?
   A. NO CHANGE
   B. bonding with the grandfather I barely knew.
   C. remembering fun times I had with relatives.
   D. trying to operate an unfamiliar machine.

2. F. NO CHANGE
   G. research. Hope to also preserve
   H. research, that hope to also preserve
   J. research, hoping to also preserve

3. A. NO CHANGE
   B. pictures, and, letters
   C. pictures and letters,
   D. pictures and letters

GO ON TO THE NEXT PAGE.

the scanner and set up the computer program. He could type documents and send e-mails, but he had never used a scanner.
4

[3]

[1] Instead of sorting through dusty boxes as I had imagined, we spent a lot of time in my grandpa's bright, tidy computer room. [2] The scanner hummed happily, turning my relatives precious memories into permanent digital images.
5
[3] A scanner is a device which makes electronic copies of actual items. [4] I worked happily while Grandpa shared stories that turned out not to be boring at all. 6

[4]

Perusing through her belongings, I felt I was opening a
7
window into the world of my relatives, a world long since gone.

Grandpa showed me a bundle of yellowed letters he had send
8
to Grandma from the front lines of World War II, and I could almost smell the gunpowder. I turned the brittle pages of my great-grandmother's recipe book and could envision her sitting in her immaculate kitchen penning meticulously every entry. All
9
of the people who had been merely names to me now had faces to match and lives lived.

[5]

I asked Grandpa to tell the story behind every picture and letter we scanned. Besides, the stories helped me not only
10
understand but also relate to my relatives. Like me, they had celebrated achievements, overcome failures, pulled silly pranks, played sports, and, attended concerts. I became so hungry for
11
more information that Grandpa needed additional props to keep

4. Which of the following choices is NOT an acceptable substitute for the underlined portion?
- **F.** e-mails but having
- **G.** e-mails, yet he had
- **H.** e-mails; however, he had
- **J.** e-mails but had

5. A. NO CHANGE
- **B.** relatives precious memory's
- **C.** relatives' precious memories
- **D.** relatives' precious memory's

6. Which of the following sentences in this paragraph is LEAST relevant to the progression of the narrative and therefore could be deleted?
- **F.** Sentence 1
- **G.** Sentence 2
- **H.** Sentence 3
- **J.** Sentence 4

7. A. NO CHANGE
- **B.** their
- **C.** one's
- **D.** there

8. F. NO CHANGE
- **G.** send
- **H.** has sent
- **J.** had sent

9. A. NO CHANGE
- **B.** kitchen, penning
- **C.** kitchen, which penned
- **D.** kitchen that penned

10. F. NO CHANGE
- **G.** Because the
- **H.** Therefore, the
- **J.** The

11. A. NO CHANGE
- **B.** sports, and
- **C.** sports and,
- **D.** sports and

GO ON TO THE NEXT PAGE.

me satisfied. He showed me a chest filled with random stuff, all covered in dust. ⬚12

[6]

As the new school year approached, Grandpa admitted, "I probably could have done this project myself. I just wanted someone to share it with." I can't thank him enough for sharing the experience and making me appreciate the family members who have made me the person I am. I will cherish family

memories and mementoes and hope that someday, I will be able to pass them down to my own grandchildren.
13

12. Which of the following true statements, if added at the beginning of this paragraph, would most successfully introduce readers to the information relayed in the paragraph?

   F. My family has been around for generations, so there were a lot of names to remember.
   G. My grandfather inundated me with items to catalogue on the computer.
   H. As I learned more about some relatives, I forgot about others.
   J. As the summer progressed, I became fascinated with my relatives' lives.

13. Which of the following provides the best conclusion to the paragraph and the essay as a whole?

   A. NO CHANGE
   B. My grandpa will teach me something new next summer.
   C. I never have to tell my mother she was right that family history isn't tedious and boring.
   D. I can figure out other ways to use my computer.

Questions 14 and 15 ask about the preceding passage as a whole.

---

14. Where should the author place Paragraph 5 in order to have a logical, coherent essay?

   F. Where it is now
   G. Before Paragraph 2
   H. Before Paragraph 3
   J. Before Paragraph 4

15. Suppose the writer's purpose had been to write an essay about some of the benefits of genealogical research. Does this essay succeed in achieving that purpose?

   A. Yes, because it describes the technological skills gained in the process of researching one's relatives.
   B. Yes, because it provides an example of how one person gained personal insights from her family history.
   C. No, because it provides only one person's research, which is susceptible to bias and cannot be reliable.
   D. No, because genealogical research require statistics in order to prove there were benefits.

Passage II

Moving to a New Life

I stand on the corner of Elm Avenue and Main Street by me, watching my parents walk away and feeling nothing but
16
apprehension about adjusting to this new town. I try not to show the passersby just how scared I really am, but it's not possible.

16. **F.** NO CHANGE
   G. me watching
   H. myself, watching
   J. myself. Watching

GO ON TO THE NEXT PAGE.

My tears start to flow, and I quickly run to my <u>new, cold,</u> bedroom.
₁₇

I know I am making a <u>complete spectacle of</u> myself, but I
₁₈

can't help it. I am an only child <u>whom has</u> never been more
₁₉
than 30 minutes away from her parents, yet here I am, on the
other side of the country, moving in to my new college dorm.

We all want to take responsibility for <u>one's own lives.</u> I just
₂₀
never realized that in order to do so, I would have to leave my
family. No longer will I wake up to Mom's Sunday breakfast of

non-pasteurized <u>milk, and fresh orange juice, fluffy</u> scrambled
₂₁
eggs and crisp bacon. I'll have to tackle the daily crossword
puzzle on my own, without Dad's carefully veiled hints.

Everything is gone. [22] Can anyone understand what I'm going
through?

As I lie crying into my pillow, <u>hearing</u> the door to the
₂₃
dorm suite open. It must be one of my two roommates. I
quickly stop crying—I couldn't stand the embarrassment

17. A. NO CHANGE
  B. new, cold
  C. new cold
  D. new cold,

18. F. NO CHANGE
  G. completely spectacle about
  H. completely spectacle of
  J. complete spectacle about

19. A. NO CHANGE
  B. whom have
  C. who has
  D. who have

20. F. NO CHANGE
  G. their own life.
  H. our own lives.
  J. your own life.

21. A. NO CHANGE
  B. milk, and fresh orange juice, fluffy,
  C. milk and fresh orange juice fluffy
  D. milk and fresh orange juice, fluffy

22. The writer is considering revising the sentence "Everything is gone" in the preceding sentence to read:

  "It feels like everything I have ever loved is being ripped away from me."

  Should the writer make this change, or keep the sentence as it is?

  F. Make the revision, because it conveys more vividly the type of emotions felt by the writer.
  G. Make the revision, because it describes the stages of emotion the writer faces as she mourns.
  H. Keep the sentence as it is, because it is already specific and does not need to be changed.
  J. Keep the sentence as it is, because it's short and more concise than the proposed revision.

23. A. NO CHANGE
  B. I was hearing
  C. I hear
  D. having heard

GO ON TO THE NEXT PAGE.

if she knew her new roommate was an emotional wreck! [24]

24. If the writer were to delete the phrase "—I couldn't stand the embarrassment if she knew her new roommate was an emotional wreck!" from the preceding sentence, the passage would primarily lose:

- **F.** a description of the uneasy relationship between the roommates.
- **G.** an insight into the reasons the writer stopped crying.
- **H.** a justification for her dissatisfaction with college.
- **J.** nothing at all, since the writer has already expressed her sadness.

Being full of surprise, I hear *her* crying as she runs to her room.
25

25.
- **A.** NO CHANGE
- **B.** Since I was surprised,
- **C.** Being surprised,
- **D.** Much to my surprise,

Curiosity overwhelming me and I tiptoe through the common
26
room to her still-open door.

26.
- **F.** NO CHANGE
- **G.** me, and I
- **H.** me, I
- **J.** me. I

I stand in the doorway for merely a second before she reacts. Slowly, her face jolts up, and her sudden shock at my
27
appearance is clearly written on her face. "Are you okay?" I

27. Given that all the choices are true, which one provides the best transition by illustrating how quickly the roommate responded to the writer's presence?

- **A.** NO CHANGE
- **B.** Abruptly,
- **C.** After several moments,
- **D.** Sluggishly,

quietly ask. "I'm sorry," she stammers. "I thought I was alone.
28
I know this must seem very childish to you. I'm just very close to my younger sister, and saying goodbye to her just now...." Her sentence trails off as she turns her face away from me. "I remember when she was born."
29

28.
- **F.** NO CHANGE
- **G.** asserts.
- **H.** quotes.
- **J.** screams.

29. Given that all the choices are true, which conclusion to this paragraph is most consistent with the writer's subsequent response?

- **A.** NO CHANGE
- **B.** "My sister has always been so fun to live with."
- **C.** "I wish that they would have left sooner."
- **D.** "It's going to be hard to adjust, that's all."

"I completely understand," I say, and I really do. "Maybe we can help each other get used to this new college life."

GO ON TO THE NEXT PAGE.

Question 30 asks about the preceding passage as a whole.

30. Suppose the writer's goal was to describe personal hardships first-time college students may experience. Does this essay successfully accomplish that goal?

F. Yes, because it gives an anecdotal account of separation anxiety experienced by the writer and her roommate.

G. Yes, because it focuses on the initial awkwardness between roommates who don't know each other.

H. No, because it focuses on the emotions of only one person instead of the experiences of many students.

J. No, because it fails to provide enough background information on the narrator's mental state before college.

GO ON TO THE NEXT PAGE.

Passage III

The following paragraphs may or may not be in the most logical order. Each paragraph is numbered in brackets, and question 45 will ask you to choose where Paragraph 2 should most logically be placed.

Thrill Seekers Wanted

[1]

Like Indiana Jones, the staid college professor who undertakes daring adventures in his spare time, my father is a businessman by day and a thrill-seeking adrenaline fanatic by night. [31] His enthusiasm rubbed off on me, and I have been lucky to be his sidekick on many an adventure. We started out small by conquering America's fastest, most twisted rollercoasters. After that, a whitewater rafting excursion through

the Grand Canyon on the majestic, if murky Colorado River
                                          32
jumpstarted our search for other extreme thrills across the globe.

[2]

Anyone who loves a challenging thrill should try canyoning. [33] Our adventure began with a 90-foot rappel

31. The writer is considering deleting the phrase "Like Indiana Jones, the staid college professor who undertakes daring adventures in his spare time," from the preceding sentence (and capitalizing the word *my*). Should the phrase be kept or deleted?

   A. Kept, because it clarifies that the writer's father is also named Indiana.
   B. Kept, because it adds a descriptive detail that heightens the thrill of the adventures described later in the passage.
   C. Deleted, because it draws attention from the paragraph's focus on the father and places it on movies.
   D. Deleted, because the information fails to specify if the writer's father is interested in archaeology.

32. F. NO CHANGE
    G. majestic if murky
    H. majestic; if murky,
    J. majestic, if murky,

33. The writer is considering deleting the phrase "who loves a challenging thrill" from the preceding sentence. Should the phrase be kept or deleted?

   A. Kept, because it clarifies the term *anyone* and contributes to the logic of the paragraph.
   B. Kept, because it indicates the paragraph's focus on people who love challenges.
   C. Deleted, because the term *anyone* describes all people and does not need clarification.
   D. Deleted, because the phrase is too long and confuses the focus of the sentence.

GO ON TO THE NEXT PAGE.

down a canyon wall into a rushing, ice-cold river, and without
wetsuits we surely would have become popsicles! Intrepidly, we
traversed the bone-chilling water toward the mouth of the river,
our final destination, where the reward for the journey would be
a panoramic view of the natural wonder of the lush Interlaken
basin.

[3]

Spectacular thrills awaited us at every corner of the world.
A remarkable activity in its own right, like skydiving was
especially momentous when performed from a helicopter over
the breathtaking Swiss Alps. We have gone spelunking in damp
and ominous Peruvian caves. [37] We have traveled to New
Zealand for *Zorb*, a strange activity in which participants enter
a giant, inflatable ball and roll down steep, grassy hills. Most
recently, in Interlaken, Switzerland, we attempted "canyoning,"

because of which was our most exhilarating adventure yet!

[4]

We had to navigate both the flowing river and the canyon
walls we became amphibious, moving seamlessly between
land and water. We slid over slick rocks at one moment,

leapt and descended from waterfalls and swam through
underwater tunnels the next. Back and forth we alternated,
scaling rope ladders before zooming down zip lines back into

34. F. NO CHANGE
G. river, without
H. river without
J. river and without

35. A. NO CHANGE
B. view naturally of the wonder
C. viewing of the wonderful nature
D. view

36. F. NO CHANGE
G. skydiving was
H. skydiving,
J. like skydiving

37. At this point, the writer is considering adding the following true statement:

> We have bungee jumped from the world's highest platform, Bloukrans Bridge in South Africa.

Should the writer make this addition here?

A. Yes, because it is an additional detail consistent with the main point of this paragraph.
B. Yes, because it helps establish the main idea that Africa has the most exciting thrills in the world.
C. No, because its focus is on a location and activity different than those in the rest of the paragraph.
D. No, because the other activities in this paragraph do not involve the use of a bungee cord.

38. F. NO CHANGE
G. and which was
H. which was
J. in which was

39. A. NO CHANGE
B. walls, we
C. walls so we
D. walls, so we

40. F. NO CHANGE
G. leapt
H. leapt in the air and descended down
J. leapt to descend

GO ON TO THE NEXT PAGE.

the fresh mountain water. Certainly, danger from possible
miscalculations were lurking in each of these activities, but that
very danger provided the rush. Canyoning was indeed one thrill
after another, from beginning to end.

[5]

While canyoning is possible only in certain locales, thrills
and adventure can be found anywhere. Our humble beginnings
in the United States showed us just that. We continue to seek
the big thrills, but in doing so, we have learned to seek lesser
forms of excitement in daily life as well. After all, we can't go
canyoning every day, and small thrills are better than none for
us thrill seekers.

41. A. NO CHANGE
B. miscalculations will be lurking
C. miscalculations was lurking
D. miscalculations lurking

42. Given that all the choices are true, which one best clarifies the distinction between the two types of activities mentioned in this paragraph?
F. NO CHANGE
G. both on rocky surfaces and in the chilly water.
H. adventure after adventure.
J. long after the waterfalls.

43. A. NO CHANGE
B. and
C. moreover,
D. furthermore,

44. Given that all the choices are true, which one concludes the paragraph with a phrase that relates to the main topic of the essay?
F. NO CHANGE
G. and that's a shame.
H. because we don't live near any canyons.
J. but it's the last thrill I'll ever need!

Question 45 asks about the preceding passage as a whole.

45. For the sake of the logic and coherence of this essay, the best placement for Paragraph 2 would be:
A. where it is now.
B. before Paragraph 1.
C. before Paragraph 4.
D. before Paragraph 5.

Passage IV

Enriching the American Tradition

The Mexican-American War, with its many conflicts and
compromises, represent a largely overlooked part of the history
of the United States, but its importance in the current shape and
culture of the United States cannot be overstated. Certainly, it
is difficult to imagine the present-day United States without

46. F. NO CHANGE
G. represents
H. have represented
J. representing

GO ON TO THE NEXT PAGE.

the list of former Mexican territories, which <u>includes</u> Texas,
⁴⁷
Arizona, California, and others, but it is equally difficult to
imagine America's vibrant multicultural society without the
influence of Mexican-Americans.

But despite the obvious richness that Mexican-Americans
have brought to American culture, one aspect of <u>their
contributions, to American arts</u> is often overlooked: literature.
⁴⁸
Although the names of many famous Mexican-Americans are
identifiable in film and music, many Americans are at a loss to
name even a single Mexican-American author. <u>Carlos Santana,
⁴⁹
a musician born and raised in Mexico, has achieved widespread
⁴⁹
popularity in the United States.</u>
⁴⁹

A major landmark in early Mexican-American literature
came in 1885, when <u>author, María Amparo Ruiz de Burton,</u>
⁵⁰
published her second novel, *The Squatter and the Don*. In
addition to being the first major novel written in English by
an author of Mexican descent, *The Squatter and the Don* was
also noteworthy for its revolutionary perspective. [51] María

Amparo Ruiz de Burton helped to <u>acquaint American readers
with and introduce them to</u> an as yet unfamiliar group through
⁵²

47. **A.** NO CHANGE
    B. includes:
    C. included,
    D. included:

48. **F.** NO CHANGE
    G. their contributions, to American arts,
    H. their contributions to American arts,
    J. their contributions to American arts

49. **A.** NO CHANGE
    B. A musician who has achieved popularity in the United
    States is Carlos Santana, who was born and raised in
    Mexico.
    C. However, many Americans can easily identify Carlos
    Santana, a popular musician born and raised in
    Mexico.
    D. DELETE the underlined portion.

50. **F.** NO CHANGE
    G. author María Amparo Ruiz de Burton
    H. author, María Amparo Ruiz de Burton
    J. author María Amparo Ruiz de Burton,

51. If the writer were to delete the phrase "In addition to being
    the first major novel written in English by an author of
    Mexican descent," from the preceding sentence, the essay
    would primarily lose:
    A. an indication of Ruiz de Burton's command of the
    English language.
    B. a fact that reveals that the novel was the first by a
    Mexican author to be read in the United States.
    C. information that helps to strengthen the sense of the
    novel's historical importance.
    D. a suggestion that María Amparo Ruiz de Burton con-
    sidered writing the novel in her native Spanish.

52. **F.** NO CHANGE
    G. give American readers a glimpse at
    H. introduce American readers unacquainted with
    Mexican-American literature to
    J. introduce American readers to

GO ON TO THE NEXT PAGE.

her fictional family, the Alamars. A family of landed gentry living in San Diego, <u>nearly all is lost to the Alamars</u> after
₅₃

53. **A.** NO CHANGE
B. the Alamars lose nearly all that they own
C. losing all that they own
D. Ruiz de Burton describes a family that loses all that they own

the American annexation of California <u>during</u> the Mexican-
₅₄
American War. As a result of the lopsided Treaty of Guadalupe Hidalgo, Mexico lost nearly forty percent of its previous territories and many, like Ruiz de Burton and her creations the Alamars, were uprooted from their previous comfort and made citizens of a new nation. Ruiz de Burton's wish <u>that</u> her
₅₅
works would speak for the many Mexican-Americans who felt

54. **F.** NO CHANGE
G. within
H. throughout
J. through

55. **A.** NO CHANGE
B. being that
C. was that
D. being

the same concerns. [56] *The Squatter and the Don* marked an early and important exploration of many themes that Mexican-

56. At this point, the writer is considering adding the following true statement:

> After the Louisiana Purchase in 1803, many people of French descent living in the United States felt displaced as well.

Should the writer make the addition here?

F. Yes, because it provides historical information about another group that deepens the reader's understanding of the difficulties faced by Mexican-Americans.
G. Yes, because it links those with French descent with the characters in *The Squatter and the Don*.
H. No, because it does not provide a direct connection between the work of María Amparo Ruiz de Burton and the work of later Mexican-American authors.
J. No, because it is clear from the essay that the Louisiana Purchase had no importance to the Mexican-American authors discussed.

American authors continue to <u>explore</u>, including themes of
₅₇
personal integrity, identity, and the relationships between individuals and collective history.

[1] Poet Ana Castillo has been publishing well-received novels and volumes of poetry prolifically since 1977, and her work has been essential in bringing issues of Mexican-American women, particularly those living in urban places such as Castillo's hometown of Chicago, to a larger audience.

57. Which of the following alternatives to the underlined portion would be LEAST acceptable?

A. investigate
B. examine
C. look into
D. solve

GO ON TO THE NEXT PAGE.

[2] Sandra Cisneros is the author of *The House on Mango Street*, which has sold over two million copies since its original publication in 1984, and her work, including the novel *Caramelo*, published in 2002, has helped give voice to the often difficult position of living between two cultures that Mexican-Americans face. [3] Ruiz de Burton's writings and that of other

58

authors remain important parts of American literature today. [59]

[4] Along with many others, these authors continue to expand

60

the boundaries of American literature, just as Mexican-Americans all over the country continue to enrich and challenge accepted notions of what we call "American culture."

58. F. NO CHANGE
  G. by
  H. those of
  J. with

59. For the sake of the logic and coherence of this paragraph, Sentence 3 should be placed:

  A. where it is now.
  B. before Sentence 1.
  C. before Sentence 2.
  D. after Sentence 4.

60. F. NO CHANGE
  G. the writers Ana Castillo and Sandra Cisneros and many other Mexican-American authors
  H. the Mexican-American authors being published today
  J. the many Mexican-American authors whose work as a whole represents them

GO ON TO THE NEXT PAGE.

Passage V

A Simple but Complex Modern Vision

Ludwig Mies van der Rohe, typically cited alongside
Walter Gropius and Le Corbusier as a pioneer of modern
architecture. Was integral to the founding and proliferation of
the "modern style" in architecture. Van der Rohe felt the design
of a building should be reflective of its age, as the Gothic and
Classical masterpieces surely were. Van der Rohe, called Mies
by friends and students, found many architects' attitudes toward
architectural design problematic, particularly these architects'
reliance on older, outdated architectural styles.

Van der Rohe, instead, sought to express through his
buildings what he feels to be the core tenets of modern
existence. The buildings based on van der Rohe's designs,
were primarily constructed with industrial steel and plate
glass—that is, only the materials of modern, twentieth-century
life and industry. By using only the bare minimum materials
produced from American and German factories, Mies sought
to cast off what he found to be one of the main problems
with contemporary architecture, and overly decorative and
ornamental structures with no "function" were wasteful uses of
space and material. Through steel and plate glass, van der Rohe
felt that he could better practice the idea of "efficiency" that he
had pulled from his earlier readings of Russian Constructivism,
and using these materials as he did to create simple, planar,
rectilinear designs, Mies invested his buildings with a strange

61. A. NO CHANGE
B. architecture. Being
C. architecture, being
D. architecture, was

62. F. NO CHANGE
G. is feeling
H. felt
J. who felt

63. A. NO CHANGE
B. buildings based on van der Rohe's designs
C. buildings, based on van der Rohe's designs
D. buildings based on van der Rohe's designs;

64. Which of the following alternatives to the underlined portion would NOT be acceptable?
F. from
G. using
H. out of
J. into

65. A. NO CHANGE
B. that is
C. this is,
D. this is

66. F. NO CHANGE
G. architecture that
H. architecture, which
J. architecture: that

GO ON TO THE NEXT PAGE.

intensity that conveyed at once the simplicity of design and
many of the buildings have been named National Historic
Landmarks.
₆₇

Van der Rohe's architectural education was unique, and many describe the architect as largely self-taught. From 1908 to 1912, under teacher Peter Behrens's guidance, Mies became a proponent of many modern and avant-garde ideas in architecture in Germany. From Behrens, van der Rohe began to see the potential of developing an architecture of ideas, and indeed, he was a "self-taught" expert in many ancient and modern philosophical concepts. This helped him to understand the character of the modern world, and with his maturing ideas of this character, van der Rohe set out to create a style truly of the twentieth century. While van der Rohe was committed to creating a philosophical, theoretical basis for his works, he helped to create a new vocabulary for the creation and study of architecture.

[1] In order to escape the oppressive Nazi regime, van der Rohe who left Germany for the United States in 1937. [2] Mies was originally invited to become head of the school and to contribute designs for the school's growing campus (which, as the Illinois Institute of Technology, continues to grow today). [3] He had two commissions waiting for him there—one in Wyoming and another at the Armour Institute of Technology in

67. Given that all the choices are true, which one would add the most effective detail to the description of the visual appeal of the buildings mentioned in the first part of the sentence?
  A. NO CHANGE
  B. the structure that had taken months, even years, to build.
  C. the complex beauty of the free-flowing structures inside.
  D. the buildings on display in many American and European cities.

68. **F.** NO CHANGE
  G. teacher, Peter Behrens's guidance,
  H. teacher Peter Behrens's guidance;
  J. teacher, Peter Behrens's guidance

69. **A.** NO CHANGE
  B. Studying philosophy
  C. Something
  D. This thing

70. **F.** NO CHANGE
  G. Even though
  H. Moreover
  J. Because

71. **A.** NO CHANGE
  B. left
  C. leaves
  D. leaving

72. Which of the following alternatives to the underlined portion would NOT be acceptable?
  F. the other
  G. one
  H. this one
  J. the other one

GO ON TO THE NEXT PAGE.

Chicago. [4] <u>Pupils learning</u> his new method and architectural
                    73
vocabulary, van der Rohe worked tirelessly as an educator, with

only limited success. [5] While many students were initially

<u>enthusiastic,</u> Mies van der Rohe's influence was eventually
        74
eclipsed by the rise of Postmodern Architecture in the early

1980s. ☐75

    There can be no doubt, though, that van der Rohe has left a

huge mark on the look of the North American city. Not only do

his buildings help to create the skylines of Chicago, New York,

and Toronto, but van der Rohe also gave architects from all over

the world a new vocabulary and set of materials with which to

create spaces for living and working, and he helped to make

architecture one of the great arts of the twentieth century.

---

73. A. NO CHANGE
    B. While pupils learn
    C. To teach pupils
    D. Pupils being taught

74. F. NO CHANGE
    G. enthusiastic and extremely excited,
    H. enthusiastic, overwhelmed with excitement,
    J. enthusiastic, thrilled,

75. For the sake of the logic and coherence of this paragraph,
Sentence 3 should be placed:

    A. where it is now.
    B. after Sentence 1.
    C. after Sentence 4.
    D. after Sentence 5.

END OF TEST 1
STOP! DO NOT TURN THE PAGE UNTIL TOLD TO DO SO.

NO TEST MATERIAL ON THIS PAGE.

MATHEMATICS TEST

60 Minutes—60 Questions

DIRECTIONS: Solve each problem, choose the correct answer, and then darken the corresponding oval on your answer sheet.

Do not linger over problems that take too much time. Solve as many as you can; then return to the others in the time you have left for this test.

You are permitted to use a calculator on this test. You may use your calculator for any problems you choose, but some of the problems may best be done without using a calculator.

Note: Unless otherwise stated, all of the following should be assumed:

1. Illustrative figures are NOT necessarily drawn to scale.
2. Geometric figures lie in a plane.
3. The word line indicates a straight line.
4. The word average indicates arithmetic mean.

---

1. Violet is baking a mixed berry pie that contains blueberries, cherries, blackberries, and raspberries. She uses three times as many blackberries as cherries, twice as many blueberries as raspberries, and the same number of blackberries and raspberries. If Violet has 10 cherries, how many of each of the other berries must she use?

	Raspberries	Blueberries	Blackberries
A.	3	2	3
B.	30	2	3
C.	30	2	30
D.	30	60	10
E.	30	60	30

2. The expression $(3x - 5)(x + 2)$ is equivalent to:

F. $3x^2 - 10$
G. $3x^2 + x + 10$
H. $3x^2 + x - 10$
J. $3x^2 + 11x - 10$
K. $3x^2 - 11x - 10$

3. A function f is defined by $f(x,y) = x - (xy - y)$. What is the value of $f(8,6)$?

A. -46
B. -34
C. 46
D. 50
E. 62

4. What is $\frac{1}{7}$ of 28% of 8,000 ?

F. 32
G. 320
H. $1,568$
J. $3,200$
K. $15,680$

DO YOUR FIGURING HERE.

GO ON TO THE NEXT PAGE.

5. If $6x + 3 = 12 + 3x$, then $x = ?$

A.   6

B.   5

C.   3

D. $\dfrac{5}{3}$

E.   1

DO YOUR FIGURING HERE.

6. The second term of an arithmetic sequence is −2, and the third term is 8. What is the first term?

(Note: An arithmetic sequence has a common difference between consecutive terms.)

F.   −12

G.   −10

H. $\dfrac{1}{2}$

J.   3

K.   10

7. Stacie has a bag of solid colored jellybeans. Each jelly-bean is orange, purple, or pink. If she randomly selects a jellybean from the bag, the probability that the jellybean is orange is $\dfrac{2}{9}$, and the probability that it is purple is $\dfrac{1}{3}$. If there are 72 jellybeans in the bag, how many pink jelly-beans are in the bag?

A.   16
B.   24
C.   32
D.   40
E.   48

8. A cellular phone company unveiled a new plan for new cus-tomers. It will charge a flat rate of $100 for initial connec-tion and service for the first two months, and $60 for service each subsequent month. If Bob subscribes to this plan for one year, how much does he pay in total for the year?

F. $600
G. $700
H. $720
J. $800
K. $820

GO ON TO THE NEXT PAGE.

9. A square and a regular pentagon (a 5-sided polygon with congruent sides and interior angles) have the same perimeter. One side of the pentagon measures 20 inches. How many inches long is one side of the square?

   A.   4
   B.   16
   C.   25
   D.   36
   E.   100

DO YOUR FIGURING HERE.

10. Two contractors bid on a job to build a brick wall in a yard. Contractor A charges a flat fee of $1,600 plus $2 per brick. Contractor B charges a flat fee of $400 plus $8 per brick. If x represents the number of bricks in the wall, which of the following equations could be solved to determine the number of bricks which would make B's charge to build the wall equal to A's charge?

   F. $1600 + 2x = 400 + 8x$
   G. $1600 + 8x = 400 + 2x$
   H. $2x + 8x = x$
   J. $2x + 8x = 1600$
   K. $2x + 8x = 400$

11. Given that $E = ABCD$, which of the following is an expression of B, in terms of $E, A, C,$ and D ?

   A. $\dfrac{ACD}{E}$

   B. $E + ACD$

   C. $E - ACD$

   D. $\dfrac{E}{ACD}$

   E. $EACD$

GO ON TO THE NEXT PAGE.

DO YOUR FIGURING HERE.

12. Lines $\overline{XV}$ and $\overline{YV}$ intersect at point V on line $\overline{WZ}$, as shown in the figure below. The measures of 2 angles are given in terms of a, in degrees. What is the measure of $\angle XVZ$ in degrees?

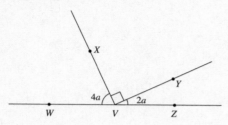

- F.   30
- G.   90
- H.   120
- J.   150
- K.   180

13. An outdoor thermometer in Hanover, NH reads 70°F. The temperature in Hanover is 25°F cooler than in New Orleans, LA. What is the temperature, C, in degrees Celsius, in New Orleans?

   (Note: $F = \dfrac{9}{5}C + 32$)

- A.   21°C
- B.   35°C
- C.   68°C
- D.   95°C
- E.   113°C

14. If $3x + 2y = 5$, what is the value of the expression $6x + 4y - 7$?

- F.   −2
- G.   3
- H.   8
- J.   10
- K.   19

GO ON TO THE NEXT PAGE.

DO YOUR FIGURING HERE.

15. Mike sold $3\frac{2}{7}$ pounds of beef at his deli on Wednesday and $2\frac{1}{3}$ pounds of beef on Saturday. Which of the following ranges includes the total amount of beef, in pounds, Mike sold during these two days?

   A. At least 5 and less than $5\frac{1}{2}$

   B. At least $5\frac{1}{2}$ and less than $5\frac{2}{3}$

   C. At least $5\frac{2}{3}$ and less than 6

   D. At least 6 and less than $6\frac{1}{2}$

   E. At least $6\frac{1}{2}$ and less than $6\frac{2}{3}$

16. Dave leaves his house and bikes directly east for 3 miles. He then turns and bikes directly south for 4 miles. How many miles is Dave from his house?

   F. 3
   G. 4
   H. 5
   J. 6
   K. 7

17. A sensor records a piece of data every .0000000038 seconds. The sensor will record 100,000,000,000 pieces of data in how many seconds?

   A. 3,800
   B. 380
   C. 38
   D. 3.8
   E. 0.0038

18. Alan has a rectangular photograph that is 20 centimeters wide by 30 centimeters long. Alan wants to reduce the area of the photograph by 264 square centimeters by decreasing the width and length by the same amount. What will be the new dimensions (width by length), in centimeters?

   F. 11 by 24
   G. 12 by 22
   H. 12 by 28
   J. 14 by 24
   K. 16 by 21

GO ON TO THE NEXT PAGE.

19. A quadrilateral has a perimeter of 36 inches. If the lengths of the sides are 4 consecutive, even integers, what is the length, in inches, of the shortest side?

   A. 2
   B. 4
   C. 6
   D. 7
   E. 8

DO YOUR FIGURING HERE.

20. In the standard (x,y) coordinate plane, what is the slope of the line with equation $7y - 3x = 21$?

   F. $-\dfrac{3}{7}$

   G. $\dfrac{3}{7}$

   H. $\dfrac{7}{3}$

   J. 3

   K. 7

21. In the figure shown below, points A, B, C, and D are collinear, and distances marked are in feet. Rectangle $ADEG$ has an area of 48 square feet. What is the area, in square feet, of the trapezoid $BCEF$?

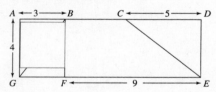

   A. 16
   B. 20
   C. 26
   D. 36
   E. 58

GO ON TO THE NEXT PAGE.

Use the following information to answer questions 22–24.

Quadrilateral *FGHJ* is shown below in the standard (x,y) coordinate plane. For this quadrilateral, $\overline{FG} = 10$, $\overline{FJ} = 6$, $\overline{HJ} = \sqrt{136}$, and $\overline{GH} = 12$.

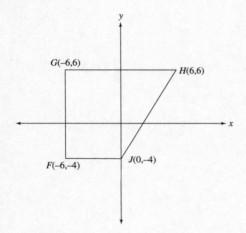

22. Which of the following is closest to the perimeter of quadrilateral *FGHJ*, in coordinate units?

F. 28.0
G. 39.7
H. 60.0
J. 108.0
K. 120.0

23. What is the length of $\overline{GJ}$, in coordinate units?

A. 4
B. 8
C. 16
D. $\sqrt{108}$
E. $\sqrt{136}$

GO ON TO THE NEXT PAGE.

24. Which of the following are the coordinates of the image of J under a 90° clockwise rotation about the origin?

   F. (–4, 0)
   G. (0, –4)
   H. (0, 0)
   J. (0, 4)
   K. (4, 0)

DO YOUR FIGURING HERE.

25. Which of the following geometric figures has at least 1 rotational symmetry and at least 1 reflectional symmetry?

(Note: The angle of rotation for the rotational symmetry must be less than 360°.)

   A.

   B.

   C.

   D.

   E.

26. What is the coefficient of x^8 in the product of the polynomials below?

$$(-x^4 + 3x^3 - 5x^2 + x - 5)(5x^4 - 2x^3 + x^2 - 5x + 2)$$

   F. 0
   G. 5
   H. 4
   J. –2
   K. –5

GO ON TO THE NEXT PAGE.

DO YOUR FIGURING HERE.

Use the following information to answer questions 27–28.

The stem-and-leaf plot below shows the scores for each golfer in a recent tournament at the Lehigh Valley Golf Club. There were 13 golfers participating in the tournament.

Stem	Leaf
6	6, 7
7	1, 2, 2, 3, 5, 7, 9
8	2, 3, 3, 7

(Note: For example, a score of 72 would have a stem value of 7 and a leaf value of 2.)

27. Which of the following is closest to the mean score of all the golfers in the tournament?

A. 72.0
B. 74.4
C. 75.0
D. 75.9
E. 83.0

28. If a score represented in the stem-and-leaf plot is selected randomly, what is the probability that the score selected is exactly 83 ?

F. $\dfrac{2}{13}$

G. $\dfrac{4}{13}$

H. $\dfrac{83}{87}$

J. $\dfrac{83}{987}$

K. $\dfrac{166}{987}$

29. What is the least common multiple of 8, 2, 3*a*, 6*b*, and 4*ab* ?

A. 16*ab*
B. 24*ab*
C. 24*a²b*
D. 54*ab*
E. 60*a²b*

GO ON TO THE NEXT PAGE.

30. Aleksandra began collecting model airplanes in May of 2008. The number of model airplanes that she owns in each month can be modeled by the function $A(m) = 2m + 2$, where $m = 0$ corresponds to May. Using this model, how many model airplanes would you expect Aleksandra to own in December of 2008 ?

   F. 2
   G. 12
   H. 14
   J. 16
   K. 18

DO YOUR FIGURING HERE.

31. In the standard (x,y) coordinate plane, line segment $\overline{CD}$ has end points $C(-3,5)$ and $D(11,-7)$. What is the midpoint of $\overline{CD}$?

   A. (14,−12)
   B. (8,   2)
   C. (7,   1)
   D. (7,   −6)
   E. (4,   −1)

32. Given $x \neq \pm 4$, which of the following is equivalent to the expression $\dfrac{x^2 - 8x + 16}{x^2 - 16}$?

   F. $\dfrac{1}{2}x - 1$

   G. $-8x$

   H. $\dfrac{x - 2}{2}$

   J. $\dfrac{1}{x + 4}$

   K. $\dfrac{x - 4}{x + 4}$

33. Evan purchased 6 boxes of sugar cookies, each box containing 10 snack bags and each bag containing 12 cookies. Evan could have purchased the same amount of cookies by buying how many family-sized packs of 30 cookies each?

   A. 12
   B. 24
   C. 48
   D. 72
   E. 180

GO ON TO THE NEXT PAGE.

34. When $\dfrac{r}{s} = -\dfrac{1}{2}$, $16r^4 - s^4 = ?$

    F.   −32
    G.   −16
    H.   0
    J.   16
    K.   32

35. Emilia is going to bake cookies. She rolls out a square of dough that is 12 inches wide by 12 inches long and cuts 9 identical circular cookies from the dough, as shown in the figure below. Each circular cut-out is tangent to the circular cut-outs next to it and tangent to the edge or edges of the square piece of dough it touches. Approximately, what is the area, in square inches, of the remaining dough, as shown in the figure?

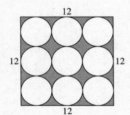

    A.   30.9
    B.   42.3
    C.   50.24
    D.   87.5
    E.   113.04

36. Which of the following lists contains only prime numbers?

    F.   63, 73, and 97
    G.   71, 87, and 91
    H.   73, 89, and 91
    J.   79, 89, and 97
    K.   81, 87, and 97

GO ON TO THE NEXT PAGE.

37. The costs of tutoring packages of different lengths, given in quarter hours, are shown in the table below.

Number of quarter hours	8	10	12	20
Cost	$200	$230	$260	$380

Each cost consists of a fixed charge and a charge per quarter hour. What is the fixed charge?

A. $15
B. $23
C. $80
D. $120
E. $380

DO YOUR FIGURING HERE.

38. At 3 P.M., the afternoon sun shines over a building and its rays hit the ground at a 34° angle. The building is 100 meters tall and is perpendicular to the ground. How long, to the nearest meter, is the building's shadow that is cast by the sun?

(Note: sin 34° ≈ 0.56, cos 34° ≈ 0.83, tan 34° ≈ 0.67)

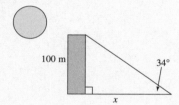

F. 56
G. 67
H. 83
J. 120
K. 148

39. In the standard (x,y) coordinate system, circle O has its center at $(4,-3)$ and a radius of 12 units. Which of the following is an equation of the circle?

A. $(x-4)^2 + (y+3)^2 = 12$
B. $(x+4)^2 + (y+3)^2 = 12$
C. $(x+4)^2 - (y+3)^2 = 12$
D. $(x-4)^2 + (y-3)^2 = 144$
E. $(x-4)^2 + (y+3)^2 = 144$

GO ON TO THE NEXT PAGE.

40. What is the least integer value of x that makes the inequality $\frac{14}{21} < \frac{x}{12}$ true?

    F. 7
    G. 8
    H. 9
    J. 10
    K. 11

41. When $f(a) = a^2 + 2a + 5$, what is the value of $f(a + b)$?

    A. $a^2 + b^2 + 2ab + 5$
    B. $a^2 + b^2 + 2a + 2b + 10$
    C. $a^2 + b^2 + 2a + 2b + 5$
    D. $(a+b)^2 + a + b + 5$
    E. $(a+b)^2 + 2a + 2b + 5$

42. In the figure below, M is on $\overline{LN}$ and O is on $\overline{NP}$. $\overline{LP}$ and $\overline{MO}$ are parallel. The dimensions given are in feet. What is the length, in feet, of $\overline{NO}$?

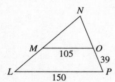

    F. 39
    G. 91
    H. 105
    J. 273
    K. 294

43. Gina watched as a plane took off from the runway and climbed to 30,000 feet. She calculated the plane's height, h feet, t seconds after takeoff to be given by $h = 1,200 + 32t$. To the nearest second, how many seconds did it take the plane to climb to a height of 2 miles? (Note: 1 mile = 5,280 feet)

    A. 37
    B. 128
    C. 293
    D. 900
    E. 1,264

GO ON TO THE NEXT PAGE.

44. In $\triangle ABC$, the measures of $\angle A$, $\angle B$, and $\angle C$ are $2x°$, $3x°$, and $5x°$, respectively. What is the measure of $\angle C$?

    F.   18°
    G.   36°
    H.   54°
    J.   90°
    K.   180°

45. A basketball player has attempted 30 free throws and made 12 of them. Starting now, if he makes every free throw attempted, what is the *least* number of additional free throws he must attempt to raise his free-throw percentage to at least 55% ?

(Note: Free-throw percentage =

$$\frac{number\ of\ free\ throws\ made}{number\ of\ free\ throws\ attempted} \times 100.)$$

    A.   5
    B.   10
    C.   16
    D.   17
    E.   29

46. If y is a negative integer, which of the following has the least value?

    F. $\sqrt[3]{y^2}$

    G. 100^y

    H. $\dfrac{\pi}{y}$

    J. $\dfrac{1}{y^2}$

    K. $\dfrac{1}{y^3}$

47. Jonathan, Ellery, and 3 other groomsmen are rehearsing for a wedding by walking down an aisle one at a time, one groomsman in front of the other. Each time all 5 walk down the aisle, the groom tells them to walk in a different order from first to last. What is the greatest number of times the groomsmen can walk down the aisle without walking in the same order twice?

    A.   3,125
    B.   720
    C.   120
    D.   100
    E.   25

DO YOUR FIGURING HERE.

GO ON TO THE NEXT PAGE.

48. In the circle below, O is the center and measures 5 inches from chord $\overline{MN}$. The area of the circle is 169π square inches. What is the length of $\overline{MN}$, in inches?

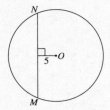

F. 12
G. 13
H. 18
J. 24
K. 26

49. What is the x–intercept of the line that passes through points $(-3,7)$ and $(6,4)$ in the standard (x,y) coordinate plane?

A. $(18,0)$

B. $(0, \dfrac{1}{3})$

C. $(0, 6)$

D. $(0,18)$

E. $(\dfrac{1}{3}, 0)$

50. Which of the following equations represents a graph that intersects the x-axis at $x = 7$?

F. $y = (x + 7)^2$
G. $y = (x - 7)^2$
H. $y = (-x - 7)^2$
J. $y - 7 = x^2$
K. $y + 7 = x^2$

GO ON TO THE NEXT PAGE.

51. If $0° < \theta < 90°$ and $\tan \theta = \dfrac{2}{9}$, what is $\sin \theta + \cos \theta$?

DO YOUR FIGURING HERE.

- **A.** $\dfrac{11}{\sqrt{85}}$

- **B.** $\dfrac{-7}{\sqrt{170}}$

- **C.** $\dfrac{11}{\sqrt{170}}$

- **D.** $\dfrac{9}{\sqrt{85}}$

- **E.** $\dfrac{2}{\sqrt{85}}$

52. In the figure below, $\overline{OA} = \overline{AB}$, and $\overline{OB}$ is a radius of the circle, having a length of 8 inches. What is the area of $\triangle OAB$, in square inches?

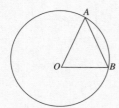

- **F.** $8\sqrt{3}$
- **G.** $16\sqrt{3}$
- **H.** 32
- **J.** $32\sqrt{3}$
- **K.** 64

GO ON TO THE NEXT PAGE.

53. In $\triangle XYZ$, shown below, $\overline{YZ} = 30$. Which of the following represents the length of $\overline{XY}$?

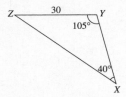

(Note: For a triangle with sides of lengths x, y, and z, and respective opposite angles measuring X, Y, and Z, it will be true that: $\dfrac{\sin X}{x} = \dfrac{\sin Y}{y} = \dfrac{\sin Z}{z}$, according to the Law of Sines.)

A. $\dfrac{30\sin 105°}{\sin 35°}$

B. $\dfrac{30\sin 105°}{\sin 40°}$

C. $\dfrac{30\sin 35°}{\sin 40°}$

D. $\dfrac{30\sin 40°}{\sin 105°}$

E. $\dfrac{30\sin 35°}{\sin 105°}$

54. Points P and Q lie on circle O with radius of 9 feet. The measure of $\angle POQ$ is 120°. What is the length, in feet, of minor arc $\overarc{PQ}$?

F. 3π
G. 6π
H. 9π
J. 18π
K. 27π

GO ON TO THE NEXT PAGE.

55.
$$\begin{bmatrix} w & x \\ y & z \end{bmatrix} - \begin{bmatrix} x & y \\ z & w \end{bmatrix} - \begin{bmatrix} \dfrac{1}{w+x} & \dfrac{1}{x+y} \\ \dfrac{1}{y+z} & \dfrac{1}{z+w} \end{bmatrix} = ?$$

DO YOUR FIGURING HERE.

A. $\begin{bmatrix} 1 & 1 \\ 1 & 1 \end{bmatrix}$

B. $\begin{bmatrix} \dfrac{w-x}{w+x} & \dfrac{x-y}{x+y} \\ \dfrac{y-z}{y+z} & \dfrac{d-a}{d+a} \end{bmatrix}$

C. $\begin{bmatrix} w-x-\dfrac{1}{w+x} & x-y-\dfrac{1}{x+y} \\ y-z-\dfrac{1}{y+z} & z-w-\dfrac{1}{z+w} \end{bmatrix}$

D. $\begin{bmatrix} \dfrac{wx}{w+x} & \dfrac{xy}{x+y} \\ \dfrac{yz}{y+z} & \dfrac{zw}{z+w} \end{bmatrix}$

E. $\begin{bmatrix} \dfrac{1}{2w-2x} & \dfrac{1}{2x-2y} \\ \dfrac{1}{2y-2z} & \dfrac{1}{2z-2w} \end{bmatrix}$

56. If function f is defined by $f(x) = -2x^3$, then what is the value of $f(f(1))$?

F. -16
G. -8
H. 4
J. 8
K. 16

GO ON TO THE NEXT PAGE.

57. The function *y* varies directly as *x* for all real numbers in the (*x*,*y*) coordinate plane. Which of the following could be the graph of *y* ?

DO YOUR FIGURING HERE.

A.

D.

B.

E.

C.

58. Gopi took 5 quizzes for which the scores are integer values ranging from 0 to 10. The median of her scores is 9. The mean of her scores is 8. The only mode of her scores is 10. Which of the following *must* be true about her quiz scores?

F. Her lowest score is 4.
G. Her lowest score is 5.
H. The median of the 3 lowest scores is 6.
J. The sum of the 5 scores is 50.
K. The sum of the 2 lowest scores is 11.

59. To make a cardboard table for her dollhouse, Ouisie uses a rectangular piece of cardboard measuring 40 inches wide and 60 inches long. She cuts out four equal-sized squares from each corner and folds down the sides at a 90° angle. If the top of the table measures 800 square inches, how tall, in inches, is the table?

A. 40
B. 30
C. 25
D. 20
E. 10

GO ON TO THE NEXT PAGE.

60. Which of the following expressions gives the area, in square feet, of ∠*ABC* shown below with the given side lengths in feet?

DO YOUR FIGURING HERE.

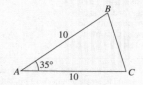

F. 50 tan 35°
G. 50 cos 35°
H. 50 sin 35°
J. 100 cos 35°
K. 100 sin 35°

END OF TEST 2
STOP! DO NOT TURN THE PAGE UNTIL TOLD TO DO SO.
DO NOT RETURN TO THE PREVIOUS TEST.

READING TEST
35 Minutes—40 Questions

DIRECTIONS: There are four passages in this test. Each passage is followed by several questions. After reading each passage, choose the best answer to each question and blacken the corresponding oval on your answer document. You may refer to the passages as often as necessary.

Passage I

PROSE FICTION: This passage is adapted from the novel *Shipwreck* by Adam C. Thomas (© 2005 by Adam Thomas).

"Let the dead bury their dead."

The words rang in the boy's ears as he trudged through the inhospitable jungle, vines snarling around his ankles. Over and over again, he heard the captain shout, "Full speed ahead,
5 let the dead bury their dead."

Now the captain was gone and the boy felt alone despite his companions, now leading him through the alien jungle. He wondered what the words meant. How can the dead do anything? How can the dead have dead of their own?

10 These thoughts circled the boy's head, intermingled with the events of the last days. Again he heard the roar of the storm, felt the ship bucking and braying beneath his feet. The typhoon had come out of nowhere, it had seemed; even the captain, who surely knew everything, was taken aback by
15 its sudden appearance.

"Avast and hold the mainsail!" he shouted to the crew. "Stay fast and let the dead bury their dead!"

The boy had held fast, even as the ship had come apart. Even as the lightning lit up the sky like the fireworks the boy
20 had heard about, but never seen. Even as the thunder filled the air, shaking the very timbers of the ship with its bellowing ferocity. The walls of water rose up, crashing over the deck, then receded for an instant of calm before rising up as a dark mountain to once again besiege the small ship.

25 These memories would come to the boy in a split-second, filling his brain before he had a chance to consciously remember what had happened. Then they would recede, just as the storm had eventually receded, and the jungle would return, the monotonous trudging, day after day amid the vines and
30 trees that were nothing like his second home on the ocean.

Sometimes, the boy would think back to before the storm, and even before the ship, to his life on land—the stultifying life on the farm where he felt landlocked before he even understood what that word signified. He thought of his mother

35 and father, frail and worn-looking. He believed his parents did all they could to create a home for him, but his mother's sad, creased face and his father's cracked hands crowded out all other childhood memories. They filled the boy's sky, just as the thunder had, and were just as devastating, in their own
40 way, as the storm.

For the boy, his birthplace's rocky ground yielded only a life he could not live and a place he could not love. But the sea was softer, a malleable place in which an enterprising lad could reinvent himself. So the boy had run off to sea. He
45 vowed to leave the land forever to live atop the ocean. Now he had learned the hardness of the sea, he thought, as he jerked his mind back to the jungle.

Soon, his thoughts drifted back to his blissful days upon the ship. Although he had come aboard as a stowaway, the
50 captain took him in and gave him daily lessons in reading the stars and plotting the ship's course. "Ignorance is dangerous, not only aboard ship but also in life," the captain warned. The eager boy soon grew familiar with the night's sky and knew the maps in the captain's quarters as well as he knew his own
55 reflection. He had felt so secure in the captain's knowledge and in his own growing understanding.

But if the captain could be caught unawares, how could the boy ever feel safe again? How could he trust that everything the captain had said wouldn't lead to the same disastrous end?

60 "Let the dead bury their dead." Well, he had seen the dead after the storm. As the remaining crew members had urged him away from the wreckage, finally having to pull him by his arms to force his legs to move, the words "Let the dead bury their dead" appeared unbidden in his mind. But what
65 did those words mean? Searching his memory, the boy was shocked to find that after the shipwreck, his mind's eye could no longer distinguish the captain from any other man—the cook, the lowest deckhand, or even the boy's father. Was that what the captain meant by "their dead"—that all the dead
70 belonged to one another?

He walked mechanically, pace after pace, leading him away from the remains of his home and the only man he had ever loved. Toward what? He had no knowledge of what lay ahead. But still his legs moved, seemingly of their own

GO ON TO THE NEXT PAGE.

75 accord, his heart continued to beat, his lungs continued to fill with air. His mind continued to retrace his life, and with the beating of his heart and the filling of his lungs, still he walked.

1. As it is used in line 32, the word *stultifying* most nearly means:

    A. stifling.
    B. strengthening.
    C. welcoming.
    D. productive.

2. The first seven paragraphs (lines 1–30) establish all of the following about the boy EXCEPT that he:

    F. had companions on the walk through the jungle.
    G. had often watched fireworks light up the sky.
    H. respected the captain.
    J. often had his thoughts filled with memories of the storm.

3. The passage states that the boy saw himself as:

    A. contented with life in the jungle.
    B. afraid of his mother.
    C. toughened by farm labor.
    D. at home on the sea.

4. The time sequence of the passage indicates that the ship-wreck takes place:

    F. after the boy leaves the farm.
    G. after the boy walks through the jungle.
    H. before the boy meets the captain.
    J. before his mother tries to protect him.

5. How does the twelfth paragraph (lines 60–70) offer one way to interpret the phrase "let the dead bury their dead," as implied by the passage?

    A. The boy remembers the captain's explanation of this phrase.
    B. The dead cannot do anything, so one should trust only the living.
    C. Death erases the distinctions that make the living unique individuals.
    D. Without his experiences, the boy cannot expect to lead a better life.

6. Compared to the captain's ideas, the boy's are:

    F. opposing; the captain is uncertain about the meaning of the phrase, "let the dead bury their dead."
    G. opposing; the captain understood why the boy's father was worn down.
    H. similar; the captain disliked the harsh life of the sea.
    J. similar; the captain valued learning and knowledge.

7. It is most reasonable to infer from the passage that the ship's remaining crewmates accompanying the boy on his walk through the jungle would agree with which of the following statements about the boy?

    A. The boy's grief over the captain's death made him unwilling to leave the scene of the shipwreck.
    B. The boy's grief over the captain's death made him run away from his companions.
    C. The boy was constantly startled by loud noises.
    D. The boy hated his life on land and had escaped to the sea to find freedom.

8. Which of the following statements best describes the actions taken by the captain on finding the boy stowed away on the ship?

    F. He scolds the boy because he did not pay the fare for passage on the ship.
    G. He teaches the boy the meaning of the phrase "let the dead bury their dead."
    H. He teaches the boy how to navigate using maps and the stars.
    J. He ignores the boy, leaving him to fend for himself.

9. According to the passage, the storm features all of the following EXCEPT:

    A. loud thunder.
    B. huge walls of water.
    C. bright lightning.
    D. ferocious hail.

10. Which of the following statements about the storm is sup-ported by the passage?

    F. It blew up without warning, taking the captain by surprise.
    G. It happened in the middle of the night.
    H. It was the most violent storm any of the crew had ever seen.
    J. It was the storm the boy's father had warned him about.

GO ON TO THE NEXT PAGE.

Passage II

SOCIAL SCIENCE: This passage is adapted from the article "Slang: Why It's Totally Sweet" by Patrick Tyrrell (© 2008 by Patrick Tyrrell).

Tony Thorne's e-mail inbox is bloated with messages from teenagers and college students around the world explicating the meaning behind local terms such as "toop," "tonk," and "chung." Why would the Director of the Language Center at
5 King's College of London concern himself with seemingly nonsensical linguistic inventions?

Thorne is busy compiling a current dictionary of slang from around the English-speaking world. Although *neologisms*, new adaptations or inventions of words, are normally
10 born out of a specific geographic and cultural context, the ease of worldwide communication ushered in by the technological age has made slang an instantly exportable commodity. College students in Iowa are just as likely to use British slang like "bum" (one's posterior) as British homemakers are to employ
15 American slang like "dust bunny," since both groups are exposed to each other's movies, TV, music, and other media.

In the world of linguistics, slang is often viewed condescendingly as an affliction of vulgar speech, its users condemned for their intellectual laziness. Early 20th century
20 linguist Oliver Wendell Holmes described slang as "at once a sign and a cause of mental atrophy." Meanwhile, Thorne points out, some legendary authors such as Walt Whitman elevated the status of slang, referring to it as "an attempt by common humanity to escape from bald literalism, and express
25 itself illimitably."

What are the origins of most slang words? Many philologists, those who attempt to study and determine the meaning of historical texts, believe that slang is created as a response to the status quo, that its usage represents a defiant opposition
30 of authority. For example, many Americans use the phrase *a cup of joe* to refer to a cup of coffee; however, few know that it originated from one Admiral Joe Daniels who in 1914 denied his sailors wine. As a result, they decided their strict leader was a fitting namesake for the terribly acidic black
35 coffee they were forced to drink instead.

Thorne, however, would point out that most slang is derived for much more innocent purposes. For example, terms like "ankle-biters" (infants), "ramping up" (on the job training), and "Googling" (searching on the Internet) do not involve
40 opposition to authority. Usually, slang evolves out of very insular groups with specific needs for informative or vibrant expressions that normal language does not encapsulate. It is the marriage of jargon, nuance, and effective imagery. While traditional hotbeds of slang have been the military, industrial
45 factories, and street markets, most modern slang comes from such arenas as corporate offices, college campuses, and users/designers of computers.

In determining the sources of slang terms, Thorne and his contemporaries repeatedly refine their definition of "slang"
50 as distinctive from "idioms," "euphemisms," "hyperbole," and other instances of conventional figurative language. Many linguists consider slang the polar opposite of formal speech, with other figurative language devices falling somewhere in between. Whereas a "colloquialism" still indicates a mea-
55 sure of respect owed to the expression's regional usefulness, "slang" brands a word as having fallen into a state of overused emptiness.

How do we know when a word has become overused or empty? Much slang is attached to some sense of style or fad
60 and therefore risks being short-lived in nature as the trend upon which it is based. However, some terms such as "punk" and "cool" have been in common use for a century or more and have completely assimilated into the acceptable mainstream dialect. Clearly, then, some words fall into a gray area
65 between slang and proper language. Although lexicologists like Thorne attempt to define and apply standard principles in their classification of slang, there is definitely some subjectivity involved in determining whether a term deserves the maligning moniker.

70 Furthermore, intellectuals who would categorically denounce slang struggle with the fact that slang, when first conceived, involves as much inherent creativity and word play as the figurative language revered in poetry. It is ultimately how the word survives, or rather who continues to use it, that
75 determines its stature as artful rhetoric or the dreaded slang. If "respectable" people continue to use an expression for its conceptual vivacity, then the word was a clever invention worth enriching a nation's lexicon. If the "common man" uses a term and uses it too liberally, the word is deemed slang,
80 and an eloquent speaker will have the tastefulness to avoid it.

Whatever slang's level of social esteem, Thorne believes that it is an essential project to compile accurate modern dictionaries of its usage. When one considers the large amount of written artifacts our present world creates on a daily basis,
85 it is reasonable to also consider providing future generations (or civilizations) of humans with an effective way of decoding our meaning, which could easily be confused by our prevalent use of slang. Imagine how much less debate there would be over the meaning of some Shakespearean verses if we had a
90 detailed description of his contemporary slang. Because of this need to inform future scholars, Thorne's dictionary of slang attempts to not only define each term but also to explain its origins, connotations, and typical conversational uses.

GO ON TO THE NEXT PAGE.

11. Based on the passage, Thorne most likely describes some slang as *innocent* (line 37) to indicate his belief that not all slang is created to be:

A. rebellious.
B. informative.
C. nuanced.
D. accusatory.

12. The author includes the information in the last paragraph primarily to:

F. criticize Thorne for being too subjective with which words he chooses to include in his dictionary.
G. illustrate how a future scholar might be able to use Thorne's dictionary as a resource.
H. identify the ways Thorne uses Shakespearean slang to describe modern terms.
J. argue that Thorne's dictionary should be the primary focus of modern linguistics.

13. All of the following groups are mentioned in the passage as related to the academic study of slang EXCEPT:

A. philologists.
B. college professors.
C. linguists.
D. lexicologists.

14. The quotation marks around the phrase "common man" in line 78 primarily serve to:

F. emphasize the subjective and somewhat derogatory process of categorizing people and the words they use.
G. reveal the author's suspicion that the man in question is not common at all.
H. introduce a demeaning term the author believes is appropriate to describe users of slang.
J. show how an inventive term may enjoy popularity briefly but ultimately does not have the proper usage to survive.

15. As it is used in line 18, the word *vulgar* most nearly means:

A. sickening.
B. malicious.
C. unsophisticated.
D. profane.

16. The passage indicates that the efforts to compile current dictionaries of slang are viewed by some as essential because these dictionaries:

F. could possibly provide future scholars with a way of deciphering the meaning of today's writings.
G. are the only way that speakers of other languages can decode the subtle meaning of English texts.
H. currently do not exist except for those chronicling Shakepeare's era.
J. will provide modern English speakers with the correct conversational uses of each slang term.

17. According to the passage, Walt Whitman seems to view the use of slang as an attempt to:

A. show civility.
B. conform to traditions.
C. broaden expression.
D. defy authority.

18. The main purpose of the first paragraph in relation to the passage is to:

F. acquaint the reader with some examples of slang.
G. establish that British scholars are the leaders in slang research.
H. introduce slang as a possibly surprising topic of academic study.
J. outline Tony Thorne's problems with managing his email inbox.

19. The author's reference to groups like the military as being *hotbeds of slang* (line 44) most nearly means that such groups are:

A. prophetic.
B. old-fashioned.
C. innovative.
D. strict.

20. The passage suggests that of the following, which one encapsulates the greatest obstacle for intellectuals who would categorically denounce slang?

F. Their own invention of some slang terms
G. Disagreement on how certain slang terms are used
H. Respect for Thorne's academic interest and tireless determination.
J. Appreciation for the creativity involved in the origination of slang

GO ON TO THE NEXT PAGE.

Passage III

HUMANITIES: Passage A is adapted from the article, "A handwritten note from Harper Lee is the politest rejection." (Used with permission of The Associated Press Copyright © 2016. All rights reserved.) Passage B is adapted from the article, "Marja Mills addresses Harper Lee controversy at literary event" by Courtney Crowder (From Chicago Tribune, July 23 © 2014 Chicago Tribune. All rights reserved. Used by permission and protected by the Copyright Laws of the United States. The printing, copying, redistribution, or retransmission of this Content without express written permission is prohibited.)

Passage A

It was, without a doubt, the nicest rejection of my journalistic career…. The author of "To Kill a Mockingbird" hadn't granted an interview in about four decades, but I figured it was worth a shot. So I crafted a letter and sent it off to Monroeville,
5 Alabama, care of attorney Alice F. Lee—the author's older sister and chief gatekeeper…. I didn't really expect a reply.

Nine days later, a letter arrived…. The note was brief. "Dear Mr. Breed: Thank you for your kind letter and its enclosures. You show much talent as a non-fiction writer!" she
10 wrote in a clear script that sloped somewhat down to the right. "I simply don't give interviews—I gave all my publisher and the movie people asked me to give long ago (before you were born), and that was it. However, if I ever decide to give another, you will be near the top of the waiting list!" There was a brief
15 postscript on the backside of the page. "My eyesight is failing, and I must look sideways to write," it read, "so please forgive the slant!" ….

In an age when people feel compelled to update their Facebook statuses constantly, Lee kept her thoughts to herself.
20 Not a post, nor a tweet. With the 2014 publication of *The Mockingbird Next Door: Life with Harper Lee*, it appeared that Lee's resolve had softened. Then in February 2015, publisher Harper announced the pending release of her *Go Set a Watchman*, even including a rare statement from Lee:
25 "I am humbled and amazed that this will now be published after all these years."

No, she did not talk with me. Yes, I would have gladly trumpeted an exclusive interview. But part of me was hoping that she'd stick to her guns and let the singular accomplishment
30 of *Mockingbird* speak for itself. We have this notion that our heroes—movie stars, athletes or authors—owe us more than just the fruits of their talents; that being public figures means they are public property. Lee was able to keep her own counsel and, along with friends and relatives, protect her privacy. I like
35 a scoop as much as the next reporter, but the idea of prying into Lee's life always felt a bit like killing a mockingbird—the bird you leave alone because all it does is sing….

Passage B

Less than a week after the publication of Marja Mills' memoir, *The Mockingbird Next Door*, her story of befriend-
40 ing the famously reclusive 88-year-old author Harper Lee, the book remains embroiled in controversy. On July 14, the day before the book's publication date, Lee, author of the American classic *To Kill a Mockingbird*, issued a statement refuting the memoir's main narrative: that Mills was allowed
45 unique access to the author and her sister, Alice Lee, 102, and that the sisters told her stories with the knowledge that Mills was going to use them in a book. "Rest assured, as long as I am alive any book purporting to be with my cooperation is a falsehood," Lee's statement said.

50 On Monday at a sold-out Tribune-sponsored book discussion at Tribune Tower, Mills, a former Tribune reporter, addressed the dispute: Lee "had always been encouraging and also quite specific about what stories that she was sharing for the book and those that were to remain private, and I did
55 respect those… I can only speak the truth, that Nelle Harper Lee and Alice F. Lee were aware I was writing this book and my friendship with both of them continued during and after my time in Monroeville." …

Mills' journey to the center of Lee's social circle began
60 in 2001, when the Tribune assigned her to capture the spirit of Monroeville, Ala., Lee's hometown, when the Chicago Public Library selected *To Kill a Mockingbird* as the first pick for the One Book, One Chicago program. After the exhaustive and meticulously researched Tribune article was published in
65 2002, Mills remained friends with the sisters, although Harper Lee, characteristically, had declined to comment for the article. In 2004, Mills moved into the house next door to them with their blessing, according to the book jacket. For the next 18 months, from fall 2004 to spring 2006, Mills accompanied
70 the sisters as they ate, explored and even did their laundry….

Mills described her book as focusing on "the last chapter of life as (the Lees) knew it." In 2007, Harper Lee had a serious stroke and had to move into an assisted-living facility. Soon after, Alice Lee also moved out of the house they had
75 both lived in for nearly all their lives. "So much that has been said about (the Lees) has been secondhand or speculated," Mills said. "I just wanted to get out of the way. I wanted to show them sitting at the kitchen table, listening to Nelle tell stories, or being in the car with them as they talked about the
80 Monroeville of 1930 versus now."

GO ON TO THE NEXT PAGE.

Questions 21–23 ask about Passage A.

21. It can most reasonably be inferred from Passage A that after Breed received Harper Lee's letter, he:

  A. had difficulty reading her writing and posted her letter on social media.

  B. felt angry that she had agreed to another reporter's request but approved of her decision.

  C. appreciated her compliment of his writing style but regretted losing the exclusive interview.

  D. felt glad that she maintained her privacy and appreciated receiving the reply.

22. Which of the following is a detail from Passage A that best supports the idea that Lee kept herself out of the public eye?

  F. Lee was worried that she might not live up to people's high expectations.

  G. Lee did not reply to interview requests.

  H. Lee announced the release of a new publication in 2014.

  J. Lee had not granted an interview for forty years.

23. Regarding the publication of *The Mockingbird Next Door*, Passage A makes clear that its appearance:

  A. seemed to show that Lee was opening up to public scrutiny after all.

  B. proved that Lee had softened her resolve.

  C. led Lee to express humility and amazement.

  D. amounted to another author prying into Lee's life.

Questions 24–27 ask about Passage B.

---

24. Based on Passage B, Harper Lee's reaction to Mills' book was:

  F. angry but also accepting that the public wanted to know more about her life.

  G. dismissive; she claimed that she had not authorized its publication.

  H. negative but also proud because people took interest in her writing.

  J. encouraging; she was pleased to give a first-hand account of her life.

25. According to Crowder, Mills' article can best be described as:

  A. controversial but exhausting.

  B. encouraging and specific.

  C. thorough and well-researched.

  D. speculative and second-hand.

26. It can most reasonably be inferred from Passage B that Mills published her book in part because she:

  F. wanted to publicize the exclusive interviews she was able to hold with the Lees.

  G. aspired to capture the spirit of Monroeville, Alabama, both in the past and in the present.

  H. felt compelled to reveal the truth about her friendship with the Lees.

  J. hoped she could provide first-hand information on the Lees' daily lives and conversations.

27. Lines 53–56 most nearly mean that Mills:

  A. acted in accordance with all of Lee's wishes regarding the book.

  B. earned the Lees' respect by sharing meals and household chores with them.

  C. censored several of Lee's stories in the final version of the book.

  D. did not include some of Lee's stories in the book.

Questions 28–30 ask about both passages.

---

28. Which statement most accurately compares the content of the two passages?

  F. Both describe first-hand accounts of contact with Lee that had different outcomes.

  G. Both analyze Lee's readers but draw different conclusions about their motivations.

  H. Both present the same anecdotes about Lee to explain her change of heart late in life.

  J. Both explore the psychological motivations for Lee's self-identification with a bird.

GO ON TO THE NEXT PAGE.

29. Based on the passages, it's most likely that Breed and Crowder would agree that Harper Lee's privacy was:

   A. secondary; her central concern was always for the reception of her novel.

   B. significant; Lee had avoided publicity since the publication of her novel.

   C. misplaced; famous people must be accountable to the public.

   D. misconstrued; reports about her concerns were mostly second-hand.

30. It can most reasonably be inferred from the passages that the author of the text referred to in lines 20–22 is:

   F. Alice F. Lee.

   G. Marja Mills.

   H. Courtney Crowder.

   J. Allan G. Breed.

GO ON TO THE NEXT PAGE.

Passage IV

NATURAL SCIENCE: This passage is excerpted from the article "Frank Drake and Project Ozma" by Arnold C. Topton (© 2004 by Crackpot Press).

On a cool April night in 1960, in Green Bank, West Virginia, Frank Drake became a scientific pioneer. Careful research had given him reason to believe that, if he tuned his radio to the correct frequency and aimed it at the correct
5 stars, he might pick up interstellar transmissions from another planet. Hoping for a breakthrough, he tuned the radio and began to listen.

So began Project Ozma, widely considered the first organized attempt to detect alien life by way of radio. Al-
10 though it was ultimately unsuccessful in its goal of finding other intelligent life in the universe, Project Ozma was hugely influential, inspiring the creation of many similar programs. The following fifty years would see a steady increase in both the sophistication and the scope of similar programs, ranging
15 from a wide-ranging but short-term program funded by NASA to the meticulously orchestrated Project Phoenix, designed to monitor carefully selected regions of space over a period of ten years. Today, many such programs are ongoing, in locations as august as the University of California at Berkeley and the
20 University of Western Sydney, both of which have reputations that draw respected scientists from around the world.

The scientists involved in the Search for Extraterrestrial Intelligence, or SETI, are far from the wide-eyed dreamers that many people associate with the field. The SETI scientists
25 are, in fact, esteemed academics, typically specializing in the areas of physics, astronomy, and engineering. Indeed, they have to be able to complete such complex tasks as calculating where to position the radios so as to achieve the best effect, deciding what messages are most likely to be understood
30 by an alien culture, and determining which stars to monitor.

Although these scientists' understanding of the origins of life on Earth is still imperfect, those involved in SETI do have some idea of what combinations of size, location, and chemical composition make a planet more likely to harbor
35 intelligent life. The general understanding is that there are two main factors that determine whether or not a planet is habitable (able to sustain life): temperature and mass. There are other factors that are often considered, such as the presence of certain chemicals, the proximity of other planets, and
40 planetary age, but temperature and mass are the initial, and most crucial, tests.

Liquid water is widely believed to be critical to the development of life, and this belief has led scientists to hypothesize that, in order to support life, a planet must experience tem-
45 peratures that fall within a range that allows for the presence

of liquid water. This, in turn, suggests that hospitable planets must be located within a certain distance of their respective suns. If a planet is too far from the sun, its temperatures will fall below that range, as in the case of Saturn. If a planet is
50 too close to the Sun, as in the case of Venus, its temperatures will be too high. Planets that fall within the range of appropriate temperatures are often called "Goldilocks Planets," since they are neither too hot nor too cold but instead "just right" to provide environments hospitable to life. However, even
55 when a planet is found that is within this range, there is still no guarantee that all of the related factors will be suitable. It is also necessary that the planet have an orbit that allows the planet to rotate at a speed and angle that prevents either side from freezing or boiling, ruling out most binary systems due
60 to their unstable orbits.

The other key to habitability is the mass of a planet. In order to sustain life, a planet must have sufficient mass to hold a gravitational field, while not having so much as to create an excessively heavy atmosphere. Truly massive planets also
65 tend to retain hydrogen gases and become "gas giants" with no solid surface. How large a planet can be, while retaining the ability to host living organisms, depends in part on that planet's distance from the Sun. Larger planets have heavier atmospheres, so they also tend to retain more heat, creat-
70 ing a greenhouse effect, wherein atmospheric gases absorb radiation, causing an increase in temperature. Therefore, a planet on the outer edge of the Goldilocks zone might be able to sustain life if its mass were great enough to hold in enough heat to bring the temperature back into the habitable
75 zone, while a smaller planet might be able to do the same on the inner edge.

The search for extraterrestrial life, and perhaps intelligence, that started in West Virginia back in 1960 continues today. The more knowledge scientists are able to gather
80 about our own galaxy, the better equipped they will be when it comes to seeking out similar planets outside our solar system. Perhaps someday Frank Drake's dream of a message from outer space will come true—once we know where to look for it.

31. According to the passage, Frank Drake:

A. was one of the first scientists to use radio technology to look for alien life.
B. successfully found signs of extraterrestrial life.
C. ran Project Phoenix from his radio telescope in West Virginia.
D. is a highly esteemed astronomer and physicist.

GO ON TO THE NEXT PAGE.

32. Which of the following would be the most appropriate characterization of Project Ozma, as portrayed by the author of the passage?

F. Its unexpected success took the scientific community by surprise, altering the face of the field.

G. Although it was a failure in one sense, it helped usher in a new era of interstellar research.

H. Drake's goals were unrealistic, given his limited knowledge and resources.

J. Without the financial support of institutions such as NASA, the Project was doomed to failure.

33. As it is used in line 19, the word *august* most nearly means:

A. summery.

B. elusive.

C. esteemed.

D. antique.

34. As conveyed in the passage, the author's attitude toward the search for life on other planets is:

F. ironic yet sympathetic.

G. scornful and angry.

H. hopeful yet pragmatic.

J. uncertain and fearful.

35. According to the passage, scientists involved in the search for life on other planets are likely to be:

A. trained in scientific disciplines such as physics, astronomy, and engineering.

B. wide-eyed dreamers prone to unrealistic expectations about space.

C. employed at institutions such as universities or NASA.

D. skilled radio mechanics, due to their work with radio telescopes.

36. The primary point of the fourth paragraph (lines 31–41) is that:

F. even today scientists do not understand why life developed on our planet.

G. liquid water is crucial to the evolution of intelligent life on any planet.

H. only planets within a "Goldilocks Zone" are able to sustain life.

J. there appear to be two crucial components in determining whether a planet may be habitable.

37. It can reasonably be inferred that, as it is used in line 46, the term *hospitable planets* is intended to mean:

A. planets with cultures that are similar to those found on our planet.

B. locations outside of our solar system that are in close proximity to the Sun.

C. binary planets with generally stable orbits and moderate temperatures.

D. places with temperatures and masses that fall within the range able to support life.

38. Based on the information in the passage, Saturn is most likely unable to sustain life because:

F. its close proximity to the Sun causes a greenhouse effect.

G. the atmosphere is too heavy to allow for liquid water to exist.

H. its distance from the Sun is too great for it to contain liquid water.

J. it is an unstable gas giant, due to the chemical combinations present.

39. The passage indicates that any new planet discovered in a location that is comparable to Venus' location, relative to the sun, would most likely be:

A. an overheated gas giant, due to its heavy atmosphere.

B. incapable of supporting life due to its lack of a gravitational field.

C. prone to the development of an unstable orbit.

D. unable to sustain life unless it were small enough not to retain too much heat.

40. According to the passage, Goldilocks Planets are characterized by:

F. temperatures that are moderate enough to allow for the existence of liquid water.

G. heavy atmospheres that retain hydrogen gases, creating a greenhouse effect.

H. either extremely hot or extremely cold temperatures, depending on proximity to the sun.

J. the presence of both liquid water and a high concentration of hydrogen gases.

END OF TEST 3.
STOP! DO NOT TURN THE PAGE UNTIL TOLD TO DO SO.
DO NOT RETURN TO A PREVIOUS TEST.

NO TEST MATERIAL ON THIS PAGE.

SCIENCE TEST
35 Minutes—40 Questions

DIRECTIONS: There are seven passages in the following section. Each passage is followed by several questions. After reading a passage, choose the best answer to each question and blacken the corresponding oval on your answer document. You may refer to the passages as often as necessary.

You are NOT permitted to use a calculator on this test.

Passage I

In recent years, the technology of magnetic levitation ("maglev") has been investigated to provide an alternative rapid transportation option. Using repulsion of magnetic fields, maglev trains can be pushed forward at speeds of up to 300 miles per hour. One specific type of magnetic levitation currently being investigated is electrodynamic suspension (EDS).

In EDS, magnetic rods are located at the bottom of the maglev train and within the track underneath the train. An electric current can induce a magnetic field in the magnets of the track. If this magnetic field can be induced to repel constantly the magnet in the maglev train, then the train will maintain a distance above the track known as an "air gap" and move forward. Theoretically, the maglev train in EDS should travel at least 4 inches above the track, so there would be virtually no energy lost to friction. If the system does lose energy, it will be in the form of thermal energy.

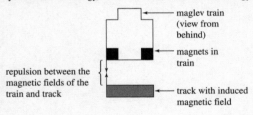

maglev train (view from behind)

magnets in train

repulsion between the magnetic fields of the train and track

track with induced magnetic field

Figure 1

Under controlled conditions, scientists conducted tests on an experimental maglev track oriented in an east-to-west direction.

Study 1

A maglev train with magnetic rods of fixed length was moved along the experimental track from east to west at various velocities v. The current I in the track required to induce these velocities was measured in amperes (A).

Table 1		
Trial	v (m/s)	I (A)
1	40	50
2	80	100
3	120	150
4	160	200
5	200	250

Study 2

The maglev train was run in five trials with varying lengths, L, of the magnetic rods, and run at a constant velocity of 40 m/s. The current I in the track required to induce this velocity given the different lengths of the rods was recorded.

Table 2		
Trial	L (m)	I (A)
6	0.6	50
7	0.8	67
8	1.0	84
9	1.2	100
10	1.4	116

Study 3

The magnetic field, B, measured in tesla (T), was varied in the maglev track. The current running through the maglev track was then measured in five new trials. Throughout these trials, the lengths of the magnetic rods and the maglev train velocities were kept constant.

GO ON TO THE NEXT PAGE.

Table 3		
Trial	B (T)	I (A)
11	5.90×10^{-4}	300
12	7.87×10^{-4}	400
13	9.84×10^{-4}	500
14	1.05×10^{-3}	600
15	1.20×10^{-3}	700

Study 4

The maglev train with magnetic rods of fixed length was moved along the experimental track from west to east at various velocities, and the current in the track required to induce these velocities was measured. The magnetic field was kept constant for each of these trials.

Table 4		
Trial	v (m/s)	I (A)
16	40	−50
17	80	−100
18	120	−150
19	160	−200
20	200	−250

1. In Study 1, I would most likely have equaled 500 A if v had been:

   A.   40 m/s.
   B.   125 m/s.
   C.   200 m/s.
   D.   400 m/s.

2. In Study 2, as the length of the magnetic rods in the maglev train increased, the amount of the current required to induce the train's velocity:

   F. increased only.
   G. decreased only.
   H. remained constant.
   J. varied, but with no consistent trend.

3. In Study 3, I would most likely have equaled 570 A if B had equaled which of the following?

   A. 6.00×10^{-4} T
   B. 8.00×10^{-4} T
   C. 1.00×10^{-3} T
   D. 1.50×10^{-3} T

4. During each trial, an electrical current moves through the magnetic track because a nonzero voltage was produced in the track. During which of the following trials in Study 3 was the voltage greatest?

   F. Trial 11
   G. Trial 12
   H. Trial 13
   J. Trial 14

5. In which of the studies, if any, did the electrical current flow in the opposite direction as compared with the other studies?

   A. Study 1 only
   B. Study 4 only
   C. Studies 1, 2, and 3 only
   D. None of these studies

6. The results of Study 3 are best represented by which of the following graphs?

F.

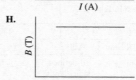

G.

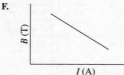

H.

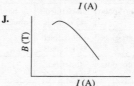

J.

GO ON TO THE NEXT PAGE.

Passage II

Bats of the family *Vespertilionidae* (Vesper bats) are commonly found in North America. A guide for identifying Vesper bats found in Utah is presented in Table 1.

		Table 1	
Step	Trait	Appearance	Result
1	If the ears are:	longer than 25 mm	go to Step 2
		shorter than 25 mm	go to Step 5
2	If the dorsum (back) has:	3 white spots	*Euderma maculotum*
		no spots	go to Step 3
3	If the ears are:	separated at the base	*Antrozous pallidus*
		not separated at the base	go to Step 4
4	If the muzzle has:	well-defined skin glands	*Idionycteris phyllotis*
		ill-defined skin glands	*Corynorhinus townsendii*
5	If the uropatagium* is:	heavily furred	go to Step 6
		not heavily furred	go to Step 7
6	If the fur color is:	pale yellow at the base	*Lasiurus cinereus*
		dark with silver tips	*Lasionycteris noctivagans*
		brick red to rust	*Lasiurus blossevillii*
7	If the tragus** is:	< 6 mm and curved	go to Step 8
		> 6 mm and straight	go to Step 9
8	If the forearm length is:	> 40 mm	*Eptesicus fuscus*
		< 40 mm	*Pipistrellus hesperus*
9	If there is an obvious fringe of fur:	on the edge of the uropatagium	*Myotis thysanodes*
		between the elbows and knees	*Myotis volans*

*Wing-like tissue between hind legs
**Cartilage structure in the ear

Students observed Vesper bats in a Utah nature reserve and recorded descriptions of them in Table 2.

				Table 2			
Bat	Ears	Dorsum	Muzzle	Uropatagium	Fur	Tragus	Forearm
I	20 mm long, separate at base	no spots	ill-defined skin glands	not heavily furred	brown	4 mm, curved	50 mm long
II	18 mm long	no spots	ill-defined skin glands	not heavily furred; only an obvious fringe of fur on its edge	brown	7 mm, straight	25 mm long
III	30 mm long, joined at base	no spots	well-defined skin glands	not heavily furred	olive	9 mm, curved	30 mm long
IV	15 mm long	no spots	ill-defined skin glands	heavily furred	black with silver tips	4 mm, curved	20 mm long

GO ON TO THE NEXT PAGE.

7. Based on the given information, which of the following characteristics distinguishes Bat IV from a *Pipistrellus hesperus*?

   A. 4 mm and curved tragus
   B. 15 mm long ears
   C. 20 mm long forearm
   D. Heavily furred uropatagium

8. Based on Table 1, Bats I and II share the same results through step:

   F. 1.
   G. 5.
   H. 7.
   J. 9.

9. Which of the following best describes the family *Vespertilionidae*?

   A. Mammals
   B. Protists
   C. Lampreys
   D. Birds

10. According to Table 1, *Lasiurus cinereus* and *Lasiurus blossevillii* could have all of the following traits in common EXCEPT:

    F. ears not separated at the base.
    G. 35 mm long ears.
    H. a heavily furred uropatagium.
    J. 20 mm long ears.

11. Based on Table 1, which of the following is likely to be most genetically similar to Bat II ?

    A. *Lasiurus blossevillii*
    B. *Idionycteris phyllotis*
    C. *Lasionyceris noctivagans*
    D. *Myotis volans*

GO ON TO THE NEXT PAGE.

Passage III

A heater was placed in a room with a measured initial temperature of 0°C. The heater was set to heat the room to 25°C, and a mercury thermometer recorded the change of the air temperature in the room over time. This process was then repeated with the heater set to heat the room to 37°C and 50°C (see Figure 1).

Next, a cooling device was placed in a tank filled with 50°C saltwater. For three separate tests, the cooler was set to cool the water to 25°C, 10°C, and 0°C, respectively, while a mercury thermometer recorded the temperature of the saltwater over time (see Figure 2).

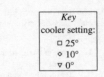

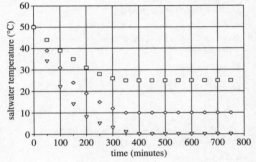

Figure 2

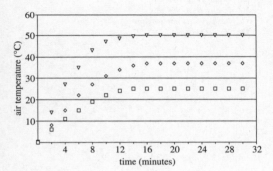

Figure 1

(Note: Assume that the temperature of the air was uniform throughout the room and that the temperature of the saltwater was uniform throughout the tank in all tests. Assume that at all times the heater and cooling device operated at full capacity.)

12. Based on the information presented in Figure 2, what was the most likely temperature of the saltwater in the 0°C setting at 220 minutes?

    F. 52°C
    G. 29°C
    H. 17°C
    J. 7°C

GO ON TO THE NEXT PAGE.

13. In the time interval from 8 minutes to 10 minutes, approximately how fast, in °C/min, was the temperature of the air changing when the heater was set to 37°C ?

   A. 0.5°C/min
   B. 2°C/min
   C. 27°C/min
   D. 31°C/min

14. When the cooling device was set to 0°C, for which of the following time periods represented in Figure 2 was the temperature of the water changing most rapidly?

   F. 0–100 min
   G. 100–200 min
   H. 200–300 min
   J. 300–400 min

15. According to Figure 2, when the cooling device was set to 25°C, at which of the following times was the average kinetic energy of the thermometer's mercury atoms the greatest?

   A. 150 min
   B. 350 min
   C. 550 min
   D. 750 min

16. Based on Figure 2, if another test were performed with the cooling device set to –10°C, approximately how long would it take for the saltwater to reach –10°C ?

   F. Greater than 400 min
   G. Between 100 and 350 min
   H. Between 10 and 50 min
   J. Less than 10 min

GO ON TO THE NEXT PAGE.

Passage IV

Pepsin is an enzyme in humans that catalyzes the digestion of proteins, like the milk protein *casein*, into smaller subunits called peptides. Pepsin is active only in acidic solutions.

The researchers prepared a solution of casein, a solution of *anserine* (a small peptide), a solution of pepsin, and various *buffer solutions* (solutions maintaining a constant pH). The following experiments were conducted using these solutions.

Experiment 1

Seven solutions were prepared in test tubes using a 5 mL solution buffered to pH 3.0. Different amounts of casein, anserine, and pepsin solutions were added to each tube, and then diluted to 10 mL with the buffer solution, so that the final pH in each test tube would be 3.0. Each tube was incubated at a constant temperature for 15 minutes, and then was monitored to determine whether there was any activity by pepsin (see Table 1).

			Table 1		
Trial	Casein (mL)	Anserine (mL)	Pepsin (mL)	Temperature (°C)	Pepsin Activity
1	1	1	1	30	No
2	1	1	1	35	Low
3	1	1	1	40	High
4	1	0	1	40	High
5	0	1	1	40	No
6	0	0	1	40	No
7	1	1	1	45	No

Experiment 2

Seven solutions were prepared in test tubes according to the same procedure as in Trial 3 of Experiment 1, and each test tube was diluted with different buffer solutions of varying pH (see Table 2).

	Table 2	
Trial	pH	Pepsin activity
8	2.5	high activity
9	3.0	high activity
10	3.5	high activity
11	4.0	low activity
12	4.5	low activity
13	5.0	low activity
14	5.5	no activity

17. Pepsin is most likely to be found in which of the following organs?

   A. Kidney
   B. Heart
   C. Stomach
   D. Spinal cord

GO ON TO THE NEXT PAGE.

18. Suppose another trial had been performed in Experiment 2, and the results showed a high level of pepsin activity. Which of the following would be the most likely pH of the buffer solution used in this new trial?

   F. 2.0
   G. 4.0
   H. 6.0
   J. 8.0

19. Which of the following is the most likely reason that Trials 3 and 4 show high levels of pepsin activity, while Trial 5 shows no pepsin activity?

   A. Pepsin activity is dependent on both casein and anserine.
   B. Pepsin activity is blocked by anserine.
   C. Pepsin is able to digest casein, but not anserine.
   D. Pepsin is able to digest anserine, but not casein.

20. According to the results from Experiment 1, which of the following trials are most likely to contain undigested casein?

   F. Trials 1, 3, 4, and 7 only
   G. Trials 1, 5, 6, and 7 only
   H. Trials 1 and 7 only
   J. Trials 5, 6, and 7 only

21. The experimental conditions for Trial 3 are most similar to those for which of the following trials?

   A. Trial 9
   B. Trial 11
   C. Trial 13
   D. Trial 14

22. According to the results from Experiments 1 and 2, which of the following best explains the relationship between pepsin activity, pH, and temperature?

   F. Pepsin digests proteins at a fast rate when the pH is greater than 4.0 and the temperature is about 40°C.
   G. Pepsin digests proteins at a fast rate when the pH is less than 4.0 and the temperature is about 40°C.
   H. Pepsin digests proteins at a fast rate when the pH is greater than 3.0 and the temperature is about 30°C.
   J. Pepsin digests proteins at a fast rate when the pH is less than 3.0 and the temperature is about 30°C.

GO ON TO THE NEXT PAGE.

Passage V

Chemical researchers studied the *viscosity* (a fluid's resistance to flow) for several liquids. Highly viscous fluids take more time to flow through a vessel than do low viscous fluids. They measured the viscosity in *centipoise* (cP) (.01 grams per centimeter per second). Some solutions were treated with chemical additives before the fluids were heated. The results are shown in Figures 1–3.

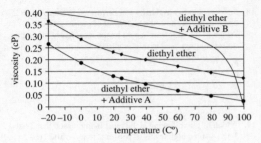

Figure 3

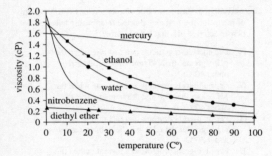

Figure 1

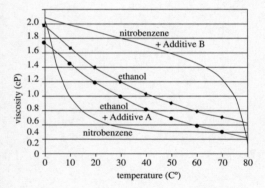

Figure 2

23. For which of the 3 figures did at least one sample fluid have a viscosity greater than 1.0 cP at a temperature of 0°C ?

A. Figure 1 only
B. Figure 3 only
C. Figures 1 and 2 only
D. Figures 1, 2, and 3

24. According to Figure 2, for the sample that contained nitrobenzene without Additive B, the greatest decrease in fluid viscosity occurred over which of the following intervals of temperature change?

F. From 0°C to 10°C
G. From 10°C to 20°C
H. From 30°C to 40°C
J. From 40°C to 50°C

GO ON TO THE NEXT PAGE.

25. According to Figure 1, after water was heated to reach a temperature of 70°C, the viscosity was closest to which of the following?

    A. 1.0 cP
    B. 0.7 cP
    C. 0.4 cP
    D. 0.2 cP

26. Based on the information given, which of the following best describes and explains the experimental results presented in Figure 2? As the temperature increased, the time required for the sample fluids to flow out of their containers:

    F. decreased, because heating the fluids increased each fluid's viscosity.
    G. decreased, because heating the fluids decreased each fluid's viscosity.
    H. increased, because heating the fluids increased each fluid's viscosity.
    J. increased, because heating the fluids decreased each fluid's viscosity.

27. A researcher hypothesized that a solution of nitrobenzene treated with Additive A would have a lower viscosity at 60°C than would untreated diethyl ether at that same temperature. Do the results in the figures confirm this hypothesis?

    A. Yes; according to Figure 2, at 60°C, nitrobenzene had a higher viscosity than did nitrobenzene treated with Additive B.
    B. Yes; according to Figure 3, at 60°C, diethyl ether had a higher viscosity than did diethyl ether treated with Additive A.
    C. No; according to Figure 2, at 60°C, nitrobenzene had a higher viscosity than did nitrobenzene treated with Additive B.
    D. No; according to Figures 1–3, samples of nitrobenzene treated with Additive A were not tested for viscosity.

GO ON TO THE NEXT PAGE.

Passage VI

Earthquakes disrupt the infrastructure of buildings and dwellings by displacing the ground beneath them as a result of surface waves. The origin of an earthquake is known as the *epicenter*. Surface waves propagate from the epicenter outward and are directly affected by the density of the ground through which they propagate. As seen in Figure 1, the strength of the wave may be characterized into three distinct types: strong, moderate, and weak.

Strong

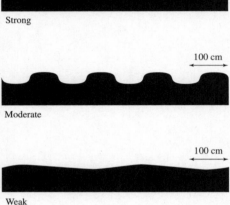

Moderate

Weak

Figure 1

In order to study the effect of ground density on wave propagation, a seismologist has assembled a circular small-scale model with varying densities. Ground density and propagation duration were controlled in the experiment. In each study, earth and clay were laid down in a circular pattern with increasing density. Seismometers were positioned to detect the type of waves propagating at specific locations. A large speaker was placed 2 m below the surface of the epicenter to mimic an earthquake and each study was conducted over a period of 2 min with a fixed frequency of 10 Hz.

Study 1

The sound source was adjusted to 60 dB to mimic the impact of a magnitude 5 earthquake. The resulting *waveform plot* (exhibits wave type as a result of varying densities and distances from the epicenter) is shown in Figure 2.

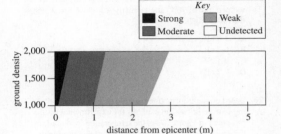

Figure 2

Study 2

Study 1 was repeated with the sound source adjusted to 80 dB to mimic the impact of a magnitude 7 earthquake. The resulting waveform plot is shown in Figure 3.

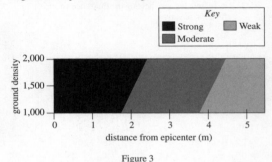

Figure 3

Study 3

The study was repeated with the sound source adjusted to 100 dB to mimic the impact of a magnitude 9 earthquake. The resulting waveform plot is shown in Figure 4.

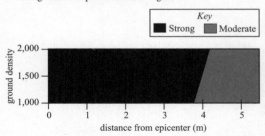

Figure 4

GO ON TO THE NEXT PAGE.

28. According to the results of Study 2, as the distance from the epicenter increases, the type of wave observed:

    F. remained strong.
    G. changed from strong to moderate.
    H. changed from moderate to strong.
    J. remained moderate.

29. According to the results of Studies 2 and 3, which of the following statements comparing the maximum distance from the epicenter for strong wave propagation and maximum distance for moderate wave propagation is true?

    A. At all ground densities studied, the maximum distance from the epicenter at which strong waves may propagate was greater than the corresponding maximum distance from the epicenter at which moderate waves propagated.
    B. At all ground densities studied, the maximum distance from the epicenter at which strong waves may propagate was less than the corresponding maximum distance from the epicenter at which moderate waves propagated.
    C. For some of the ground densities studied, the maximum distance from the epicenter at which strong waves may propagate was greater than the corresponding maximum distance from the epicenter at which moderate waves propagated.
    D. For some of the ground densities studied, the maximum distance from the epicenter at which strong waves may propagate was less than the corresponding maximum distance from the epicenter at which moderate waves propagated.

30. Which of the following factors in the seismologist's studies was NOT directly controlled?

    F. Sound intensity (in dB)
    G. Ground density
    H. Propagation duration
    J. Wave type

31. Consider the relative wavelengths of a moderate wave and a weak wave, as shown in Figure 1. Which, if either, is less than 100 cm ?

    A. The wavelength of a moderate wave only
    B. The wavelength of a weak wave only
    C. Both the wavelength of the moderate wave and the wavelength of the weak wave
    D. Neither the wavelength of the moderate wave nor the wavelength of the weak wave

32. Suppose Study 1 were repeated using a sound intensity of 70 dB. The resulting waveform plot would include which of the wave types referred to in the passage?

    F. Strong only
    G. Strong and weak waves only
    H. Strong and moderate waves only
    J. Strong, moderate, and weak waves

33. A study was conducted using a sound intensity between 75 dB and 85 dB. The minimum ground density where strong waves began propagating ranged from 1,000 kg/m^3 to 2,000 kg/m^3. Based on the information presented, the distance from the epicenter was most likely:

    A. less than 2.5 m.
    B. between 2.5 and 3.5 m.
    C. between 3.5 and 4.5 m.
    D. greater than 4.5 m.

GO ON TO THE NEXT PAGE.

Passage VII

A *solution* results from dissolving a *solute* into a *solvent*. The van 't Hoff factor (*i*) is the number of moles (1 mole = 6.02×10^{23} entities such as molecules, ions, or atoms) of particles produced in solution for every 1 mole of solute dissolved.

The temperature at which a solution changes state from liquid to solid is the *freezing point*. Two scientists observed that the freezing point of H_2O decreased after adding KCl to it. To explore this further, they conducted an experiment and each scientist provided separate explanations of the results.

Experiment

One mole each of fructose, KCl, and $MgCl_2$ were separately dissolved in 1 kg of pure water. The concentration of each solution was thus 1.0 mole/kg. In addition, 1 kg of pure water only was placed in a fourth container. The containers were placed in a cooling device. The temperature was gradually decreased and the freezing point of each solution was recorded. The results are shown in Table 1.

			Table 1	
Solution	Solute	*i*	Solution properties	Freezing point
1	—	—	Pure water only	0°C
2	fructose	1	1 dissolved neutral particle	–1.9°C
3	KCl	2	2 dissolved charged particles (K^+ and Cl^-)	–3.8°C
4	$MgCl_2$	3	3 dissolved charged particles (Mg^{2+} and 2 Cl^-)	–5.7°C

Scientist 1

For a solvent to freeze, its molecules must arrange in an orderly fashion relative to each other. When a solute is added, the dissolved solute molecules are attracted to the solvent molecules by the intermolecular force of charge. The attraction of the solute particles to the solvent particles interferes with the orderly arrangement of solvent molecules, and the net effect is that the freezing point is lowered. This decrease in freezing point is related only to the charge of the solute particles and occurs with solutes that form charged particles in solution.

Scientist 2

The freezing point of a solvent is the temperature at which the liquid and solid states of that solvent have equivalent energetic potentials. Below the freezing point, the solvent has a lower energetic potential in the solid state. When a solute is dissolved in a solvent, the energetic potential of the liquid phase is decreased more than the energetic potential of the solid phase. Because of the different energetic potentials, it takes a larger drop in temperature for the liquid to freeze. Thus, the size of the decrease in freezing point is in direct proportion with the van 't Hoff factor. This decrease in freezing point is related only to the concentration of particles, not to the identity or properties of each individual particle.

34. Based on the results in Table 1, how did the concentration of dissolved particles in Solution 4 compare with the concentration of dissolved particles in Solution 2? Solution 4 contained:

  F. fewer particles in solution than did Solution 2, resulting in a lower freezing point.
  G. more particles in solution than did Solution 2, resulting in a lower freezing point.
  H. fewer particles in solution than did Solution 2, resulting in a higher freezing point.
  J. more particles in solution than did Solution 2, resulting in a higher freezing point.

GO ON TO THE NEXT PAGE.

35. The freezing point of benzene is lowered with the addition of the solute naphthalene ($C_{10}H_8$), which has no charge. According to the information in the passage, this observation *disagrees* with the explanation provided by:

   A. Scientist 1, who argued that only charged particles can have an effect on the freezing point of a solution.
   B. Scientist 1, who argued that any solute is capable of increasing the stability of the liquid phase of a solvent.
   C. Scientist 2, who argued that only charged particles can have an effect on the freezing point of a solution.
   D. Scientist 2, who argued that any solute is capable of increasing the stability of the liquid phase of a solvent.

36. With which of the following statements about solutes would both scientists agree? Adding to a liquid a substance that has:

   F. a positive or negative charge will decrease the liquid's freezing point.
   G. a positive or negative charge will increase the liquid's freezing point.
   H. no charge will decrease the liquid's freezing point.
   J. no charge will increase the liquid's freezing point.

37. Suppose an experiment showed that adding the positively-charged solute $NaClO_4$ to the solvent H_2O but holding the concentration of the solution constant, the freezing point was significantly lower than an equally concentrated uncharged solution of $NaClO_4$ in pure H_2O. This finding would support the explanation(s) of which of the scientists, if either?

   A. Scientist 1 only
   B. Scientist 2 only
   C. Both Scientists 1 and 2
   D. Neither Scientist

38. Of the following diagrams, which best illustrates how Scientist 1 would describe the results after a charged solute (•) has been added to H_2O (×) ?

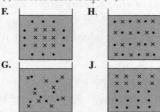

39. Do the scientists offer different explanations for the impact of a solute's physical properties, such as solute charge, on the decrease in freezing point of a solution?

   A. Yes, Scientist 1 states that solute physical properties have an impact, but Scientist 2 states they do not.
   B. Yes, Scientist 2 states that solute physical properties have an impact, but Scientist 1 states they do not.
   C. No, both scientists state that solute physical properties have an impact on solution freezing point.
   D. No, neither Scientist discusses the impact of solute physical properties on solution freezing point.

40. Assume the following for the addition of a substance to a pure liquid: k is a constant, ΔT is the decrease in freezing point, and i is the van 't Hoff factor. Which of the following equations is most consistent with Scientist 2's explanation?

   F. $\Delta T = k/i$
   G. $\Delta T = ki^2$
   H. $\Delta T = k/i^2$
   J. $\Delta T = ki$

END OF TEST 4
STOP! DO NOT RETURN TO ANY OTHER TEST.

Directions

This is a test of your writing skills. You will have forty (40) minutes to read the prompt, plan your response, and write an essay in English. Before you begin working, read all material in this test booklet carefully to understand exactly what you are being asked to do.

You will write your answer on the lined pages in the answer document provided. Your writing on those pages will be scored. You may use the unlined pages in this test booklet to plan your essay. Your work on these pages will not be scored.

Your essay will be evaluated based on the evidence it provides of your ability to:

- clearly state your own perspective on a complex issue and analyze the relationship between your perspective and at least one other perspective
- develop and support your ideas with reasoning and examples
- organize your ideas clearly and logically
- communicate your ideas effectively in standard written English

Lay your pencil down immediately when time is called.

DO NOT OPEN THIS BOOK UNTIL YOU ARE TOLD TO DO SO.

Composition paper for the essay can be found beginning on page 177.

More Food Is Better

Foods that have had their DNA altered are known as genetically modified foods. This technology is used to make crops disease- and pest-resistant, produce more food with fewer chemicals, and increase the nutritional value of foods. Advocates of this approach maintain that it allows more people to be fed, food to be grown in various climates, and many other benefits. Opponents voice their concerns about environmental issues and safety to human consumption.

Read and carefully consider these perspectives. Each suggests a particular way of thinking about the conflict over genetically modified foods.

Perspective One	Perspective Two	Perspective Three
Genetically modified foods are unnecessary. The problem of world hunger is real and must be solved, but it is the result of an unequal distribution of food, not a lack of it.	Genetically modified foods are better for the environment. Because these foods have already been engineered to be pest resistant, there is no need to treat them with dangerous chemical pesticides.	Genetically modified foods can make people sick. When the natural components of a crop are restructured, this can cause someone who ingests something not originally contained in the food to have an allergic reaction.

Essay Task

Write a unified, coherent essay in which you evaluate multiple perspectives on the use of genetically modified foods. In your essay, be sure to:

- clearly state your own perspective on the issue and analyze the relationship between your perspective and at least one other perspective
- develop and support your ideas with reasoning and examples
- organize your ideas clearly and logically
- communicate your ideas effectively in standard written English

Your perspective may be in full agreement with any of the others, in partial agreement, or wholly different. Whatever the case, support your ideas with logical reasoning and detailed, persuasive examples.

The Princeton Review®

ACT Diagnostic Test Form

USE A SOFT LEAD NO. 2 PENCIL ONLY.
(Do NOT use a mechanical pencil, ink,
ballpoint, correction fluid, or felt-tip pen.)

E-MAIL: _____

PHONE NO.: _____
(Print)

SCHOOL: _____

CLASS OF: _____

IMPORTANT: Please fill in these boxes exactly
as shown on the back cover of your tests book.

2. TEST FORM
_____

3. TEST CODE

⓪ ⓪ ⓪ ⓪
① ① ① ①
② ② ② ②
③ ③ ③ ③
④ ④ ④ ④
⑤ ⑤ ⑤ ⑤
⑥ ⑥ ⑥ ⑥
⑦ ⑦ ⑦ ⑦
⑧ ⑧ ⑧ ⑧
⑨ ⑨ ⑨ ⑨

ALL examinees must complete Blocks A, B, C, and D – please print.

A NAME, MAILING ADDRESS, AND TELEPHONE
(Please print.)

Last Name   First Name   MI (Middle Initial)

House Number & Street (Apt. No.); or PO Box & No.; or RR & No.

City   State/Province   ZIP/Postal Code

Area Code   Number   Country

B MATCH NAME
(First 5 letters of last name)

Ⓐ Ⓐ Ⓐ Ⓐ Ⓐ
Ⓑ Ⓑ Ⓑ Ⓑ Ⓑ
Ⓒ Ⓒ Ⓒ Ⓒ Ⓒ
Ⓓ Ⓓ Ⓓ Ⓓ Ⓓ
Ⓔ Ⓔ Ⓔ Ⓔ Ⓔ
Ⓕ Ⓕ Ⓕ Ⓕ Ⓕ
Ⓖ Ⓖ Ⓖ Ⓖ Ⓖ
Ⓗ Ⓗ Ⓗ Ⓗ Ⓗ
Ⓘ Ⓘ Ⓘ Ⓘ Ⓘ
Ⓚ Ⓚ Ⓚ Ⓚ Ⓚ
Ⓛ Ⓛ Ⓛ Ⓛ Ⓛ
Ⓜ Ⓜ Ⓜ Ⓜ Ⓜ
Ⓝ Ⓝ Ⓝ Ⓝ Ⓝ
Ⓞ Ⓞ Ⓞ Ⓞ Ⓞ
Ⓟ Ⓟ Ⓟ Ⓟ Ⓟ
Ⓠ Ⓠ Ⓠ Ⓠ Ⓠ
Ⓡ Ⓡ Ⓡ Ⓡ Ⓡ
Ⓢ Ⓢ Ⓢ Ⓢ Ⓢ
Ⓣ Ⓣ Ⓣ Ⓣ Ⓣ
Ⓤ Ⓤ Ⓤ Ⓤ Ⓤ
Ⓥ Ⓥ Ⓥ Ⓥ Ⓥ
Ⓦ Ⓦ Ⓦ Ⓦ Ⓦ
Ⓧ Ⓧ Ⓧ Ⓧ Ⓧ
Ⓨ Ⓨ Ⓨ Ⓨ Ⓨ
Ⓩ Ⓩ Ⓩ Ⓩ Ⓩ

C MATCH NUMBER

① ① ① ① ①   ① ① ① ① ①
② ② ② ② ②   ② ② ② ② ②
③ ③ ③ ③ ③   ③ ③ ③ ③ ③
④ ④ ④ ④ ④   ④ ④ ④ ④ ④
⑤ ⑤ ⑤ ⑤ ⑤   ⑤ ⑤ ⑤ ⑤ ⑤
⑥ ⑥ ⑥ ⑥ ⑥   ⑥ ⑥ ⑥ ⑥ ⑥
⑦ ⑦ ⑦ ⑦ ⑦   ⑦ ⑦ ⑦ ⑦ ⑦
⑧ ⑧ ⑧ ⑧ ⑧   ⑧ ⑧ ⑧ ⑧ ⑧
⑨ ⑨ ⑨ ⑨ ⑨   ⑨ ⑨ ⑨ ⑨ ⑨
⓪ ⓪ ⓪ ⓪ ⓪   ⓪ ⓪ ⓪ ⓪ ⓪

D DATE OF BIRTH

Month	Day	Year
○ January		
○ February		
○ March	① ①	① ①
○ April	② ②	② ②
○ May	③ ③	③ ③
○ June	④	④ ④
○ July	⑤	⑤ ⑤
○ August	⑥	⑥ ⑥
○ September	⑦	⑦ ⑦
○ October	⑧	⑧ ⑧
○ November	⑨	⑨ ⑨
○ December	⓪	⓪ ⓪

Marking Directions: Mark only **one** oval for
each question. Fill in response completely.
Erase errors cleanly without smudging.

Correct mark: ○ ● ○ ○

Do **NOT** use these *incorrect* or *bad* marks.

Incorrect marks: ⊘ ⊗ ⊙ ⊜
Overlapping mark: ○ ○ ◖◗ ○
Cross-out mark: ○ ⊗ ○ ○
Smudged erasure: ○ ○ ◐ ○
Mark is too light: ◔ ○ ○ ○

BOOKLET NUMBER

① ① ① ① ① ①
② ② ② ② ② ②
③ ③ ③ ③ ③ ③
④ ④ ④ ④ ④ ④
⑤ ⑤ ⑤ ⑤ ⑤ ⑤
⑥ ⑥ ⑥ ⑥ ⑥ ⑥
⑦ ⑦ ⑦ ⑦ ⑦ ⑦
⑧ ⑧ ⑧ ⑧ ⑧ ⑧
⑨ ⑨ ⑨ ⑨ ⑨ ⑨
⓪ ⓪ ⓪ ⓪ ⓪ ⓪

FORM

Print your
3-character
Test Form in
the boxes
above and
fill in the
corresponding
oval at the
right

BE SURE TO FILL IN THE CORRECT FORM OVAL.

PRE ○

THIS PAGE INTENTIONALLY LEFT BLANK

The Princeton Review
Diagnostic ACT Form

TEST 1: ENGLISH

1 Ⓐ Ⓑ Ⓒ Ⓓ	14 Ⓕ Ⓖ Ⓗ Ⓙ	27 Ⓐ Ⓑ Ⓒ Ⓓ	40 Ⓕ Ⓖ Ⓗ Ⓙ	53 Ⓐ Ⓑ Ⓒ Ⓓ	66 Ⓕ Ⓖ Ⓗ Ⓙ
2 Ⓕ Ⓖ Ⓗ Ⓙ	15 Ⓐ Ⓑ Ⓒ Ⓓ	28 Ⓕ Ⓖ Ⓗ Ⓙ	41 Ⓐ Ⓑ Ⓒ Ⓓ	54 Ⓕ Ⓖ Ⓗ Ⓙ	67 Ⓐ Ⓑ Ⓒ Ⓓ
3 Ⓐ Ⓑ Ⓒ Ⓓ	16 Ⓕ Ⓖ Ⓗ Ⓙ	29 Ⓐ Ⓑ Ⓒ Ⓓ	42 Ⓕ Ⓖ Ⓗ Ⓙ	55 Ⓐ Ⓑ Ⓒ Ⓓ	68 Ⓕ Ⓖ Ⓗ Ⓙ
4 Ⓕ Ⓖ Ⓗ Ⓙ	17 Ⓐ Ⓑ Ⓒ Ⓓ	30 Ⓕ Ⓖ Ⓗ Ⓙ	43 Ⓐ Ⓑ Ⓒ Ⓓ	56 Ⓕ Ⓖ Ⓗ Ⓙ	69 Ⓐ Ⓑ Ⓒ Ⓓ
5 Ⓐ Ⓑ Ⓒ Ⓓ	18 Ⓕ Ⓖ Ⓗ Ⓙ	31 Ⓐ Ⓑ Ⓒ Ⓓ	44 Ⓕ Ⓖ Ⓗ Ⓙ	57 Ⓐ Ⓑ Ⓒ Ⓓ	70 Ⓕ Ⓖ Ⓗ Ⓙ
6 Ⓕ Ⓖ Ⓗ Ⓙ	19 Ⓐ Ⓑ Ⓒ Ⓓ	32 Ⓕ Ⓖ Ⓗ Ⓙ	45 Ⓐ Ⓑ Ⓒ Ⓓ	58 Ⓕ Ⓖ Ⓗ Ⓙ	71 Ⓐ Ⓑ Ⓒ Ⓓ
7 Ⓐ Ⓑ Ⓒ Ⓓ	20 Ⓕ Ⓖ Ⓗ Ⓙ	33 Ⓐ Ⓑ Ⓒ Ⓓ	46 Ⓕ Ⓖ Ⓗ Ⓙ	59 Ⓐ Ⓑ Ⓒ Ⓓ	72 Ⓕ Ⓖ Ⓗ Ⓙ
8 Ⓕ Ⓖ Ⓗ Ⓙ	21 Ⓐ Ⓑ Ⓒ Ⓓ	34 Ⓕ Ⓖ Ⓗ Ⓙ	47 Ⓐ Ⓑ Ⓒ Ⓓ	60 Ⓕ Ⓖ Ⓗ Ⓙ	73 Ⓐ Ⓑ Ⓒ Ⓓ
9 Ⓐ Ⓑ Ⓒ Ⓓ	22 Ⓕ Ⓖ Ⓗ Ⓙ	35 Ⓐ Ⓑ Ⓒ Ⓓ	48 Ⓕ Ⓖ Ⓗ Ⓙ	61 Ⓐ Ⓑ Ⓒ Ⓓ	74 Ⓕ Ⓖ Ⓗ Ⓙ
10 Ⓕ Ⓖ Ⓗ Ⓙ	23 Ⓐ Ⓑ Ⓒ Ⓓ	36 Ⓕ Ⓖ Ⓗ Ⓙ	49 Ⓐ Ⓑ Ⓒ Ⓓ	62 Ⓕ Ⓖ Ⓗ Ⓙ	75 Ⓐ Ⓑ Ⓒ Ⓓ
11 Ⓐ Ⓑ Ⓒ Ⓓ	24 Ⓕ Ⓖ Ⓗ Ⓙ	37 Ⓐ Ⓑ Ⓒ Ⓓ	50 Ⓕ Ⓖ Ⓗ Ⓙ	63 Ⓐ Ⓑ Ⓒ Ⓓ	
12 Ⓕ Ⓖ Ⓗ Ⓙ	25 Ⓐ Ⓑ Ⓒ Ⓓ	38 Ⓕ Ⓖ Ⓗ Ⓙ	51 Ⓐ Ⓑ Ⓒ Ⓓ	64 Ⓕ Ⓖ Ⓗ Ⓙ	
13 Ⓐ Ⓑ Ⓒ Ⓓ	26 Ⓕ Ⓖ Ⓗ Ⓙ	39 Ⓐ Ⓑ Ⓒ Ⓓ	52 Ⓕ Ⓖ Ⓗ Ⓙ	65 Ⓐ Ⓑ Ⓒ Ⓓ	

TEST 2: MATHEMATICS

1 Ⓐ Ⓑ Ⓒ Ⓓ Ⓔ	11 Ⓐ Ⓑ Ⓒ Ⓓ Ⓔ	21 Ⓐ Ⓑ Ⓒ Ⓓ Ⓔ	31 Ⓐ Ⓑ Ⓒ Ⓓ Ⓔ	41 Ⓐ Ⓑ Ⓒ Ⓓ Ⓔ	51 Ⓐ Ⓑ Ⓒ Ⓓ Ⓔ
2 Ⓕ Ⓖ Ⓗ Ⓙ Ⓚ	12 Ⓕ Ⓖ Ⓗ Ⓙ Ⓚ	22 Ⓕ Ⓖ Ⓗ Ⓙ Ⓚ	32 Ⓕ Ⓖ Ⓗ Ⓙ Ⓚ	42 Ⓕ Ⓖ Ⓗ Ⓙ Ⓚ	52 Ⓕ Ⓖ Ⓗ Ⓙ Ⓚ
3 Ⓐ Ⓑ Ⓒ Ⓓ Ⓔ	13 Ⓐ Ⓑ Ⓒ Ⓓ Ⓔ	23 Ⓐ Ⓑ Ⓒ Ⓓ Ⓔ	33 Ⓐ Ⓑ Ⓒ Ⓓ Ⓔ	43 Ⓐ Ⓑ Ⓒ Ⓓ Ⓔ	53 Ⓐ Ⓑ Ⓒ Ⓓ Ⓔ
4 Ⓕ Ⓖ Ⓗ Ⓙ Ⓚ	14 Ⓕ Ⓖ Ⓗ Ⓙ Ⓚ	24 Ⓕ Ⓖ Ⓗ Ⓙ Ⓚ	34 Ⓕ Ⓖ Ⓗ Ⓙ Ⓚ	44 Ⓕ Ⓖ Ⓗ Ⓙ Ⓚ	54 Ⓕ Ⓖ Ⓗ Ⓙ Ⓚ
5 Ⓐ Ⓑ Ⓒ Ⓓ Ⓔ	15 Ⓐ Ⓑ Ⓒ Ⓓ Ⓔ	25 Ⓐ Ⓑ Ⓒ Ⓓ Ⓔ	35 Ⓐ Ⓑ Ⓒ Ⓓ Ⓔ	45 Ⓐ Ⓑ Ⓒ Ⓓ Ⓔ	55 Ⓐ Ⓑ Ⓒ Ⓓ Ⓔ
6 Ⓕ Ⓖ Ⓗ Ⓙ Ⓚ	16 Ⓕ Ⓖ Ⓗ Ⓙ Ⓚ	26 Ⓕ Ⓖ Ⓗ Ⓙ Ⓚ	36 Ⓕ Ⓖ Ⓗ Ⓙ Ⓚ	46 Ⓕ Ⓖ Ⓗ Ⓙ Ⓚ	56 Ⓕ Ⓖ Ⓗ Ⓙ Ⓚ
7 Ⓐ Ⓑ Ⓒ Ⓓ Ⓔ	17 Ⓐ Ⓑ Ⓒ Ⓓ Ⓔ	27 Ⓐ Ⓑ Ⓒ Ⓓ Ⓔ	37 Ⓐ Ⓑ Ⓒ Ⓓ Ⓔ	47 Ⓐ Ⓑ Ⓒ Ⓓ Ⓔ	57 Ⓐ Ⓑ Ⓒ Ⓓ Ⓔ
8 Ⓕ Ⓖ Ⓗ Ⓙ Ⓚ	18 Ⓕ Ⓖ Ⓗ Ⓙ Ⓚ	28 Ⓕ Ⓖ Ⓗ Ⓙ Ⓚ	38 Ⓕ Ⓖ Ⓗ Ⓙ Ⓚ	48 Ⓕ Ⓖ Ⓗ Ⓙ Ⓚ	58 Ⓕ Ⓖ Ⓗ Ⓙ Ⓚ
9 Ⓐ Ⓑ Ⓒ Ⓓ Ⓔ	19 Ⓐ Ⓑ Ⓒ Ⓓ Ⓔ	29 Ⓐ Ⓑ Ⓒ Ⓓ Ⓔ	39 Ⓐ Ⓑ Ⓒ Ⓓ Ⓔ	49 Ⓐ Ⓑ Ⓒ Ⓓ Ⓔ	59 Ⓐ Ⓑ Ⓒ Ⓓ Ⓔ
10 Ⓕ Ⓖ Ⓗ Ⓙ Ⓚ	20 Ⓕ Ⓖ Ⓗ Ⓙ Ⓚ	30 Ⓕ Ⓖ Ⓗ Ⓙ Ⓚ	40 Ⓕ Ⓖ Ⓗ Ⓙ Ⓚ	50 Ⓕ Ⓖ Ⓗ Ⓙ Ⓚ	60 Ⓕ Ⓖ Ⓗ Ⓙ Ⓚ

The Princeton Review
Diagnostic ACT Form

TEST 3: READING

1 Ⓐ Ⓑ Ⓒ Ⓓ	8 Ⓕ Ⓖ Ⓗ Ⓙ	15 Ⓐ Ⓑ Ⓒ Ⓓ	22 Ⓕ Ⓖ Ⓗ Ⓙ	29 Ⓐ Ⓑ Ⓒ Ⓓ	36 Ⓕ Ⓖ Ⓗ Ⓙ
2 Ⓕ Ⓖ Ⓗ Ⓙ	9 Ⓐ Ⓑ Ⓒ Ⓓ	16 Ⓕ Ⓖ Ⓗ Ⓙ	23 Ⓐ Ⓑ Ⓒ Ⓓ	30 Ⓕ Ⓖ Ⓗ Ⓙ	37 Ⓐ Ⓑ Ⓒ Ⓓ
3 Ⓐ Ⓑ Ⓒ Ⓓ	10 Ⓕ Ⓖ Ⓗ Ⓙ	17 Ⓐ Ⓑ Ⓒ Ⓓ	24 Ⓕ Ⓖ Ⓗ Ⓙ	31 Ⓐ Ⓑ Ⓒ Ⓓ	38 Ⓕ Ⓖ Ⓗ Ⓙ
4 Ⓕ Ⓖ Ⓗ Ⓙ	11 Ⓐ Ⓑ Ⓒ Ⓓ	18 Ⓕ Ⓖ Ⓗ Ⓙ	25 Ⓐ Ⓑ Ⓒ Ⓓ	32 Ⓕ Ⓖ Ⓗ Ⓙ	39 Ⓐ Ⓑ Ⓒ Ⓓ
5 Ⓐ Ⓑ Ⓒ Ⓓ	12 Ⓕ Ⓖ Ⓗ Ⓙ	19 Ⓐ Ⓑ Ⓒ Ⓓ	26 Ⓕ Ⓖ Ⓗ Ⓙ	33 Ⓐ Ⓑ Ⓒ Ⓓ	40 Ⓕ Ⓖ Ⓗ Ⓙ
6 Ⓕ Ⓖ Ⓗ Ⓙ	13 Ⓐ Ⓑ Ⓒ Ⓓ	20 Ⓕ Ⓖ Ⓗ Ⓙ	27 Ⓐ Ⓑ Ⓒ Ⓓ	34 Ⓕ Ⓖ Ⓗ Ⓙ	
7 Ⓐ Ⓑ Ⓒ Ⓓ	14 Ⓕ Ⓖ Ⓗ Ⓙ	21 Ⓐ Ⓑ Ⓒ Ⓓ	28 Ⓕ Ⓖ Ⓗ Ⓙ	35 Ⓐ Ⓑ Ⓒ Ⓓ	

TEST 4: SCIENCE

1 Ⓐ Ⓑ Ⓒ Ⓓ	8 Ⓕ Ⓖ Ⓗ Ⓙ	15 Ⓐ Ⓑ Ⓒ Ⓓ	22 Ⓕ Ⓖ Ⓗ Ⓙ	29 Ⓐ Ⓑ Ⓒ Ⓓ	36 Ⓕ Ⓖ Ⓗ Ⓙ
2 Ⓐ Ⓑ Ⓒ Ⓓ	9 Ⓐ Ⓑ Ⓒ Ⓓ	16 Ⓕ Ⓖ Ⓗ Ⓙ	23 Ⓐ Ⓑ Ⓒ Ⓓ	30 Ⓕ Ⓖ Ⓗ Ⓙ	37 Ⓐ Ⓑ Ⓒ Ⓓ
3 Ⓐ Ⓑ Ⓒ Ⓓ	10 Ⓕ Ⓖ Ⓗ Ⓙ	17 Ⓐ Ⓑ Ⓒ Ⓓ	24 Ⓕ Ⓖ Ⓗ Ⓙ	31 Ⓐ Ⓑ Ⓒ Ⓓ	38 Ⓕ Ⓖ Ⓗ Ⓙ
4 Ⓕ Ⓖ Ⓗ Ⓙ	11 Ⓐ Ⓑ Ⓒ Ⓓ	18 Ⓕ Ⓖ Ⓗ Ⓙ	25 Ⓐ Ⓑ Ⓒ Ⓓ	32 Ⓕ Ⓖ Ⓗ Ⓙ	39 Ⓐ Ⓑ Ⓒ Ⓓ
5 Ⓐ Ⓑ Ⓒ Ⓓ	12 Ⓕ Ⓖ Ⓗ Ⓙ	19 Ⓐ Ⓑ Ⓒ Ⓓ	26 Ⓕ Ⓖ Ⓗ Ⓙ	33 Ⓐ Ⓑ Ⓒ Ⓓ	40 Ⓕ Ⓖ Ⓗ Ⓙ
6 Ⓕ Ⓖ Ⓗ Ⓙ	13 Ⓐ Ⓑ Ⓒ Ⓓ	20 Ⓕ Ⓖ Ⓗ Ⓙ	27 Ⓐ Ⓑ Ⓒ Ⓓ	34 Ⓕ Ⓖ Ⓗ Ⓙ	
7 Ⓐ Ⓑ Ⓒ Ⓓ	14 Ⓕ Ⓖ Ⓗ Ⓙ	21 Ⓐ Ⓑ Ⓒ Ⓓ	28 Ⓕ Ⓖ Ⓗ Ⓙ	35 Ⓐ Ⓑ Ⓒ Ⓓ	

The Princeton Review
Diagnostic ACT Form

ESSAY

Begin your essay on this side. If necessary, continue on the opposite side.

Continue on the opposite side if necessary.

The Princeton Review
Diagnostic ACT Form

Continued from previous page.

The Princeton Review
Diagnostic ACT Form

Continued from previous page.

_____
_____
_____
_____
_____
_____
_____
_____
_____
_____
_____
_____
_____
_____
_____
_____
_____
_____
_____
_____
_____
_____
_____
_____

PLEASE PRINT
YOUR INITIALS

| First | Middle | Last |

The Princeton Review
Diagnostic ACT Form

Continued from previous page.

PLEASE PRINT
YOUR INITIALS

First   Middle   Last

Chapter 5
Test 2: Answers
and Explanations

TEST 2 ENGLISH ANSWERS

1.	A	48.	J
2.	J	49.	D
3.	D	50.	G
4.	F	51.	C
5.	C	52.	J
6.	H	53.	B
7.	B	54.	F
8.	J	55.	C
9.	B	56.	H
10.	J	57.	D
11.	B	58.	H
12.	J	59.	B
13.	A	60.	F
14.	J	61.	D
15.	B	62.	H
16.	H	63.	B
17.	B	64.	J
18.	F	65.	A
19.	C	66.	J
20.	H	67.	C
21.	D	68.	F
22.	F	69.	B
23.	C	70.	J
24.	G	71.	B
25.	D	72.	H
26.	H	73.	C
27.	B	74.	F
28.	F	75.	B
29.	D		
30.	F		
31.	B		
32.	J		
33.	A		

TEST 2 MATH ANSWERS

34.	F	1.	E
35.	D	2.	H
36.	G	3.	B
37.	A	4.	G
38.	H	5.	C
39.	D	6.	F
40.	G	7.	C
41.	C	8.	G
42.	G	9.	C
43.	A	10.	F
44.	F	11.	D
45.	C	12.	H
46.	G	13.	B
47.	A	14.	G

15.	B
16.	H
17.	B
18.	J
19.	C
20.	G
21.	C
22.	G
23.	E
24.	F
25.	C
26.	K
27.	D
28.	F
29.	B
30.	J
31.	E
32.	K
33.	B
34.	H
35.	A
36.	J
37.	C
38.	K
39.	E
40.	H
41.	E
42.	G
43.	C
44.	J
45.	B
46.	H
47.	C
48.	J
49.	A
50.	G
51.	A
52.	G
53.	C
54.	G
55.	C
56.	K
57.	A
58.	K
59.	E
60.	H

TEST 2 READING ANSWERS

1.	A
2.	G
3.	D
4.	F
5.	C
6.	J
7.	A
8.	H
9.	D
10.	F
11.	A
12.	G
13.	B
14.	F
15.	C
16.	F
17.	C
18.	H
19.	C
20.	J
21.	D
22.	J
23.	A
24.	G
25.	C
26.	J
27.	D
28.	F
29.	B
30.	G
31.	A
32.	G
33.	C
34.	H
35.	A
36.	J
37.	D
38.	H
39.	D
40.	F

TEST 2 SCIENCE ANSWERS

1. D
2. F
3. C
4. J
5. B
6. G
7. D
8. G
9. A
10. G
11. D
12. J
13. B
14. F
15. A
16. F
17. C
18. F
19. C
20. H
21. A
22. G
23. C
24. F
25. C
26. G
27. D
28. G
29. B
30. J
31. D
32. J
33. A
34. G
35. A
36. F
37. A
38. G
39. A
40. J

SCORING YOUR PRACTICE EXAM

Step A
Count the number of correct answers for each section and record the number in the space provided for your raw score on the Score Conversion Worksheet below.

Step B
Using the Score Conversion Chart on the next page, convert your raw scores on each section to scaled scores. Then compute your composite ACT score by averaging the four subject scores. Add them up and divide by four. Don't worry about the essay score; it is not included in your composite score.

Score Conversion Worksheet		
Section	Raw Score	Scaled Score
1	_____/75	_____
2	_____/60	_____
3	_____/40	_____
4	_____/40	_____

SCORE CONVERSION CHART

Scaled Score	Raw Score			
	English	Mathematics	Reading	Science
36	75	60	39–40	40
35	74	59	38	39
34	72–73	58	37	38
33	71	57	36	—
32	70	55–56	35	37
31	69	53–54	34	36
30	67–68	52	33	—
29	65–66	50–51	32	35
28	62–64	46–49	30–31	33–34
27	59–61	43–45	28–29	31–32
26	57–58	41–42	27	30
25	55–56	39–40	26	29
24	52–54	37–38	25	28
23	50–51	35–36	24	27–26
22	49	33–34	23	25
21	48	31–32	21–22	24
20	45–47	29–30	20	23
19	43–44	27–28	19	22
18	40–42	24–26	18	20–21
17	38–39	21–23	17	18–19
16	35–37	18–20	16	16–17
15	32–34	16–17	15	15
14	29–31	13–15	14	13–14
13	27–28	11–12	12–13	12
12	24–26	9–10	11	11
11	21–23	7–8	9–10	10
10	18–20	6	8	9
9	15–17	5	7	7–8
8	13–14	4	—	6
7	11–12	—	6	5
6	9–10	3	5	—
5	7–8	2	4	4
4	5–6	—	3	3
3	3–4	1	2	2
2	2	—	1	1
1	0	0	0	0

TEST 2 ENGLISH EXPLANATIONS

1. **A** The mother says that the author will be surprised to find that *family histories can be very interesting*, which implies that the author currently believes the opposite. Choice (A) is the best answer, expressing boredom and disinterest. Choices (B) and (C) are too optimistic, and (D) is irrelevant in this paragraph.

2. **J** Choice (F) creates a fragment because *hoping* begins an incomplete thought. Choice (G) creates a fragment because there is no subject for the verb *hope*. Choice (J) is the best answer because it corrects the sentence fragment error by connecting the incomplete thought to the complete one before it with a comma. Choice (H) confuses the meaning of the sentence.

3. **D** *Pictures and letters* is a list of only two items, so no commas are needed before the *and*, eliminating (A) and (B). Choice (C) also has an unnecessary comma after *letters*, interrupting the flow of the sentence.

4. **F** In EXCEPT/LEAST/NOT questions, the underlined portion of the sentence is correct. Choice (G) has the same structure and meaning as the original, since *yet* and *but* are both coordinating conjunctions, which, with a comma, can join two complete ideas. Choice (H) is acceptable because a semicolon is an appropriate punctuation to separate two complete thoughts. Choices (F) and (J) eliminate the need for punctuation by deleting *he* and making the second half of the sentence incomplete. However, (F) uses an incorrect tense and is NOT acceptable.

5. **C** Choice (C) correctly uses the apostrophe to show possession. An apostrophe after *relatives* is necessary to indicate more than one relative has the memories, eliminating (A) and (B). *Memory* does not possess *into;* thus, (D) is incorrect.

6. **H** Sentences 1 and 2 continue the narrative by providing a setting and the scanner's activity. Sentence 4 shows an important shift in the author's attitude from reluctance to happiness. Sentence 3 offers information that can be figured out from the context and is therefore the least relevant to the telling of the story.

7. **B** The word *belongings* refers to the relatives, which is plural, so you can eliminate (A) and (C). The correct answer is (B), not (D); *there* refers to a place and *their* is the plural possessive pronoun.

8. **J** Choice (J) gives the past perfect form of the verb *to send*; this form is needed because the letters were sent in the distant past. Choices (G) and (H) are in the wrong tense, and (F) does not use the proper past participle form of the verb *send*.

9. **B** A pause is necessary between *kitchen* and *penning* to clarify that the great-grandmother, not the kitchen, was *penning* the entries, which makes (B) better than (A). Choices (C) and (D) can also be eliminated because *which* and *that* refer to the closest preceding noun, which is *kitchen*, and create the same error in meaning.

10. **J** This sentence continues the same attitude about stories that is expressed in the previous sentence, so you can eliminate (F) for incorrect direction. *Because* makes the phrase after incomplete, so (G) is incorrect because it creates a sentence fragment. *Therefore* indicates the correct direction but doesn't link the ideas in a logical way. The best answer is (J).

11. **B** A comma should precede the last *and* in a list of 3 or more things, eliminating (C) and (D). Choice (A) has an unnecessary comma after the *and*, so the correct answer is (B).

12. **J** The best answer is (J) because it clearly introduces the paragraph's focus on the author's growing interest in her family. Choices (F) and (H) mention the relatives; however, the focus is not on how many names and relatives the writer needs to keep track of. Choice (G) revisits the idea of using the computer to preserve family memories but does not match this paragraph's main idea.

13. **A** Paragraph 6 discusses what the writer gained from her experience, and the conclusion should continue that idea. Choice (A) is the best choice because it discusses what the writer plans to do with what she gained and emphasizes the important relationship between grandfather and grandchild seen in this narrative. Choices (B), (C), and (D) digress from the main point of the essay about the significance of the experience.

14. **J** Paragraph 5 discusses the writer's positive view of her grandfather's stories. Her change in attitude is first introduced at the end of Paragraph 3. Paragraph 5 then concludes by introducing the chest of stuff, which explains what the *belongings* are in the beginning of Paragraph 4. Therefore, the best placement of Paragraph 5 should be between Paragraphs 3 and 4.

15. **B** The writer concludes the essay by stating how much she appreciates family memories and mementoes after helping her grandfather research their family lineage; thus, her purpose has been achieved, eliminating (C) and (D). Choice (A) is not true because the computer skills are not the benefit the writer gained from her experience.

16. **H** The writer is trying to state that she is standing alone; thus, the correct pronoun is *myself* not *me*, eliminating (F) and (G). The phrase after *myself* is incomplete and cannot be separated by a period, eliminating (J). A comma can be used to connect a complete thought to an incomplete thought.

17. **B** The words *new* and *cold* are both adjectives describing *bedroom* and should be separated by a comma, eliminating (C) and (D). A comma after *cold* is unnecessary and disruptive to the flow of the sentence, eliminating (A).

18. **F** The writer is trying to describe *spectacle,* which is a noun, so *complete* should be an adjective, eliminating (G) and (H). The correct idiomatic expression is *to make a spectacle of,* so (F) is better than (J).

19. **C** Since the action *has never been more than 30 minutes away* refers to *only child*, the pronoun should be in subject case *who*, eliminating (A) and (B). Choice (D) incorrectly uses the plural verb form, rather than the singular.

20. **H** The pronoun *one's* does not agree with the subject *we* earlier in the sentence. Only (H) uses the correct possessive pronoun of *we*, which is *our.*

21. **D** The sentence is listing two different pairs of breakfast items—milk and juice, eggs and bacon. There should not be a comma after *milk* because the *and* is used to connect two nouns, *milk* and *juice*, not to list 3 or more items. You can eliminate (A) and (B). The comma is necessary between *juice* and *fluffy* in order to separate the two different pairs of items.

22. **F** Choice (F) clearly articulates the angst she feels and clarifies that she misses her old way of life. Choice (G) is incorrect because the different stages of mourning are not described. Although the original sentence is short and concise, it is too literal and does not accurately describe her emotional state. Eliminate (H) and (J).

23. **C** Because the first half of the sentence is an incomplete thought, the underlined portion must include a subject to make the second half a complete thought, eliminating (A) and (D). Choice (C) uses the present tense of the verb, which fits better in the context of the story than the present perfect tense in (B).

24. **G** Choice (G) is correct, because the phrase does clarify why the writer stops crying in the first half of the sentence. There is no evidence to support a strained roommate relationship, so (F) is incorrect. Choice (H) is incorrect because the phrase does not show that the writer is right to feel sad. The phrase does give new understanding into what the author is thinking and feeling, so (J) is incorrect.

25. **D** Choices (A), (B), and (C) imply that the writer hears her roommate crying because she is surprised, which is not the intended meaning. The writer is surprised to hear her roommate cry, making (D) correct.

26. **H** The conjunction *and* is not the correct link between the incomplete thought *Curiosity overwhelming me* and the complete second half the sentence, eliminating (F) and (G). Choice (J) is incorrect because a period cannot come after an incomplete thought.

27. **B** Choice (B) is the only transition listed that suggests a quick, unexpected reaction from the roommate. Choices (A), (C), and (D) all indicate that some time passes before the roommate responds.

28. **F** Choice (F) is the only appropriate verb that is consistent in meaning with the description of the roommate as shaken up and surprised by the presence of the writer. Choice (G) means to state confidently, (H) means to use another person's words, and (J) means to yell loudly.

29. **D** Choice (D) both captures the roommate's emotion and explains why the writer responds by suggesting they adjust to college life together. Choices (A) and (B) are not consistent with the writer's response. Choice (C) completely disagrees with the emotions of both the writer and the roommate.

30. **F** The passage is a personal account of the writer, a first-time college student who is worried after moving away from home, and of the writer's roommate, who feels similar emotions. Thus, (F) is the best answer.

31. **B** Choice (B) is the best answer here because the analogy provides vivid detail. The reasons provided in (A), (C), and (D) are not compelling.

32. **J** The phrase *if murky* is unnecessary information, so it should be offset by commas. Thus, (J) is correct. Choice (G) has no pauses to offset this information, which confuses the flow of the sentence. Choices (F) and (H) create sentence fragments.

33. **A** The phrase clarifies the term *anyone* by describing the kind of people who should try canyoning, so (A) is correct. Choice (B) is incorrect because the paragraph focuses on canyoning, not people. Choice (C) is extreme and not logical. Choice (D) is incorrect because the phrase does not confuse the focus of the sentence in any way.

34. **F** The word *river* ends a complete thought, and the word *without* begins a second complete thought. Choice (F) correctly uses a comma with a coordinating conjunction to link two complete thoughts. Choices (G), (H), and (J) create run-on sentences and do not provide proper punctuation to link two complete thoughts.

35. **D** Choice (D) is the most concise answer that conveys the correct meaning. Choices (A), (B), and (C) are wordy and unclear.

36. **G** Because *A remarkable activity in its own right* is a modifier, the *activity*—skydiving—must be named immediately after the modifier. Thus, (F) and (J) are wrong. Choice (H) omits the sentence's verb and also treats skydiving as unnecessary information by setting it off with commas. Choice (G) is the answer.

37. **A** Choice (A) is correct because the statement describes an additional thrilling activity in an exotic location, which is the focus of this paragraph. Choice (B) does not correctly describe the main idea of the paragraph. Choice (C) is incorrect because the locations and activities are different in each scenario, not just this one. Choice (D) is too narrowly focused and strays from the main idea.

38. **H** The phrase *because of which was our most exhilarating adventure yet* is intended to describe (modify) *canyoning*. Thus, the phrase should begin with the word *which*, as in (H). The remaining answer choices are unclear and create fragments.

39. **D** The word *walls* ends a complete thought, and the word *we* begins a second complete thought. Choice (D) correctly uses a comma with a coordinating conjunction to link two complete thoughts. Choices (A), (B), and (C) create run-on sentences and do not provide proper punctuation to link two complete thoughts.

40. **G** Choice (G) is the most concise answer that conveys the correct meaning, since *leaping* naturally implies a following descent. Choices (F), (H), and (J) are redundant.

41. **C** The subject of the sentence is the word *danger*, so its verb must be singular to agree with it, as with (C). Choice (A) contains a plural form of the verb, so it does not agree with the subject. Choice (B) contains a future tense, so it does not agree with the past tense of this sentence and of the passage. Choice (D) uses a gerund form incorrectly.

42. **G** A clear distinction between water and land activities is made in this paragraph, so (G) best clarifies this distinction with its mention of *rocky surfaces* and *chilly water*. Choices (F), (H), and (J) do not address the distinction at all.

43. **A** The word *thrills* begins a complete thought that switches the direction of the sentence, so an opposite direction conjunction is necessary at the beginning of the thought preceding it. Choice (A) provides the correct conjunction. Choices (C) and (D) are adverbs that indicate the ideas are going in the same direction, so you can eliminate those choices.

44. **F** The essay focuses on the enjoyment of thrills, so (F) is correct. Choices (G) and (H) do not mention thrills at all. Choice (J) mentions thrills but with a tone opposite to that of the entire essay.

45. **C** The best location for Paragraph 2 is before Paragraph 4, (C), because Paragraph 3 introduces the activity of *canyoning* discussed in the first sentence of Paragraph 2. There is also a logical sequence from the introduction and description of the river in Paragraph 2 to its navigation in the beginning of Paragraph 5.

46. **G** Note that the subject of this sentence—*Mexican-American War*—is singular. Don't be thrown off by the words *conflicts* and *compromises*, which, although closer to the verb, are not the main subjects of the sentence. Since *Mexican-American War* is singular, you can eliminate (F) and (H), and (J) creates a sentence fragment. Only (G) works.

47. **A** Two main things are changing in the answer choices here. First, the verb in the sentence changes from the present *include* to the past *included*, but this sentence discusses the Mexican-American War as being *overlooked* in the present (and note the mention of the *current shape and culture* in the following sentence), so you'll want to keep *include*. Moreover, if you're going to use a colon (:), you must have, at the very least, a complete idea before it, which you do not in this case.

48. **J** Choices (F) and (H) break the flow of the sentence unnecessarily, so they can be eliminated easily, but to determine whether you need the commas around the phrase *to American arts,* determine whether the sentence makes sense without this piece of information. As you can see, without this phrase, the word *contributions* is not clearly defined in the text. Accordingly, *to American arts* is an essential part of the sentence and should not be set off by commas.

49. **D** Choices (A), (B), and (C) all rewrite the same sentence—only (D) gives a completely different option. If you check (D) first, you can save yourself a lot of work. In this case, you can DELETE this sentence because it is inappropriately placed in the paragraph. While Mexican-American musicians are mentioned earlier in the paragraph, the previous sentence represents an important transition to the following paragraphs discussing Mexican-American authors.

50. **G** To determine whether or not a selection should be set off by commas, as *María Amparo Ruiz de Burton* is in this sentence, see if the sentence makes sense without that selection. In this case, it does not make sense to say, *A major landmark in early Mexican-American literature came in 1885, when author published her first novel...* The author's name is an essential part of this sentence and so cannot be set off by commas.

51. **C** Choices (A) and (D) are out, because neither is indicated elsewhere in the passage. Choice (B) is deceptive—the paragraph says this novel was the first to be written in English by an author of Mexican descent, not that it was the first by a Mexican author to be read in the United States. Only (C) captures the historical importance of the novel having been the first written in English by an author of Mexican descent.

52. **J** Since all of these answer choices ultimately say the same thing, pick the most concise answer that preserves the meaning of the original sentence. This definitely eliminates (F) and (H), and while (G) seems similar in length to (J), (G) is unclear and awkward in its construction, not least because *give a glimpse at* is idiomatically incorrect.

53. **B** Because *A family of landed gentry living in San Diego* is a modifier, the *family*—the Alamars—must be named immediately after the modifier. Thus, (A), (C), and (D) are wrong, and (B) is the answer.

54. **F** The sentence discusses a single event that took place during the Mexican-American War, so (H), which implies that the event was continuous, must be eliminated. Choices (G) and (J) alter the meaning of the sentence and are idiomatically incorrect. Only (F) works appropriately.

55. **C** Choices (A), (B), and (D) all create sentence fragments. Only (C) contains a verb, *was,* that can make this sentence complete.

56. **H** You need to determine here whether the sentence should be added to or kept out of the paragraph. If you're not sure whether to answer Yes or No, look at the reasons in each answer choice. Choice (F) can't work because the sentence discusses individuals of French descent, and there is no indication that the writer is drawing any kind of parallel between individuals of French descent and those of Mexican descent. Choice (G) can't work because the sentence does not give any indication that it is meant to be connected to *The Squatter and the Don*. Choice (J) can't work because the reaction of Mexican-Americans to the Louisiana Purchase is never discussed. Only (H) indicates that the sentence does not provide information relevant to this paragraph.

57. **D** In EXCEPT/LEAST/NOT questions, the underlined portion of the sentence is correct. In this case, the words in (A), (B), and (C)—*investigate*, *examine*, and *look into*—are all roughly synonyms for *explore*. Choice (D), *solve*, has a meaning different than *explore* and its synonyms and changes the meaning of the sentence. Thus, (D) is the LEAST acceptable solution and the correct answer to this question.

58. **H** Choices (G) and (J) are both idiomatically incorrect and change the meaning of the sentence, so all you really need to decide is whether to use the relative pronoun *that* or *those*. To determine this, find which word or words the pronoun will be replacing. In this case, the word replaced is *writings*, a plural noun, which can be replaced only by the plural pronoun *those*.

59. **B** Sentence 3 introduces *other authors* for the first time in the passage. Sentences 1 and 2 provide examples of two other authors who are important. Therefore, Sentence 3 must come before Sentence 1. Choice (B) is correct.

60. **F** Because all four answer choices have the same meaning, select the most clear and concise. Choice (F) is the most clear and concise.

61. **D** Note the context of this sentence. The underlined portion ends a portion of the sentence that should be set off by commas—*typically cited alongside Walter Gropius and Le Corbusier as a pioneer of modern architecture*, so you can eliminate (A) and (B). The word *being*, as in (C), creates a sentence fragment, so the best answer is (D).

62. **H** Note the other verb in this sentence, *sought*. Since this is in the past tense, the other verbs in this sentence must be in the past tense. For the underlined portion, only (H) and (J) are written in the past tense, and (J) creates a sentence fragment with its use of the relative pronoun *who*.

63. **B** The easiest answer to eliminate is (D), as the semicolon would improperly separate two incomplete ideas. The phrase *based on van der Rohe's designs* is a necessary part of the sentence, so it should not be set off by commas. Likewise, it is not part of an introductory clause, so it should not be followed by a comma. Choice (B) correctly omits any commas.

64. **J** In EXCEPT/LEAST/NOT questions, the underlined portion of the sentence is correct. Choice (J) is NOT acceptable, because it changes the meaning of the sentence by suggesting that something is being made *into* steel and glass, when in fact the buildings are constructed *out of* steel and glass.

65. **A** The phrase *that is* is an introductory clause and therefore is properly followed by a comma. The part of the sentence after the dash serves to elaborate upon the sentence's earlier mention of the materials, and *that is* (an idiomatically shortened form of *that is to say*) functions in the same way that expressions like *for example* or *in this case* might in another sentence.

66. **J**   Of the choices available here, only the colon is appropriate. The latter part of the sentence gives an example of *one of the problems* mentioned earlier in the passage. Accordingly, only (J) can be appropriate. Also note, when using a colon, make sure there is a complete sentence before it, as there is in (J).

67. **C**   Choices (A) and (B) don't directly discuss the visual elements of the buildings, merely how long they took to construct or their historical importance. Choice (D) gets closer by mentioning that the buildings are *on display* in various cities, but only (C) really discusses the buildings' *visual appeal* in its description of the buildings' *complex beauty*.

68. **F**   The easiest answer to eliminate is (H), as the semicolon would improperly separate two incomplete ideas. Because the phrase *under teacher Peter Behrens's guidance* is unnecessary to the sentence as a whole, it should be set off by commas. Therefore, (F) is correct. Choice (J) is wrong because it eliminates the comma needed at the end of an unnecessary phrase and it incorrectly inserts a comma after *teacher*. Choice (G) is wrong because, while the entire phrase as a whole may be unnecessary, *Peter Behrens's guidance* is a necessary part of the phrase, so the comma following *teacher* is inappropriate.

69. **B**   In the sentence as written, it is unclear what the pronoun *This* refers to, so to fix this pronoun ambiguity, you'll need a substitute that is more specific. Choices (C) and (D) are no more specific than is (A); only (B) fixes the problem by giving a specific subject.

70. **J**   First, consider whether the last sentence of the paragraph provides a contrast to or a continuation of the prior sentence. Both sentences concern van der Rohe's development of a new style, so contrasting (F) and (G) are wrong. Choice (H) is wrong because it would transform an incomplete sentence followed by a comma and a complete sentence into two complete sentences separated by a comma. Choice (J) is grammatically correct and clear.

71. **B**   Since this sentence refers to an event that occurred in 1937, the sentence must be in the past tense (note, also, that the other sentences in the paragraph are in the past tense). Only (A) and (B) satisfy this condition, but (A) creates a sentence fragment by introducing the relative pronoun *who*.

72. **H**   In EXCEPT/LEAST/NOT questions, the underlined portion of the sentence is correct. Choices (F), (G), and (J) all preserve the meaning of the original sentence. Choice (H) changes the meaning of the sentence and, moreover, contains a pronoun, *this,* that does not refer to any noun. Choice (H) is thus NOT an acceptable substitution.

73. **C**   Choices (A) and (D) create a misplaced modifier—since *van der Rohe* comes directly after the introductory phrase, the introductory phrase must properly refer to *van der Rohe*, and must be modifying this subject in some way. The word *while* in (B) suggests that a contradiction will come later in the sentence, but none does. Only (C) functions properly to modify the actions of van der Rohe.

74. **F**   Since all the answer choices are roughly synonymous, choose the most concise that preserves the meaning. Choices (G), (H), and (J) all contain some redundancy and do not contain any essential information beyond the word *enthusiastic*.

75. **B** Look for clues in Sentence 3 that might give you some hints as to its proper placement. The main clue is the word *there*, which suggests that a previous sentence will contain some mention of a place. Sentence 2 discusses the Illinois Institute of Technology, but look closely, the end of Sentence 3 indicates that this is one of the commissions awaiting him there, so it is still unclear of what *there* is. In Sentence 1, however, you see that the architect is discussed as moving from Germany to the United States, so Sentence 3 should clearly be placed after Sentence 1 because the *there* in this situation clearly refers to the United States.

TEST 2 MATH EXPLANATIONS

1. **E**   Use Process of Elimination aggressively. Since Violet has 10 cherries, she uses *three times* 10 = 30 blackberries, eliminating (A), (B), and (D). Thus, she also uses 30 raspberries and *twice* 30 = 60 blueberries. Choice (C) lists 2 rather than 2 × 30 for the number of blueberries.

2. **H**   Expand the equation with FOIL (first, outside, inside, last): $(3x)(x) + (3x)(2) + (-5)(x) + (-5)(2) = 3x^2 + 6x + (-5x) + (-10)$. Combine the middle terms to get the simplified expression $3x^2 + x - 10$. Choices (G), (J), and (K) are the results of confusing the signs. Choice (F) only multiplies the first terms and the last terms, which is not the correct way to multiply binomials.

3. **B**   Substitute 8 and 6 for x and y, respectively, into the equation $f(x,y)$, to get $f(8,6) = 8 - [(8 \times 6) - 6] = 8 - 42 = -34$. Choices (A), (C), (D), and (E) are wrong because they do not distribute the negative correctly.

4. **G**   Use the words in the problem to create an equation: *percent* means "divide by 100," *of* means "multiply," and *what number* means "use a variable." The equation is $x = \frac{1}{7} \times \frac{28}{100} \times 8,000$. So, $x =$ 320. Choice (H) is $7 \times \frac{28}{100} \times 8,000$, a common fraction mistake.

5. **C**   When you have numbers in the answer choices and variables in the question, you can plug the answer choices into the variables in the question to find out which answer choice makes the equation true. Start with (C) when plugging in the answer choices because it is the middle value and will sometimes tell you whether you need a bigger or smaller number if (C) is not the correct answer. Does 6(3) + 3 = 12 + 3(3)? Simplify both sides: 18 + 3 = 12 + 9 and 21 = 21, so this works!

6. **F**   First, calculate the difference of the third and second terms: 8 – (–2) = 10. The first term, therefore, is the second term minus the difference: (–2) – 10 = –12. Choices (G) and (K) are variations of the actual common difference, rather than the value of the first term. Choice (H) calculates the first term in a geometric, rather than arithmetic, sequence. Choice (J) incorrectly calculates –2 as the first term, rather than the second.

7. **C**   Probability is equal to $\frac{number\ of\ favorable\ outcomes}{number\ of\ total\ possible\ outcomes}$. If you find a common denominator between the two probabilities, you can determine the number of unfavorable outcomes. The least common denominator between $\frac{2}{9}$ and $\frac{1}{3}$ is 9. The probability that the jellybean is NOT pink is $\frac{5}{9}$, so the probability that the jellybean is pink is $\frac{4}{9}$. Now, multiply $\frac{4}{9}$ by the total number of jellybeans, 72, to find the bag contains 32 pink jellybeans, (C).

8.   **G**   Because the flat rate of $100 includes the first two months, Bob will be billed $60/month for only 10 months out of the year. The total cost is $100 + $60 (10) = $700, so (G) is correct. Choice (F) results if you incorrectly charge $100 for every two-month period. The flat rate applies only for the first two months. Choice (H) calculates the total without the flat rate. Choice (J) incorrectly charges the flat rate twice for the first two months. Choice (K) adds 12, rather than 10, months of service charges to the flat rate.

9.   **C**   If one side of the pentagon measures 20 inches, the perimeter of the pentagon is 100 inches (20 × 5). Because the pentagon and the square have the same perimeter, the square also has a perimeter of 100 inches. Each side of the square is then 25 inches (100 ÷ 4). Choice (E) is wrong because it is equal to the perimeter of both the square and the pentagon, which is not what the question asks for. Choices (A), (B), and (D) give a perimeter that is not equal to the target of 100 inches.

10. **F**   Translate the words into an equation, making x the number of bricks. Contractor A charges $1,600 *plus* $2 *times* the number of bricks, 1,600 + 2x. Contractor B charges $400 plus $8 times the number of bricks, 400 + 8x. Set the expressions equal to each other to get 1,600 + 2x = 400 + 8x. Choice (G) sets each contractor's flat rate plus the other contractor's per brick charge equal. Choice (H) sets the sum of each contractor's per brick charges and the number of bricks equal. Choices (J) and (K) set the per brick charges equal to Contractor A's and B's flat rates, respectively.

11. **D**   Solve for B. Divide both sides of the equation by ACD to get $B = \dfrac{E}{ACD}$.

12. **H**   You need to remember some things about angles and lines: A straight line, in this case $\angle WVZ$, measures 180°, and $\angle XVY$ measures 90° because it is marked as a right angle. The sum of the measures of $\angle WVX$ and $\angle YVZ$ = 180° − 90° = 90°. Since $\angle WVX$ and $\angle YVZ$ measure 4a and 2a respectively, 6a = 90° so a = 15°. Therefore, $\angle YVZ$ = 30° and $\angle XVY$ = 90° + 30° = 120°. Choice (F) is the value of $\angle YVZ$. Choice (J) is the sum of $\angle WVX$ and $\angle WVY$. Choice (K) is too big because $\angle VVZ$ is not a straight line.

13. **B**   First, find the temperature of New Orleans in °F by adding 25°F to 70°F to get 95°F. Your answer choices give you different values of °C. You can start with the middle answer choice, 68°C, and substitute this value for C in the equation to see if you get 95°F. Choice (C) gives $\dfrac{9}{5}$(68) + 32 = 154°F. Since this value is too large, you can eliminate (C), (D), and (E). Choice (B) gives $\dfrac{9}{5}$(35) + 32 = 95°F.

14. **G**   The factored form of the expression is 2(3x + 2y) − 7, so you can substitute 5 for 3x + 2y to get 2(5) − 7 = 3. Choice (F) results if you forget to multiply 3x + 2y by 2, and (J) forgets to subtract 7. Choices (H) and (K) incorrectly use the coefficients of x and y to determine the value.

15. **B**   The total amount of beef in pounds would be $3\dfrac{2}{7} + 2\dfrac{1}{3} = 5\dfrac{13}{21}$. This number falls in the range "At least $5\dfrac{1}{2}$ and less than $5\dfrac{2}{3}$." Choices (A), (C), (D), and (E) are incorrect because $5\dfrac{13}{21}$ does not fall within those ranges.

16. **H** Draw a picture. Since Dave went directly east and then directly south, the distance to his house can be found using a right triangle. The distance is $d = \sqrt{3^2 + 4^2} = 5$. Careful not to select (K), which is the sum of the two legs of the triangle!

17. **B** The rate at which the sensor records—1 piece of data every .0000000038 seconds, or $\dfrac{1}{.0000000038}$

—is constant, and therefore the ratio of pieces of data recorded per second will be equal for any given number of pieces of data or seconds. Set $\dfrac{1}{.0000000038}$ equal to the ratio 100,000,000,000

pieces of data every x seconds: $\dfrac{1}{.0000000038} = \dfrac{100,000,000,000}{x}$. Solve for x by multiplying

diagonally across the equation: $x \times 1 = 100,000,000,000 \times .0000000038$, so $x = 380$.

18. **J** Use the answers: Since the width and length are reduced by the same amount, you can eliminate any that do not use the same difference between original and new dimensions, (F), (H), and (K). Then, calculate the original area of the photograph: $A = l \times w = 20 \times 30 = 600$ cm². The final area of the photo, therefore, equals $600 - 264 = 336$ cm². Choice (G) gives you $12 \times 22 = 264$ cm². The correct answer is (J), $14 \times 24 = 336$.

19. **C** The perimeter is the sum of all 4 side lengths of the quadrilateral. The answer choices give you the length of the shortest side, so you can work backwards by adding the three larger consecutive even numbers to each answer choice. You can immediately eliminate (D) because 7 is not an even number. Choice (C) correctly gives you $6 + 8 + 10 + 12 = 36$. Choices (A), (B), and (E) do not give you a sum of 36.

20. **G** Rearrange the equation into the slope-intercept form, $y = mx + b$. The resulting equation is $y = \dfrac{3}{7}$ $x + 3$, with slope m of $\dfrac{3}{7}$. Choice (F) confuses the signs. Choice (H) results if you rearrange the equation into "$x =$" form, which does not indicate slope. Choice (J) is the y-intercept of the line.

21. **C** To find the area of the trapezoid *BCEF*, subtract the area of triangle *CDE* from rectangle *BDEF*. The area of rectangle *BDEF* is 36 square feet (9 × 4), and the area of triangle *CDE* is 10 square feet [(5 × 4) ÷ 2]; therefore, the area of the trapezoid *BCEF* is 26 square feet (36 – 10). Choice (A) is incorrect because it finds the area of the square with sides *BC* and *BF*. Choice (D) is incorrect because it is only solving for the area of the rectangle *BDEF*.

22. **G** Make sure you read the given information carefully. You don't have to do any figuring aside from approximating $\sqrt{136}$ because all the other values are given to you. Because $\sqrt{136} \approx 11.7$, to find the perimeter, simply add the sides: 11.7 + 10 + 6 + 12 = 39.7. If you chose (F), you may have forgotten to include the diagonal in your calculation. If you chose (J), you did too much work—this is the area!

23. **E** Use the Pythagorean Theorem, $a^2 + b^2 = c^2$. Since $\overline{FG} = 10$ and $\overline{FJ} = 6$, $(10)^2 + (6)^2 = \overline{GGJ}^2$, and $\overline{GJ} = \sqrt{136}$. If you chose (B), you may have confused this with a 6:8:10 triangle, but be careful—$\overline{FG}$ and $\overline{FJ}$ are just the legs in this triangle. If this were a 6:8:10 triangle, the longest side would have to be 10. Also note, that because point J shares a y-coordinate with the midpoint of $\overline{GH}$, $\overline{GJ} = \overline{HJ}$.

24. **F** Since the graph is rotating clockwise, the point will be moving 90° and will have a new point on the x-axis. Any point on the x-axis must have a y-coordinate of 0, so you can eliminate (G) and (J) immediately. If you chose (K), be careful—you may have rotated the graph in a *counter*clockwise direction rather than a clockwise direction.

25. **C** A geometric figure has rotational symmetry if it looks the same after a certain amount of rotation. A geometric figure has reflectional symmetry when one half is the reflection of the other half. Choice (C) is the only figure that has rotational and reflectional symmetry.

26. **K** Expand the equation with FOIL (First, Outside, Inside, Last) and you will see that only the first term in each polynomial has exponents that add together to become x^8: $-x^4 \cdot 5x^4 = -5x^8$. Choice (F) wrongly assumes the absence of a x^8 term. Choice (G) confuses the sign; (H) incorrectly adds the coefficients; (J) multiplies the wrong terms.

27. **D** To find the mean, add up all the scores: $66 + 67 + 71 + 72 + 72 + 73 + 75 + 77 + 79 + 82 + 83 + 83 + 87 = 987$. Divide this number by the total number of scores, 13, to find $\frac{987}{13} \approx 75.9$. If you selected (C), be careful—this is the median. If you chose (B), you may have taken the means of the stems and leaves separately and added them together.

28. **F** To find the probability, determine the number of desirable outcomes divided by the number of total possible outcomes. Since you want a score of exactly 83, go to the stem-and-leaf plot to see that two of the golfers had a score of 83. Since there were 13 total golfers, the probability that an 83 would be selected out of the whole group is $\frac{2}{13}$. If you chose either (J) or (K), be careful—this question is asking about the probability of selecting a certain score; the actual numerical value of that score is not relevant.

29. **B** First, factor each number. In this problem, the given numbers are all products of 2, 3, *a*, and *b*. To find the lowest common multiple of the given values, you need to figure out the maximum number of times each component (2, 3, *a*, and *b*) appears in any one of the given values. $8 = 2 \times 2 \times 2$, so the lowest common multiple must have $2 \times 2 \times 2$ as a factor. No value has more than one factor of 3, so the number is only required to have one factor of 3. Finally, the least common multiple must have one *a* and one *b*. Multiply the mandatory factors together, $2 \times 2 \times 2 \times 3 \times a \times b$, to get $24ab$.

30. **J** To solve for the function, you need to determine the value of *m* in December. Since December is 7 months after May and $m = 0$ in May, $m = 7$ in December. Substitute 7 for m in the function to get $A(7) = 2(7) + 2$, so Aleksandra will have 16 model airplanes. Choice (F) is the number of airplanes she had in May. Choices (G), (H), and (K) result if you use the wrong value of *m* for December.

31. **E** The midpoint of a line is $(\frac{x_1 + x_2}{2})$, $(\frac{y_1 + y_2}{2})$. Thus, the x-coordinate of the midpoint $= \frac{-3+11}{2} = 4$, eliminating (A), (B), (C), and (D). The only remaining choice is (E), which also has the correct y-coordinate $= \frac{5-7}{2} = -1$. Be careful not to subtract x_2 from x_1, which would give you an x-coordinate of 7. Choices (A) and (B) merely add or subtract the x- and y-coordinates, rather than finding their averages.

32. **K** Factor the numerator and denominator separately: $\frac{(x-4)(x-4)}{(x+4)(x-4)}$. The factor $(x-4)$ on both the top and the bottom of the fraction cancel each other out, so you're left with (K). Choices (F), (G), and (H) are all the result of incorrectly canceling out terms without factoring. Choice (J) cancels both factors from the numerator, which is not possible with only one $(x-4)$ in the denominator.

33. **B** If Evan purchased 6 boxes, with 10 bags in each box, and 12 cookies in each bag, he will have purchased 720 cookies ($6 \times 10 \times 12$). Dividing 720 by 30 will give you the number of family packs with 30 cookies that he could have purchased instead. $720 \div 30 = 24$. Choices (A), (B), (C), and (E) are wrong because they do not result in the target amount of total cookies.

34. **H** If $\frac{r}{s} = -\frac{1}{2}$, then $s = -2r$. Substitute $-2r$ for s in the given expression: $16r^4 - (-2r)^4 = 16r^4 - 16r^4 = 0$. If you selected (K) you may have made a sign error.

35. **A** Because the nine circles fit into the square "as shown," quickly estimate the area that remains to eliminate any answer choices that couldn't possibly be correct. Roughly, it appears that $\frac{1}{4}$ of the square remains. Since the total area of the square is 144 square inches, and $144 \div 4 = 36$, (C), (D), and (E) are out because they are too big. Choice (A) is slightly closer to the estimate than (B), but if you have time, do the math. Since the circles are identical and are tangent to all adjacent circles and to the edges, the diameter of any circle must be $\frac{1}{3}$ of a 12-inch side, or 4 inches, and the radius of any circle must be 2 . The area of each circle is $\pi \times$ the radius squared, or 3.14×4, or 12.56. Multiply 12.56 square inches by 9 cookie cut-outs to get 113.04 square inches cut out, and 30.96 square inches remaining. You can also make this problem fast if you know that the area of a circle inscribed in a square is always equal to $\frac{\pi}{4} \times$ the area of the square, and can see that the area remaining in each of the small squares is proportional to the area remaining in the big square: $144 - (\frac{\pi}{4} \times 144) = 30.9$.

36. **J** Use the answer choices and Process of Elimination. Remember that a prime number has only two distinct factors, itself and 1. The number 63 is divisible by 3, 7, 9, and 21, eliminating (F). The number 91 is divisible by 7 and 13, eliminating (G) and (H). The number 81 is divisible by 3, 9, and 27, eliminating (K).

37. **C** First, determine the cost per quarter hour using the rate formula: $rate = \dfrac{change\ in\ cost}{change\ in\ quarter - hours}$. Pick two different packages: $\dfrac{\$230 - \$200}{10 - 8} = \dfrac{\$30}{2}$ to find the rate that is \$15 per quarter-hour. Now use the 8 quarter-hour package: fixed cost + $\$15 \times 8 = \$200$ to find that the fixed cost is \$80. Choice (B) finds the rate for the 10-quarter-hour package without a fixed cost. Choice (D) is a partial answer.

38. **K** Because you know the height of the building *opposite* the angle and want to find the shadow length *adjacent* the angle, use SOHCAHTOA: $\tan(45°) = 1 = \dfrac{Opposite}{Adjacent} = \dfrac{100}{x}$, thus $x = 100/\tan$ $34° \approx 100/0.67 \approx 148$. Choices (F), (H), and (J) are the result if you use the wrong trigonometric function. Choice (G) is the result if you incorrectly set up $\tan \theta = \dfrac{adjacent}{opposite}$.

39. **E** The general equation for a circle with center (h,k) and radius r, is $(x - h)^2 + (y - k)^2 = r^2$. Because $h = 4$, $k = -3$, and $r = 12$, the equation for this circle is $(x - 4)^2 + (y + 3)^2 = 144$. Choices (A), (B), and (C) are incorrect because they do not square r. Choice (D) is incorrect because it does not distribute the negative in the $(y - k)^2$ term.

40. **H** Use your calculator to make the comparisons easier: $\dfrac{14}{21} = 0.\overline{66}$. Now, test the answers. Choice (F) is $\dfrac{7}{12} = 0.58\overline{3}$, which is less than $0.\overline{66}$, and (G) is $\dfrac{8}{12} = 0.\overline{66}$, which makes the two fractions equal. Choice (H) is $\dfrac{9}{12} = 0.75$, which makes the inequality true. Choices (J) and (K) also make the inequality true but neither is the *least* integer that makes the inequality true.

41. **E** Substitute $(a + b)$ for a. Square the quantity $(a + b)$, distribute the 2 within $(a + b)$ by multiplying a and b both by 2, and add 5.

42. **G** Since lines $\overline{MO}$ and $\overline{LP}$ are parallel, $\angle NMO \cong \angle NLP$ and $\angle NOM \cong \angle NPL$. Thus, $\triangle MNO$ and $\triangle LNP$ are similar triangles with congruent angles and proportional sides. To find the length of $\overline{NO}$, set up a proportion: $\dfrac{\overline{MO}}{\overline{LP}} = \dfrac{\overline{NO}}{\overline{NP}}$. Using x for $\overline{NO}$, solve for x: $\dfrac{105}{150} = \dfrac{x}{x + 39}$. $\overline{NO}$ = 91 feet. Choice (F) gives the length of $\overline{OP}$. Choice (K) is the sum of the three side lengths.

43. **C** First, convert 2 miles to feet, $2\,miles \times \dfrac{5{,}280\,feet}{1\,mile} = 10{,}560\,feet$, because height, h, is given in feet in the equation. Now, substitute the answer choices for the value of t to see which choice equals 10,560 feet. Choice (C) gives you: $1{,}200 + 32(293) = 10{,}576$. The precise answer is 292.5 seconds, but the question asked for the nearest second.

44. **J** The sum of the three angles of a triangle will always equal 180°, so $2x + 3x + 5x = 180$. Since $\angle C = 5x$ and $x = 18°$, $\angle C = 5(18°) = 90$. Choices (F) and (K) are partial answers. Choices (G) and (H) give the measures for the wrong angles.

45. **B** If the basketball player made 12 out of his 30 shots, he currently has a free-throw percentage of 40%. Use the answers to calculate the least number of additional free throws he must make. Make sure you add the number to both the numerator and denomination, since any additional free throws are both attempted and made. Choice (B) gives you $\dfrac{12+10}{30+10} \times 100 = 55\%$. Choice (A) is the result of adding 5 only to the numerator. Choices (C) and (D) approximate 55% to 56% of 30 free throws. Choice (E) incorrectly raises the percentage *by* 55% rather than *to* 55%.

46. **H** Pick a number in the provided range and try out the answers. If $y = -2$, (F), (G), and (J) yield positive results. Choice (H) is approximately $-\dfrac{3}{2}$, which is less than the result of (K), $-\dfrac{1}{8}$.

47. **C** Draw five placeholders for the positions of each of the 5 groomsmen: ___ ___ ___ ___ ___ How many groomsmen could possibly walk in the first position? Five. Write a 5 in the 1st position. Next, if one groomsman takes the first position, how many possible groomsmen are left to take the second position? Four. Write a 4 in the second position, and multiply the 5 possibilities for the first position by the 4 possibilities for the second position (each of the 5 possible groomsmen in the 1st position could be with 4 different other groomsmen in the 2nd position). After another of the groomsmen is chosen for the 2nd position, there are 3 possible groomsmen for the 3rd position, then 2 possible groomsmen for the 4th position, and finally only 1 possible groomsman for the 5th position. _5_ × _4_ × _3_ × _2_ × _1_ = 120 total possible orderings.

48. **J** As with all circle problems, it is helpful to first calculate and draw the radius. Given the area of the circle is 169π square inches, use the area formula: $A = 169\pi = \pi r^2$, so $r = 13$. Radii $\overline{MO}$ and $\overline{NO}$ form two right triangles with chord $\overline{MN}$, so you can use the Pythagorean Theorem to find the length of the two missing legs: $5^2 + b^2 = 13^2$, so $b = 12$. The length of the chord is $2 \times 12 = 24$ inches. Choice (F) gives only half the length of the chord. Choices (G) and (K) give the radius and diameter of the circle, rather than the chord. Choice (H) is the sum of 5 and 13, which is not the correct operation to calculate lengths of a right triangle.

49. **A** The x-intercept occurs where $y = 0$, eliminating (B), (C), and (D). Next, find the slope of the

line: $\dfrac{rise}{run} = \dfrac{4-7}{6+3} = -\dfrac{3}{9}$, or $-\dfrac{1}{3}$. The line to the x-intercept must have the same slope. The slope

between choice (A) and $(-3,7)$ is $\dfrac{7-0}{-3-18} = -\dfrac{1}{3}$. Careful not to select (C), which is the y-intercept.

50. **G** Intercepting the x-axis at $x = 7$ means the equation must satisfy the coordinate $(7,0)$. The only equation that does this is (G). Choices (F) and (H) incorrectly give x-intercepts at $(-7,0)$. Choice (J) gives the y-intercept at $y = 7$, and (K) gives the y-intercept at $(0,-7)$.

51. **A** If the $\tan \theta = \dfrac{2}{9}$, the side opposite to θ is 2, and the side adjacent is 9. Therefore, the hypotenuse is

$\sqrt{85}$ $(h = \sqrt{2^2 + 9^2})$, so $\cos \theta = \dfrac{9}{\sqrt{85}}$ and $\sin \theta = \dfrac{2}{\sqrt{85}}$, and $\cos \theta + \sin \theta = \dfrac{11}{\sqrt{85}}$.

52. **G** Triangle OAB is equilateral since OA and OB are both radii of the circle and $OA = AB$. The for-

mula for the area of a triangle is $A = \dfrac{1}{2}bh$. The base of $\triangle OAB$ is 8. To find the height of $\triangle OAB$,

draw a line from A that is perpendicular to OB, creating two 30°-60°-90° triangles. Using the rela-

tionship $a : a\sqrt{3} : 2a$, the height of $\triangle OAB$ is $4\sqrt{3}$. So, $A = \dfrac{1}{2}(8)(4\sqrt{3}) = 16\sqrt{3}$. Choice (F) uses 4

for the base. If you chose (J), you probably forgot the $\dfrac{1}{2}$ in the area formula. Choice (H) uses 8 for

both the base and the height of the triangle.

53. **C** Use the formula given and replace variables with values from the diagram. You will also need to

find the degree measure of angle Z, since the problem asks for the length of the side opposite Z.

Given that there are 180° in a triangle, subtract 105° and 40° from 180° to get 35° for angle Z.

Now plug in all of the information in the equation: $\dfrac{\sin 40°}{30} = \dfrac{\sin 35°}{z}$. Solve for z by multiplying

both sides by z and by 30 to get: $z \sin 40° = 30 \sin 35°$. Divide both sides by $\sin 40°$.

54. **G** To find arc length, use a ratio of $\dfrac{sector}{circle} : \dfrac{central\ angle}{360°} = \dfrac{arc\ length}{circumference}$. Since the radius is 9 ft., the

circumference is $C = 2\pi(9) = 18\pi$. Now, fill known values into the ratio: $\dfrac{120°}{360°} = \dfrac{arc\ PQ}{18\pi}$. Cross-

multiply and solve to find the length of the arc is 6π. Choice (J) is a partial answer that gives the

circumference rather than arc length. Choice (K) is the sector's area, rather than arc length.

55. **C** In order to subtract these matrices, you must combine the corresponding elements from each matrix. That is, you subtract the first row, first column numbers in the second and third matrices from the first row, first column number in the first matrix. Thus, the matrix

$$\begin{bmatrix} w - x - \dfrac{1}{w+x} & x - y - \dfrac{1}{x+y} \\ y - z - \dfrac{1}{y+z} & z - w - \dfrac{1}{z+w} \end{bmatrix}$$, (C), is the best answer. Choices (A), (B), and (E) all improperly

subtract fractions and integers. Choice (D) uses multiplication rather than subtraction.

56. **K** To deal with compound functions, the trick is to work inside out. First, determine the value of the inside $f(1) = -2(1)^3 = -2$. The value of $f(1)$ becomes the new x-value for the outside f function, so determine $f(-2) = -2(-2)^3 = -2(-8) = 16$. Remember that a negative number raised to an odd integer stays negative; (F) and (G) are wrong because they confuse the signs. Choice (H) is the value of $-x^3$, rather than $-2x^3$. Choice (H) is the result of multiplying $f(x)$ by $f(x)$, which is not the same operation as compound functions.

57. **A** If a function y varies directly with x, this means that as x increases, y increases proportionally, eliminating (B) and (D). This proportionality means that the function must be a straight line, eliminating (E), with the equation $y = kx$, where k is a constant. This line must then pass through the origin, because if $x = 0$, then $y = 0$. Choice (C) is incorrect because it does not pass through the origin.

58. **K** If the quiz scores are listed from lowest to highest, the middle score, the median, is 9. The two highest scores are both 10. Since the only mode of the quiz scores is 10, the remaining two scores must be distinct integers. The mean of the 5 scores is 8, so the sum of the five scores is $8 \times 5 = 40$. The sum of the two lowest scores must be $40 - (9 + 10 + 10) = 11$. Choices (F), (G) and (H) *could* be true because the quiz scores could be (3, 8, 9, 10, 10), (4, 7, 9, 10, 10), or (5, 6, 9, 10, 10). Choice (J) is the number of scores multiplied by the mode.

59. **E** First, draw a picture and fill in as much information as you can from the problem. Two opposite sides of the cardboard are 60 inches, and two opposite sides are 40 inches. Since you're looking for the height of the table and the answer choices are numbers, not variables, representing the height of the table, use the answer choices to fill in the diagram further. Try labeling the height of the table starting with (C), the middle value. Given that the width of the cardboard is 40 inches, a height of 25 inches on either side of the tabletop is not possible—50 inches is greater than the size of the paper. Try the next smallest number, 20 inches, in (D). 20 inches is too big: If the paper table were 20 inches tall on either side, the top of the table would be a line. Choice (E), 10 inches, must be the correct answer.

60. **H** To find the area of a triangle, use the formula $A = \frac{1}{2} base \times height$. You already know the base is 10, but you need to find the height. Draw a line from point B that is perpendicular to line $\overline{AC}$. Use SOHCAHTOA: $\sin 35° = \frac{height}{AB}$, so the height of this triangle is $10 \sin 35°$. The area is $A = \frac{1}{2}(10)(10 \sin 35°) = 50 \sin 35°$. Choices (F), (G), and (H) use the wrong trigonometric functions. Choice (K) does not take $\frac{1}{2}$ the product of $\overline{AB}$ and $\overline{AC}$.

TEST 2 READING EXPLANATIONS

Passage I

1. **A** The use of the word *stultifying* refers to the boy's experience of life on his family's farm; later in the sentence, the passage tells us that the boy felt *landlocked* by this life, so something like trapped would fit well. Therefore, you can eliminate (B) and (C), because *strengthening* and *welcoming* don't match this description. Choice (D) is incorrect because nothing in the passage implies productivity.

2. **G** Line 20 shows that the boy had only heard about but never seen fireworks. Line 7 shows that the boy has companions who lead him through the jungle, so (F) is incorrect; line 55 implies that the boy respects the captain's knowledge, so (H) can be eliminated. Line 25 shows that memories of the storm often intruded in the boy's thoughts, so (J) doesn't work.

3. **D** Line 30 refers to the boy's second home on the ocean, the idea presented in (D). Line 3 refers to the jungle as *inhospitable* and mentions the *snarling* vines in the jungle, making (A) incorrect; (B) is incorrect because the passage portrays the boy's mother only as *frail and worn-looking* (line 35), not frightening; and (C) is incorrect because the passage doesn't note that the boy feels positive about any aspect of farm life.

4. **F** Choice (F) is correct because the passage about the boy leaving the farm is a flashback, as shown in line 44. Choice (G) is incorrect because the boy is remembering his past life while he continues to walk through the jungle; (H) doesn't work because the boy meets the captain and sets sail before the captain is killed and the ship is destroyed in the wreck; (J) is incorrect because his parents *create a home for him* (line 36) on the farm, before he goes off to sea.

5. **C** Choice (C) is correct because the boy follows his question about what the phrase means with an acknowledgment that he can't distinguish the captain from the other men in his mind (lines 63–67). Choice (A) is incorrect because the passage up to this point has shown the boy wondering about the meaning behind the captain's words, implying that the captain hadn't explained the phrase previously; (B) is incorrect because, although the boy wonders what the dead can do earlier in the passage, his thoughts here are focused on the captain; (D) is incorrect because there is no indication that the boy's experiences will lead him to a better life.

6. **J** Choice (J) is correct because the boy was eager to learn about navigation from the captain, as seen in lines 52–55, and the passage shows us the captain's dislike of ignorance, which he sees as *dangerous* (line 51). Choice (F) is incorrect because the boy wonders what the words mean at the beginning and end of the passage (lines 60–70); (G) is incorrect because the passage contains no evidence that the captain even knew the boy's father was *worn down*; (H) is incorrect because the passage contains no evidence about the captain's view of life at sea.

7. **A** Choice (A) is correct because lines 61–63 show the crewmates urging the boy (and finally pulling him) away from the scene of the wreck, showing his reluctance to leave. Choice (B) is incorrect because lines 6–7 shows the boy continuing to walk with his companions—no running away here; (C) is incorrect because, although lines 10–12 say that unpleasant memories of the storm often filled his thoughts, there is nothing in the passage that describes his reaction to loud noises; (D) is incorrect because the passage contains no evidence that the crewmates know about the boy's feelings about life on the farm.

8. **H** Choice (H) is correct because the passage shows the captain teaching the boy about navigation (lines 49–51). Choice (F) is incorrect because the passage never describes the captain scolding the boy for stowing away; (G) is incorrect because the boy wonders what the phrase means even at the end of the story, as shown in lines 68–70; (J) is incorrect because lines 48–56 show the captain paying attention to the boy by teaching him navigation.

9. **D** Choice (D) is correct because the passage does not mention hail. *Thunder* is described in lines 20–22, the *walls of water* are mentioned in line 22, and *lightning* is described in lines 19–20, making (A), (B), and (C) incorrect.

10. **F** Choice (F) is correct because lines 13–15 show the unexpectedness of the storm. Choice (G) is incorrect because the passage does not mention the time at which the storm arrived; (H) is incorrect because the passage does not mention how the crew responded to the storm; (J) is incorrect because the passage does not contain any reference to the boy's father mentioning a storm.

Passage II

11. **A** The *however* at the beginning of this sentence tells you that Thorne's comment is in direct contrast to the paragraph that came before, which identified the typical understanding of slang as something that is said in *defiant opposition of authority*. Choice (A) is most relevant to undermining that generalization. Choices (B) and (C) do not relate to defying authority, and rather they represent Thorne's attempts to provide counterexamples to the claim that all slang is intended to be against the status quo. Choice (D) is unsupportable anywhere in the passage; it is a trap answer based on the normal association of the contrast between *accusing* someone of guilt and his/her *innocence*.

12. **G** The final paragraph establishes the need to compile a slang dictionary so that people of future eras will have a way to understand our current forms of communication. The details regarding how Thorne's dictionary will explain each term and the analogy to modern attempts to decipher Shakespearean slang support (G). There is nothing critical in tone in this paragraph to support (F). The passage does not say that Thorne uses Shakespearean slang in his dictionary, as (H) states. While the author does agree that a dictionary of slang would be useful to future generations, he does not argue that the project of compiling such a dictionary is the *primary* goal of modern linguistics, as (J) states.

13. **B** Choice (B) is correct because college professors, while possibly involved in the study of slang, are never mentioned in the passage. Choices (A), (C), and (D) are all mentioned in the passage.

14. **F** The quotation marks around *common man* highlight the fact that this is a questionable term that is being applied by someone else's point of view. This paragraph discusses how a word becomes viewed as slang based on a very subjective assessment of the people who use that word. The parallelism of the two sentences tells you that *common man* must be the opposite of the *respectable* people

mentioned in the previous sentence. Choice (F) correctly relates the derogatory classification of slang to its less respected users. Choice (G) is not supported anywhere in the passage. Choice (H) incorrectly identifies a point of view held by *intellectuals who would categorically denounce slang* as the author's own. Choice (J), while related to this paragraph, is too extreme in wording and does not answer the question of the intended effect of adding quotation marks around a certain term.

15. **C** The context of this sentence tells you that slang is viewed *condescendingly* and as a signal of *intellectual laziness*. Choice (C) reinforces these ideas by identifying vulgar speech as containing something (slang) that sophisticated speech would not include. Choices (A), (B), and (D) are all correctly negative in tone but to an unfairly severe and specific degree. Certain uses of slang may be *sickening, malicious,* or *profane,* but this sentence is concerned with the way linguists view ALL slang as being uneducated in tone.

16. **F** According to the final paragraph, Thorne believes that in order for *future generations* or *civilization* to be able to decode the meaning contained in all our written artifacts, we need to provide them with a way of understanding our usage of slang. Choice (F) correctly identifies this purpose. Choice (G) suggests the purpose is for foreign language learners, (H) suggests the purpose is to write the first-ever slang dictionary, and (J) suggests the purpose is to provide a current how-to-use manual of slang. All three are unsupported and do not address the stated need for this sort of resource.

17. **C** The quote from Whitman describes slang as an attempt to escape from *bald literalism*, meaning an attempt to find more colorful ways of saying what one means, and as humanity's attempt to *express itself illimitably*, meaning to have limitless expression. Choice (C) is a fair paraphrase of those ideas. Choice (A) is irrelevant and unsupportable. Choices (B) and (D) are stated elsewhere in the passage as reasons for slang but not attributable to Whitman or related to his quote.

18. **H** The first paragraph attempts to make a contrast between unscholarly sounding words and a man of great academic distinction. The rhetorical question at the end of the paragraph attempts to invite the reader's curiosity as to why these two things would go together. Choice (H) effectively ties the first paragraph's anecdote to the purpose of the passage as a whole, discussing the academic treatment of slang. Choices (F) and (J) are too narrow in scope, failing to explain the first paragraph's relation to the passage as a whole. Choice (G) has an extreme claim that British scholars are the *leaders*, which is unsupported by the passage.

19. **C** The parallelism of this sentence indicates that while *most modern slang comes from* groups like corporate office workers, students, and computer users, previously most slang came from groups like the military. In describing groups such as the military as *hotbeds of slang*, the author is saying that such groups are likely inventors of slang. Choice (C) correctly matches this concept. Choice (A) means to predict the future, which is not supported by the passage. Choices (B) and (D) are unsupportable and make use of the trap language association between *traditionally* and *old-fashioned* as well as *the military* and *strict*.

20. **J** The passage indicates that most intellectuals do not completely reject slang because they *realize almost all slang* initially *involves as much inherent creativity* as the admired word play of poetry. Choice (J) addresses this detail. Choices (F), (G), and (H) are not supported anywhere in the passage.

Passage III

21. **D** The question asks what happened *after Breed received Harper Lee's letter* according to Passage A. Look for the lead word *letter* in the passage, which first appears in line 7. It says that Breed *crafted a letter and sent it off* to Harper Lee. According to the first sentence of the subsequent paragraph, *nine days later (another) letter arrived*, this time from Lee to Breed. The remainder of the second paragraph describes the contents of Lee's letter. The third paragraph provides context for how *Lee kept her thoughts to herself*, before the final paragraph expresses Breed's appreciation for how *Lee was able to keep her own counsel and protect her privacy*. So it can be predicted that *after Breed received Harper Lee's letter*, he was not surprised by the rejection, and was even glad she maintained her dedication to privacy. *Social media* is mentioned as something Lee doesn't use, not a place *Breed posted her letter*, so eliminate (A). There is no indication that Breed *felt angry*, so eliminate (B). There is no indication that Breed *appreciated her compliment of his writing style*, so eliminate (C). *Felt glad that she maintained her privacy and appreciated receiving the reply* matches the prediction. The correct answer is (D).

22. **J** The question asks about *a detail that supports the idea that Lee kept herself out of the public eye*. According to Lee's letter, she *simply (didn't) give interviews*. So it can be predicted that her lack of interviews supports the idea she kept to herself. There is no indication of how Lee felt about *people's high expectations*, so eliminate (F). At first glance, the fact that *Lee did not reply to interview requests* might seem like it matches the prediction. However, this answer is extreme, because if she never replied to such requests, she would not have replied to Breed; eliminate (G). The 2014 publication mentioned in Passage A is *The Mockingbird Next Door: Life with Harper Lee*, not a new publication by Lee; eliminate (H). In the second sentence of the first paragraph (Lines 2–4) Breed states that *the author of "To Kill a Mockingbird" hadn't granted an interview in about four decades*. The correct answer is (J).

23. **A** The question asks about a detail *regarding the publication of The Mockingbird Next Door*. Look for the lead words *The Mockingbird Next Door* in the passage, which appear in lines 20–21. The answer should come from a window of approximately lines 18–26. According to the window, *Lee kept her thoughts to herself. Not a post, nor a tweet. With the 2014 publication of The Mockingbird Next Door: Life with Harper Lee, it appeared that Lee's resolve had softened*. So it can be predicted from this information that Lee had opened herself up to some public interaction. Choice (A) matches this prediction, so keep it. Choice (B) is deceptive language. Just because it *appeared Lee's resolve had softened* does not necessarily prove that it had, so eliminate (B). It was the release of *Go Set a Watchman* that led Lee to release a statement *to express humility and amazement*, not *The Mockingbird Next Door*; eliminate (C). Choice (D) refers to information found in Passage B, not Passage A, so eliminate (D). The correct answer is (A).

24. **G** The question asks about *Harper Lee's reaction to Mills' book*, according to Passage B. The first paragraph of Passage B states that *the day before the book's publication date, Lee…issued a statement refuting the memoir's main narrative. "Rest assured, as long as I am alive any book purporting to be with my cooperation is a falsehood."* Therefore, it can be predicted that Lee reacted very negatively to Mills' book, basically calling it fake. Lee was neither *accepting, proud*, nor, *pleased*, so eliminate (F), (H), and (J). *Dismissive* and *claimed that she had not authorized its publication* matches the prediction. The correct answer is (G).

25. **C**   The question asks how *Mills' article can be described* according to Crowder, the author of Passage B. Look for the lead word *article* in Passage B, which appears in line 65. The answer should come from a window of approximately lines 61–70. According to the window, *after the exhaustive and meticulously researched Tribune article was published in 2002, Mills remained friends with the sisters*. From this information it can be predicted that Crowder describes the Tribune article as *exhaustive and meticulously researched*. *Controversial* is supported by the passage, but *exhausting* means "completely consuming" as opposed to *exhaustive* which means just "complete"; eliminate (A). *Specific* means "precise," and *meticulously* means "precisely," but there is nothing to show that Crowder finds the article *encouraging*; eliminate (B). *Thorough and well-researched* matches *exhaustive and meticulously researched*, so keep (C). *Speculative and second-hand* is a reversal of the prediction, as well as a deceptive use of language from the last paragraph, so eliminate (D). The correct answer is (C).

26. **J**   The question asks why *Mills published her book,* according to Passage B. Mills' perspective on the book is provided in the fourth paragraph, which begins, *Mills described her book as focusing on "the last chapter of life as (the Lees) knew it."* From this information it can be predicted that Mills published her book at least in part to share *life as (the Lees) knew it*. Neither *exclusive interviews* nor being *compelled to reveal the truth about her friendship with the Lees* are cited as reasons by Mills, so eliminate (F) and (H). According to the opening sentence of the third paragraph, *the Tribune assigned (Mills) to capture the spirit of Monroeville* in the article. Mills herself never mentions aspirations *to capture the spirit of Monroeville*, so eliminate (G). That Mills *hoped she could provide first-hand information on the Lees' daily lives and conversations* matches the prediction. The correct answer is (J).

27. **D**   The question asks what the sentence in lines 53–56 means about Mills. The sentence is a quote in which Mills says that *Lee "had always been encouraging and also quite specific about stories that she was sharing for the book and those that were to remain private, and I did respect those."* So it can be predicted that Mills left some of Lee's stories private. Choice (A) is extreme because it cannot be inferred that Mills *acted in accordance with all of Lee's wishes regarding the book*, so eliminate (A). There is no mention of *meals and household chores*, so eliminate (B). While the prediction says some stories were left private, there is no indication that Mills *censored several of Lee's stories*; eliminate (C). That Mills *did not include some of Lee's stories* matches the prediction. The correct answer is (D).

28. **F**   The question asks *which accurately compares the content of the two passages*. Because this is a general question about both passages, it should be done after all of the specific questions and general questions for each individual passage. Both passages discuss personal interactions of journalists with the reclusive author Harper Lee. The author of Passage 1, although he did not get the interview he sought, became sympathetic to Lee's privacy. The author of Passage 2 recounts the controversy around Marja Mills's memoir *The Mockingbird Next Door* and how Mills and Lee came to be at odds because of the book's publishing. So, it can be predicted that the answer will reflect this information. *Both describe first-hand accounts of contact with Lee that had different outcomes* matches the prediction; keep (F). There is no mention of Lee's readers, so eliminate (G). The passages involve different interactions with Lee, so eliminate (H). Lee does not self-identify with a bird, so eliminate (J). The correct answer is (F).

29. **B** The question asks about what the two authors would agree upon in regard to *Harper Lee's privacy*. Because this is a general question about both passages, it should be done after all of the specific questions and general questions for each individual passage. The author of Passage 1, although he did not get the interview he sought, became sympathetic to Lee's privacy. The author of Passage 2 recounts the controversy around Marja Mills' memoir *The Mockingbird Next Door* and how Mills and Lee came to be at odds because of the book's publishing. So it can be predicted that something both authors would agree about Harper Lee's privacy would be that it was very important to her. *Secondary, misplaced,* and *misconstrued* each do not match that her privacy was important; eliminate (A), (C), and (D). The correct answer is (B).

30. **G** The question asks who the author of the text in lines 20–22 is. *The Mockingbird Next Door* is the text referred to in the line reference. From the first sentence of Passage B, it can be predicted that *The Mockingbird Next Door* is *Marja Mills' memoir*. Choice (G) matches this prediction. The correct answer is (G).

Passage IV

31. **A** Frank Drake is primarily discussed in the first paragraph and briefly mentioned during the conclusion. He is described as the person in charge of Project Ozma, which is in turn called *the first organized attempt to detect alien life by way of radio*. The correct answer, (A), correctly summarizes this information. The project was unsuccessful in its search for alien life, making (B) incorrect. Choice (C) confuses Project Ozma with Project Phoenix, which is not mentioned in connection with Drake. The passage does not explicitly state Drake's education or position, as in (D).

32. **G** Project Ozma is discussed in the second paragraph, immediately after the description of Frank Drake's experiment. The passage states that the project was a failure in the sense that it failed to find signs of intelligent life but a success in terms of leading to other similar programs. Therefore, (G) is the best answer. Choice (F) is incorrect because the project was not a success. The passage does not call Drake's goals unrealistic, as in (H), nor does it discuss NASA at this time, as in (J).

33. **C** The word *august* is used to describe two colleges, the University of California at Berkeley and the University of Western Sydney. Those programs are then described as having *reputations that draw respected scientists from around the world*. Therefore, a good word to replace *august* would be respected. Choice (C), *esteemed*, is a good synonym for respected. Choice (A), *summery*, might sound like it's related to *august*, but it doesn't mean respected.

34. **H** The author concludes the passage by stating that *Perhaps someday Frank Drake's dream of a message from outer space will come true once we know where to look for it.* This implies a certain hopefulness about the search while acknowledging that there are difficulties yet to be overcome. Therefore, the best answer is (H). There is no evidence that the author is *ironic*, as in (F), or *angry*, as in (G). Choice (J) goes too far, since the author is inclined to be hopeful, not fearful.

35. **A** The passage describes scientists in this field in the third paragraph. They are described as *esteemed academics, typically specializing in the areas of physics, astronomy, and engineering*. Choice (A), the best answer, is a good paraphrase of this information. Choice (B) includes words from the passage, but goes against the information given. Choice (C) mentions specific places of employment. Although the passage does mention such institutions, it does not discuss these researchers as specifically employed there. Choice (D) incorrectly focuses on *radio mechanics*, instead of interstellar research.

36. **J** The fourth paragraph serves as a bridge between the introductory paragraphs, which discuss the search for extraterrestrial life in general terms, and the rest of the passage, which goes into greater detail about two of the relevant factors in determining various planets' habitability. Choice (J) is the best answer because it correctly identifies the shift to the two factors as the primary point of the paragraph. Choice (F) incorrectly identifies a minor point in the first sentence as the main idea. Liquid water is not discussed until paragraph five, ruling out (G). *Goldilocks Zones* are not mentioned until paragraph six, ruling out (H).

37. **D** The term *hospitable planets* is used in the fifth paragraph, during the discussion of temperature and liquid water. The sentence states that *hospitable planets must be located within a certain distance of their respective suns.* This sentence falls in the middle of the discussion of what conditions will allow for life, so a good phrase to replace *hospitable planets* with would be *life-supporting* or, to use another term introduced in the passage, *life-sustaining*. Choice (D) is the best answer, since it is the best match for *life-supporting*. Choice (A) refers to *cultures*, which are not within the scope of this passage. Choice (B) incorrectly focuses on distance from the Sun, which does not necessarily mean *life-supporting*. Choice (C) goes against the information in the passage.

38. **H** Saturn is mentioned in paragraph five, as an example of a planet that is too far from the Sun to have temperatures conducive to life. Choice (H) correctly connects this statement to the earlier statement that planets too far away from the Sun cannot sustain liquid water, making it the best answer. Choice (F) incorrectly states that Saturn is too close to the Sun. Choice (G) incorrectly associates distance from the Sun with a heavy atmosphere, a link not discussed in this passage. Choice (J) mentions *gas giants,* which the passage does not discuss until the following paragraph, and not in connection with Saturn.

39. **D** This question asks you to find a situation analogous to that of Venus. The passage mentions Venus in the fifth paragraph, as an example of a planet that is too close to the Sun, and thus too hot, to support life. Later in the passage, the author also notes that the size of a planet may alter this rule, since smaller planets retain less heat and can thus be closer to the Sun. The correct answer, (D), correctly connects these facts. The passage never describes Venus as a *gas giant*, as in (A), nor does it state that Venus lacks a *gravitational field*, as in (B). Choice (C) incorrectly identifies Venus as having an *unstable orbit*.

40. **F** Goldilocks Planets are discussed in the fifth paragraph and are described as *planets that fall within the range of appropriate temperatures*. Therefore, (F) is the best answer. Choice (G) incorrectly discusses *atmospheres*, while (H) has the opposite information as the passage. Choice (J) incorrectly mentions *hydrogen gases*, which are not mentioned in this part of the passage.

TEST 2 SCIENCE EXPLANATIONS

Passage I

1. **D** In Table 1, when the current doubles, the velocity of the train also doubles. Therefore, a current of 500 A must be associated with a train velocity of 2×200 m/s = 400 m/s.

2. **F** Table 2 shows that the current consistently increases as the length of the magnetic rods increases, so (F) is the best answer.

3. **C** When $B = 9.84 \times 10^{-4}$ T, I = 500 A, and when $B = 1.05 \times 10^{-3}$ T, $I = 600$ A. Therefore, $I = 570$ A would be produced by a magnetic field with a values in between these two B values. Choice (C) is the only option that fits.

4. **J** The question suggests that an increasing electrical current results from an increasing voltage. Of the options listed, Trial 14 has the greatest electrical current, so it must also have the greatest voltage.

5. **B** Study 4 stands out because all of the values for electrical current are negative. Therefore, (B) is the correct answer.

6. **G** In Study 3, both current (I) and magnetic field (B) increase with a direct relationship. Choice (G) shows this direct increasing linear relationship.

Passage II

7. **D** Using Figure 1, determine the features of a *Pipistrellus hesperus* starting at Step 8 and work backwards. Step 8 describes it to have a *forearm length < 40 mm*. Step 7 describes it to have a *tragus < 6 mm and curved*. Step 5 describes it to have a *uropatagium not heavily furred*, and Step 1 describes it to have *ears shorter than 25 mm*. Only (D) refers to a feature of Bat IV, *uropatagium heavily furred*, that differs from those of *Pipistrellus hesperus* found using the above method. Alternatively, you could use the features of Bat IV from Table 1 and find the point on Figure 1 where the result differs from the path necessary to get to *Pipistrellus hesperus*.

8. **G** Follow Figure 1 step by step using the descriptions for Bats I and II from Table 1 until you find the last step with the same result. Starting at Step 1, both bats have ears *shorter than 25 mm* making Step 5 next. Therefore, (F) must be wrong. Both bats have a uropatagium that is *not heavily furred*, making Step 7 next. Bat I has a *4 mm, curved* tragus, and Bat II has a *7 mm, straight* tragus. Therefore, the results of Step 7 differ making (H) and (J) wrong. This leaves (G), Step 5, as the last point where the bats had similar traits. Note that the *obvious fringe of fur* on the uropatagium of Bat II does not come into play until Step 9 of Figure 1.

9. **A** All of the choices are in the kingdom Animalia and phylum Chordata. Vesper bats, like all bats, belong to the class Mammalia. Mammals are vertebrates with sweat glands, hair, and similar middle ear structures that give birth to live young (except monotremes which lay eggs).

10. **G** Both species are found at Step 6 in Figure 1. Step 6 can only be reached from having *heavily furred* uropatagium in Step 5, eliminating (H). Step 5 can only be reached from having *shorter than 25 mm* ears in Step 1, eliminating (J). Choice (F) refers to Step 3 which is not part of the path for either species, meaning it may or may not be a common trait. Choice (G) is more definitive because it refers to the only feature that neither species can have according to Figure 1. It is not possible to get to Step 6 if the ears are greater than 25 mm long.

11. **D** Using the features listed in Table 1 for Bat II, follow the steps in Figure 1. Bat II's *18 mm long* ears lead from Step 1 to Step 5 in Figure 1. The uropatagium overall is *not heavily furred*, which then leads to Step 7. The tragus is *7 mm* and *straight*, leading next to Step 9. Since there is an *obvious fringe of fur* on the edge of the uropatgium, Bat II is *Myotis thysanodes*. Choice (D), *Myotis volans*, is most likely the closest genetic relative because it is in the same genus, has very similar features, and is adjacent on Figure 1.

Passage III

12. **J** Looking at Figure 2, the 0°C setting is the lowest curve, represented by triangles. At 200 min. the saltwater temperature is about 8°C, and at 250 min. the temperature is about 5°C. Therefore, at 220 min., you should expect the temperature to be between 5°C and 8°C.

13. **B** Since you are asked about a heater and a 37°C trial, Figure 1 will be the relevant chart. At 8 min. the air temperature is about 27°C, and at 10 min. the temperature is about 31°C. If the air changes 4°C in 2 minutes, divide 4 by 2 to get the answer: 2°C/min.

14. **F** For every temperature setting in each figure, the temperature changes fastest in the beginning and slower as time progresses. The 0°C cooling trial is no different: from 0–100 min. the saltwater temperature goes from 50°C to about 22°C, a change of 28°C, a much greater change than those recorded in any of the other 100-minute intervals listed in the answer choices.

15. **A** Average kinetic energy is directly proportional to temperature. That is, when temperature is high, average kinetic energy is high, and when temperature is low, average kinetic energy is low. Choice (A) corresponds to the highest temperature. However, you don't need to know what kinetic energy is to answer the question. Choices (B), (C), and (D) all yield the same temperature (25°C), and since there is no other variable in either figure to which average kinetic energy could be related, if one of them were correct, they would all have to be correct. Therefore, by Process of Elimination, (A) is the only possibility.

16. **F** The lower the cooling device's temperature setting, the longer it takes for the saltwater to reach that temperature. It takes the cooling device about 300 min. to reach the 25°C setting; about 350 min. to reach the 10°C setting, and about 400 min. to reach the 0°C. Therefore, you should expect the cooler to take more than 400 min. to reach an even lower setting, such as –10°C.

Passage IV

17. **C** Pepsin is described as an enzyme that is involved with protein breakdown, and that is active in an acidic environment. Of the choices listed, only (C) is a component of the digestive system, which is responsible for the breakdown of nutrients. Also, the stomach is an organ with a highly acidic environment.

18. **F** Note where the Pepsin Activity in Table 2 is High. There is no evidence on the table that Pepsin activity is high at any pH higher than 3.5, so you can only be sure of (F).

19. **C** Pepsin is capable of high activity in the absence of anserine in Trial 4, thus (A) cannot be correct. Pepsin activity is also high in the presence of anserine in Trial 3, thus (B) cannot be correct. Casein is described as a protein that can be digested by pepsin, so (D) cannot be correct. This leaves (C) as the only possible answer. Another way to approach this problem is to notice that what makes Trial 5 different from Trials 3 and 4 is that it does not contain casein. If no pepsin activity is seen when casein is absent, it would follow that casein is a substance that can be digested by pepsin, supporting (C).

20. **H** In order for casein to remain undigested, casein must first be present in the solution. Trials 5 and 6 do not contain casein, so (G) and (J) can be eliminated. Choice (H) is a better choice than (F) because the high pepsin activity in Trials 3 and 4 would break casein down into the smaller peptides.

21. **A** Trial 3 in Experiment 1 is conducted at a pH of 3.0 and at a temperature of 40°C. While all of answer choices feature Experiment 2 trials conducted at a temperature of 40°C, only Trial 9 is conducted at a similar pH of 3.0. Therefore, (A) is the best answer.

22. **G** The results from Experiment 1 show high activity of pepsin, meaning a fast rate of protein digestion by pepsin, at a temperature of 40°C, which excludes (C) and (D). The results from Experiment 2 show high activity of pepsin at pH values that are less than 4.0, so (B) is the best answer.

Passage V

23. **C** Read the vertical axes in all 3 figures when $T = 0$°C. The only fluid whose viscosity is less than 1.0 cP is diethyl ether, eliminating (B) and (D). Ethanol, water, mercury, and nitrobenzene are all found in both Figures 1 and 2, so the correct answer is (C).

24. **F** The nitrobenzene line in Figure 2 has a sharp initial decrease and then plateaus. Thus, (F) has the greatest decrease in viscosity of approximately 1.1 cP. Choice (G) has only a decrease of approximately 0.25 cP. Choices (H) and (J) both decreases less than 0.1 cP.

25. **C** Figure 1 shows that the viscosity of water at 70°C is approximately 0.4 cP. Although (A), (B), and (D) provide values that are represented in the figure, they are all values for temperatures other than the specified 70°C.

26. **G** Figure 2 demonstrates that viscosity decreased with an increase in temperature, eliminating (F) and (H). The introduction states that the greater the viscosity, the greater the resistance to flow, the greater time it would take for a fluid to move out of its container. Given Figure 2 shows decreasing viscosity, the time for the fluids to leave their containers would also decrease. Thus, (G) is the correct answer.

27. **D** To assess the hypothesis, you would require values for viscosity at 60°C for nitrobenzene with Additive A and untreated diethyl ether. Although Figure 2 provides the viscosity for nitrobenzene treated with Additive B, no figure shows the viscosity value for nitrobenzene blended with chemical Additive A. Figure 1 shows that nitrobenzene has a viscosity higher than that of diethyl ether, and Figures 2 and 3 show that Additive A lowers the viscosity of both ethanol and diethyl ether; however, you cannot assume that treatment of nitrobenzene with Additive A would lower its viscosity below 0.07cP. Thus, (D) is the best option.

Passage VI

28. **G** Examine Figure 3 along the *x*-axis. Notice how the farther you go to the right along the *x*-axis, the weaker the wave type becomes. Only (G) accurately describes this phenomenon.

29. **B** First, examine Figures 3 and 4 closely. In both figures, the transition lines show that at densities between 1,000 and 2,000 kg/m^3, strong waves appear always to begin to propagate at shorter distances from the epicenter than moderate waves. Thus, (C) and (D) may be eliminated. Since the maximum distance from the epicenter is less for strong waves than moderate waves, (A) may also be eliminated.

30. **J** Look at the passage closely; the passage states that *ground density and propagation duration were controlled in the experiment*. Thus, (G) and (H) may be eliminated. Choice (F) may be eliminated because in each experiment, the sound intensity was controlled. The wave type formed in the experiments was not controlled as it varied with distance and density.

31. **D** Examine Figure 1 closely. A wavelength constitutes the distance from one hump to the next. The moderate wave is approximately 150 cm, and the weak wave is approximately 500 cm. Subsequently, neither wave type exhibits a wavelength of less than 100 cm.

32. **J** From the passage, Studies 1 and 2 were conducted using sound intensities of 60 and 80 dB, respectively. Accordingly, the resulting waveform plot of study using 70 dB should exhibit wave types reminiscent of Figures 2 and 3. Both figures exhibit all three types of waves; therefore, (J) is the best answer. The waveform plot of Study 3 does not include weak waves, but its sound intensity was set to 100 dB, well above the sound intensity of 70 dB given in this question.

33. **A** Use the range of sound intensities given in the passage to determine which waveform plot you need to use. Since this range is 75 dB to 85 dB, you can confidently use the waveform plot from Study 2, which has as its sound intensity 80 dB. Using Figure 3 (Study 2), therefore, note the range of distances from the epicenter for strong waves: roughly 0 m to 2.3 m. Accordingly, any distance from the epicenter for strong waves between sound intensities of 75 dB and 85 dB can be reasonably expected to have a distance shorter than 2.5 m.

Passage VII

34. **G** The information in Table 1 indicates that Solution 4 contained three dissolved particles, while Solution 2 contained only one dissolved particle. Solution 4 thus had more dissolved particles, enabling you to eliminate (F) and (H). Now compare the respective freezing point of each solution. The freezing point of Solution 2 was −1.9°C, while the freezing point of Solution 4 was lower at −5.7°C. Be careful here—a large negative number is smaller than a small one!

35. **A** Scientist 2 states that the change in freezing point is NOT related *to the identity or properties* of the solute dissolved. The observation that a solute with no charge such as naphthalene can still lower the freezing point of a solvent does not contradict Scientist 2's viewpoint, so (C) and (D) are incorrect. Scientist 1 specifically states that a change in freezing point *only occurs with solutes that form charged particles in solution*. Therefore, the fact that naphthalene causes a change in the freezing point of benzene directly contradicts Scientist 1's viewpoint, as stated in (A).

36. **F** Use Process of Elimination. Scientist 2 argues that any increase in the concentration of a solution will lower its freezing point, so you can eliminate (G) and (J). Scientist 1 argues that only charged solvents can have an influence on the freezing point, so you can eliminate (H) as well. This leaves you only with (F), which agrees with the hypotheses of both scientists.

37. **A** Scientist 2 states that only the concentration of a solution can change its freezing point, and since the concentration here is held constant, (B) and (C) are not the best answers. Scientist 1 states that *the decrease in freezing point is related only to the charge of the solute particles*, a hypothesis supported by the observations in the question.

38. **G** Scientist 1 states that *solute molecules are attracted to the solvent molecules by intermolecular forces* and interfere *with the orderly arrangement of solvent molecules*. Choices (F) and (J) are eliminated because they do not depict attraction between solute and solvent molecules, and both show a very orderly arrangement of solvent molecules. Choices (G) and (H) demonstrate attraction between solute and solvent, but only (G) illustrates interference with non-orderly arrangement of solvent molecules.

39. **A** Only Scientist 1 states that the physical properties (charge) of the solute have an impact on changing the freezing point of a solvent. This eliminates (B) and (D). Scientist 2 states that the physical properties of the solute do not have an effect on freezing point depression. Therefore, (C) is eliminated and (A) is correct.

40. **J** Scientist 2 states that the decrease in temperature *is in direct proportion with the van 't Hoff factor*. Choices (F) and (H) show the decrease in temperature and the van 't Hoff factor in an inverse proportion, so they can be eliminated. Choice (G) can also be eliminated because there is no indication that the van 't Hoff factor should be squared in the proportion. Only (J) shows decrease in temperature (ΔT) and the van 't Hoff factor (i) in direction proportion with one another.

WRITING TEST

Essay Checklist

- ☐ Clearly state your own perspective

- ☐ Reference the ideas of all 3 perspectives

- ☐ Use examples to explain your point of view

- ☐ Have 2–3 body paragraphs with 5–7 sentences each

- ☐ Have an introduction and a conclusion paragraph

- ☐ Write neatly

- ☐ Use a formal tone and mature level of vocabulary

- ☐ Avoid spelling and grammar errors

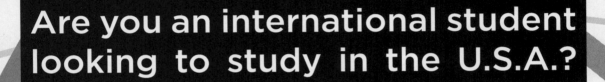